# Other publications by Van Haren Publishing

Van Haren Publishing (VHP) specializes in titles on Best Practices, methods and standards within four domains:

- IT management,
- Architecture (Enterprise and IT),
- Business management and
- Project management

These publications are grouped in series, eg: *ITSM Library*, *Best Practice* and *IT Management Topics*. VHP is also publisher on behalf of leading companies and institutions, eg The Open Group, IPMA-NL, PMI-NL, CA, Getronics, Pink Elephant.

Topics are (per domain):

| IT (Service) Management / IT Governance | Architecture (Enterprise and IT) | Project/Programme/ Risk Management |
|---|---|---|
| ASL | Archimate | A4 Project management |
| BiSL | TOGAF™ | ICB |
| CATS | | MINCE® |
| CMMI | **Business Management** | M_o_R® |
| CObiT | EFQM | MSP |
| ISO 17799 | ISA-95 | PMBoK |
| ISO 27001 | ISO 9000 | PRINCE2® |
| ISO/IEC 20000 | ISO 9001:2000 | |
| ISPL | SixSigma | |
| IT Service CMM | SOX | |
| ITIL® V2 | SqEME® | |
| ITIL® V3 | | |
| ITSM | | |
| MOF | | |
| MSF | | |

For the latest information on VHP publications, visit our website: www.vanharen.net.

# IT Financial Management
## Best Practice

Van Haren
PUBLISHING

# Colophon

| | |
|---|---|
| Title: | IT Financial Management: Best Practice |
| Authors: | Maxime Sottini |
| Editors: | Jan van Bon (Inform-IT, Managing Editor) |
| | Ruby Tjassing (Inform-IT, managing editor) |
| Copy editor: | Jane Chittenden |
| Publisher: | Van Haren Publishing, Zaltbommel, www.vanharen.net |
| Design & layout: | CO2 Premedia bv, Amersfoort – NL |
| ISBN: | 9789087535018 |
| Edition: | First edition, first impression, March 2009 |

For any further enquiries about Van Haren Publishing, please send an e-mail to:
info@vanharen.net

# Foreword

Financial Management is not the first function an IT organization will try to cover. Normally we see that topics like Change Management, Incident Management and Service Level Management are among the very first to be tackled in quality improvement projects. But sooner or later the organization will need to get in control of that very core attribute of the IT services: the cost! Managing the financial aspects of IT service management is so very essential to the organization, that it cannot escape to be subject to the management system.

There is a wealth of technical books on financial management out there, ranging from academic study books to 'finance for dummies'. Unfortunately, IT managers are not financial managers, and they normally are not deeply trained in 'the art of financial management'. The same goes for most financial managers: they know little of IT. Available information in frameworks like ITIL was also limited to a rather abstract level. Given this lack of existing guidance, a book on IT financial management, scoped at the needs of IT managers, would be of great practical value.

The same situation applies to many other IT service management topics: a lot of information is available in sources like COBIT, ITIL and MOF, but additional guidance for practitioners is in high demand. This was the reason for developing a series of books that complemented the available sources of best practices. The series is being published in the ITSM Library, the independent set of books that cover *global best practices*. Publications in the ITSM Library result from global projects, covering experts from all kinds of disciplines, and from many corners of the world. These publications are always very instructive, and offer practical guidance for practitioners. They all are titled 'Best Practices'.

The remarkable lack of practical guidance on IT financial management is the reason that this book is one of the very first titles to be developed in the Best Practices subseries of the ITSM Library. As this is part of a bigger project, a lot of attention is paid to the design of the Best Practices subseries, and to the structure of each book in this subseries. All topics covered are described from a clear architecture, in terms of People, Process and Technology, sharing the same philosophy on IT service management. Specifically, each book makes clear whether the topic described is a process or a function: there are important differences that need to be respected on implementation.
In this respect, IT financial management is a clear example of a function, using several other well-known IT service management processes.

We expect that this book will be a very useful practical guide that supports the reader in understanding more on financial management in IT service organizations, offering a good structure and lots of practical tips, templates and checklists, on a topic that will have to be tackled sooner or later…

Jan van Bon
Managing Editor

# Contents

Foreword . . . . . . . . . . . . . . . . . . . . . . . . . . . . . . . . . . . . . . . . . . . . . . . . . . . . . . V

**1 Context for IT financial management** . . . . . . . . . . . . . . . . . . . . . . . . . . . . . . 1
    1.1    Setting the scene . . . . . . . . . . . . . . . . . . . . . . . . . . . . . . . . . . . . . . . . . 1
    1.2    IT services and cost . . . . . . . . . . . . . . . . . . . . . . . . . . . . . . . . . . . . . . . 1
    1.3    The nature of IT financial management . . . . . . . . . . . . . . . . . . . . . . . . 3
    1.4    IT financial management and the evolution of ITIL . . . . . . . . . . . . . . . . 5
    1.5    Parameters influencing IT financial management . . . . . . . . . . . . . . . . . 6
    1.6    IT financial management maturity . . . . . . . . . . . . . . . . . . . . . . . . . . . . 8
    1.7    ITSM drivers . . . . . . . . . . . . . . . . . . . . . . . . . . . . . . . . . . . . . . . . . . . 8

**2 What is IT financial management?** . . . . . . . . . . . . . . . . . . . . . . . . . . . . . . . . 9
    2.1    Definition . . . . . . . . . . . . . . . . . . . . . . . . . . . . . . . . . . . . . . . . . . . . . 9
    2.2    Goals and objectives . . . . . . . . . . . . . . . . . . . . . . . . . . . . . . . . . . . . . 10
    2.3    IT financial management maturity levels . . . . . . . . . . . . . . . . . . . . . . 12
    2.4    Scope . . . . . . . . . . . . . . . . . . . . . . . . . . . . . . . . . . . . . . . . . . . . . . . . 16
    2.5    Specific elements of IT financial management . . . . . . . . . . . . . . . . . . . 17

**3 Perspectives and benefits of IT financial management** . . . . . . . . . . . . . . . . . 19
    3.1    Perspectives and benefits of IT financial management . . . . . . . . . . . . . 19
    3.2    Costs of IT financial management . . . . . . . . . . . . . . . . . . . . . . . . . . . 24
    3.3    More quantifiable benefits or costs? . . . . . . . . . . . . . . . . . . . . . . . . . . 28

**4 Description of financial management activities** . . . . . . . . . . . . . . . . . . . . . . 31
    4.1    Strategy . . . . . . . . . . . . . . . . . . . . . . . . . . . . . . . . . . . . . . . . . . . . . . 33
    4.2    Budgeting . . . . . . . . . . . . . . . . . . . . . . . . . . . . . . . . . . . . . . . . . . . . 44
    4.3    Accounting . . . . . . . . . . . . . . . . . . . . . . . . . . . . . . . . . . . . . . . . . . . 57
    4.4    Charging . . . . . . . . . . . . . . . . . . . . . . . . . . . . . . . . . . . . . . . . . . . . . 62
    4.5    Relationships with other functions, processes and practices . . . . . . . . . 65
    4.6    IT financial management and the service lifecycle . . . . . . . . . . . . . . . . 75

**5 Roles of IT financial management** . . . . . . . . . . . . . . . . . . . . . . . . . . . . . . . 77
    5.1    Overview of roles . . . . . . . . . . . . . . . . . . . . . . . . . . . . . . . . . . . . . . . 77
    5.2    Roles for Scenario 1: IT financial management for internal IT departments . . . . . 77
    5.3    Roles for Scenario 2: IT financial management for internal IT providers . . . . . . 78
    5.4    Roles for Scenario 3: IT financial management for market IT providers . . . . . . 80
    5.5    Details of roles . . . . . . . . . . . . . . . . . . . . . . . . . . . . . . . . . . . . . . . . 81

**6 Planning and implementing IT financial management** . . . . . . . . . . . . . . . . . 87
    6.1    Continual service improvement . . . . . . . . . . . . . . . . . . . . . . . . . . . . . 87
    6.2    An example of an improvement project . . . . . . . . . . . . . . . . . . . . . . . 91
    6.3    Continuous improvement . . . . . . . . . . . . . . . . . . . . . . . . . . . . . . . . . 99

| | 6.4 | Organizational change management | 104 |
| | 6.5 | Design topics | 107 |
| | 6.6 | Challenges, possible problems, critical success factors and risks | 153 |

| **7** | **Managing finances** | | **157** |
| | 7.1 | Operational management | 157 |
| | 7.2 | Controls | 160 |
| | 7.3 | Metrics for IT financial management | 163 |

| **8** | **Tooling** | | **177** |
| | 8.1 | Requirements for IT financial management tools | 177 |
| | 8.2 | Architecture and options for IT financial management tools | 179 |
| | 8.3 | How to evaluate and select a tool | 181 |

| **9** | **Terminology and definitions** | | **183** |
| | 9.1 | Definitions list | 183 |
| | 9.2 | Acronyms list | 193 |

| **10** | **Templates** | | **195** |
| | 10.1 | Levels of maturity according to the Process Maturity Framework | 195 |
| | 10.2 | ISO/IEC 20000 for IT financial management | 197 |
| | 10.3 | CobiT and IT financial management | 198 |
| | 10.4 | Techniques enabling improvement | 200 |

| **Appendix A. Basic concepts for IT service management** | | | **207** |
| | A1. | Good Practice | 207 |
| | A2. | Service | 207 |
| | A3. | Value | 208 |
| | A4. | Service management | 208 |
| | A5. | Systems | 208 |
| | A6. | Processes versus functions | 208 |
| | A7. | Process models | 210 |
| | A8. | Processes, procedures and work instructions | 213 |
| | A9. | Process and line in a matrix organization | 215 |
| | A10. | Process and maturity | 217 |
| | A11. | Core processes of a service provider | 220 |
| | A12. | Setting up functions in the service provider's organization | 221 |

| **Appendix B. Sources** | | | **225** |

| **Index** | | | **227** |

# Introduction

This book is intended to provide the reader with some general background and a little technical detail as regards the practice of IT financial management. It is assumed that the reader has an understanding of IT infrastructure and may well have read the relevant parts of the IT Infrastructure Library (ITIL). No matter which version of ITIL has been read, the material amounts to some fifty pages of general description of the activities involved in financial management for IT services. If the reader has read the financial management requirements identified in the ISO/IEC 20000 standard, they will appreciate that is a one page summary of the expected deliverables of the practice. This book extends the description of the practice to over 200 pages and goes into quite a bit more depth.

The target audience is anyone involved with IT financial management, whether as a practitioner or as a manager or working in related areas and seeking a better understanding of it. It should be recommended reading for those in any ITIL activity, be it strategic, tactical, or operational, as well as for customers (ITIL's term for end-user managers paying for the IT service). The book provides general descriptions of all the related activities and deliverables as well as many checklists going into some detail of tasks and data involved. Thus the book could be read from start to end but it is anticipated that for many readers a lot of value will lie in the individual checklists, the structures and graphics presented, and in the templates and appendices. It is entirely within the spirit of ITIL, and most authorities on the subject, that the reader chooses at will whether to adopt or adapt any part of this book. Take it or leave it. That was true of the first version of ITIL and is still true today.

The book is structured into ten chapters. The first chapter provides an introduction to IT financial management practices in the context of IT service management and chapter two expands on its background.

Chapter three reviews the benefits gained by adopting the practice of IT financial management.

Chapter four is one of the two longest chapters and outlines the activities, inputs, processing and outputs involved in IT financial management, and its relationships to other functions and processes.

Chapter five summarizes different perspectives of IT financial management.

Chapter six is the other very long chapter, discussing implementation issues.

Chapter seven outlines the management of the IT financial management practice and chapter eight describes the supporting tools.

Chapter nine presents the set of terms and definitions used throughout this book

Finally, chapter ten deals with maturity, and presents a series of checklists and templates that support the use of IT financial management, as well as a number of relevant frameworks.

Appendix A is essential to this book, as it provides the basic concepts for IT service management, and is the common philosophy for all books in the Best Practices series. It is important that anyone not fully aware of the differences between processes and functions reads this Appendix to avoid conceptual errors in the embedding of IT financial management in their organization. ITIL and IT service management are most often related to process-based approaches, and IT financial management can follow that approach. IT financial management in itself, however, clearly is a function (or 'practice'), an organizational capability, using people, processes and technology to accomplish its targets. In larger organizations it often is a department. This Appendix explains the approach to make that work.

Appendix B provides a list of useful sources for information on IT financial management.

At the end of this book you'll find an index to keywords and their location within the book.

# Acknowledgements

Following feedback from expert review, guidance on IT financial management has been high on the list for many professionals for a long time. The fact that existing publications offered limited information has led to many requests for more detailed and practical guidance. In the field, IT financial management is still one of the least-developed areas in IT service management.

So when we discussed this with Maxime Sottini, we were delighted to receive his offer to share his experience in this specific field, and extend the information on IT financial management with a practical guide. With his deep level of expertise, Maxime Sottini took the role of author in a team of expert editors of the ITSM Library. To ensure international knowledge and experience was reflected in the resulting guidance, a broad panel of experts was installed as a Review Team. This editorial team set the scope of the book by agreeing on an initial Table of Contents.

The project was then turned over to the author: he gathered the best practices on IT financial management, using his own experiences, existing literature and information from peers. The Review Team then added their personal experience and knowledge to the manuscript, ensuring that it was a balanced result, and reflected the knowledge of the entire editorial team. The result is this book: a thorough introduction to the field of IT financial management, with a lot of practical guidance.

We sincerely thank Maxime Sottini for his enthusiasm and persistence, and his willingness to listen to the reviewers and to seriously consider their issues. This has enabled us to develop a true *best practice* on IT financial management.

We also wish to thank our international Review Team that has contributed their experience and knowledge. They provided encouragement, criticism and useful new ideas, to ensure that the book reflects the very best practice.

A special thanks goes out to Kevin Holland who was a big help to us in the important preview phase of this book and the Best practice series as a whole.

The Review Team consisted of:
- Michael Busch, it SolutionCrew GmbH, Switzerland
- Rob Benyon, Rhodes University, South Africa
- Pierre Bernard, Pink Elephant Inc., Canada
- Janaki Chakravarthy, Infosys Technologies Limited, India
- Oscar A. Corbelli, New Horizons Madrid, Spain
- Kevin Ellis, Bank of Montreal, Canada
- Robert Falkowitz, Concentric Circle Consulting, Switzerland
- Simone Fuchs, SAP, Germany
- Kevin Holland, National Health Service, UK
- Brian Johnson, CA, USA

- Steve Tremblay, Excelsa Technologies Consulting Inc., Canada
- Antonio Valle Salas, G2 Gobierno y Gestión de TI, SL, Spain
- Jos de Vos, IBM, The Netherlands

Jan van Bon, Managing Editor

# 1 Context for IT financial management

## 1.1 Setting the scene

The importance of IT has dramatically grown in the past decades and is probably still growing. Many businesses are depending on IT to improve their efficiency and effectiveness, if not for surviving. As a consequence the IT budgets of most companies have increased substantially (Hitt, et al., 2002). In this scenario it has been proven (Kellar and Akel, 2003) that larger companies tend to invest more than smaller ones. This seems intuitive as, for example, in large organization the opportunity to improve efficiency by automating repetitive processes is higher and an important driver.

When it comes to understanding the link between IT investments and companies' performance, the situation becomes much less clear. By the end of 2000, research (Brynjolfsson, 1998) demonstrated that computerization did not lead to improved productivity. This result was known as the "productivity paradox". Possible explanations were given to justify this result but later studies (CSC, 2001; Brynjolfsson and Hitt, 1996; McKinsley and Company, 2002) have questioned the validity of the paradox. Analyzing the relationship between IT investments and companies' profitability did not lead to better results and, again, literature shows contradictory results. What seems evident is that, in all business sectors, some firms are more successful than others in transforming IT investments into value for the business (Kellar and Akel, 2003).

So, while the absolute value of IT investments is growing, the ability to profit from investments varies tremendously from firm to firm. IT financial management deals with the amount, the funding, the question how it is spent and the control of the money that organizations put in IT. Therefore, IT financial management is an important discipline for understanding and improving the capability to wisely spend this money and therefore to improve the profitability of the business.

The need to better plan, control and evaluate IT investments and spending is also boosted by globalization and growing competition. This is a very well-known topic and it brings, as a consequence, the need to quest and carefully control all investments and to put them into competition one against the other: only those that clearly contribute to achieving the goals of the organization should find adequate funding.

## 1.2 IT services and cost

In the perspective of IT services, IT financial management is certainly dealing with costs, which are often perceived as being related to quality of services (see Figure 1.1).

Without the introduction of innovative business models, products or services, there is a performance barrier which can't be crossed. This barrier establishes a relationship between costs and service quality (Fig. 1.2). IT organizations shall define how they want to position themselves,

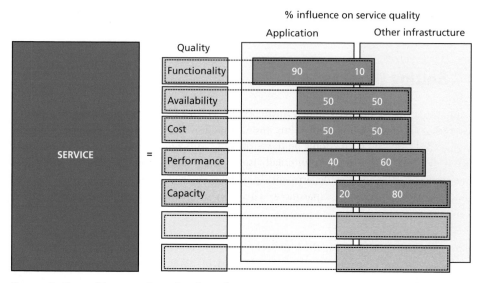

Figure 1.1 Cost is one of the core attributes of service quality

opting for low, average or high quality of services. They then have to control costs and minimize them as much as possible. This means trying to reach the performance barrier at the desired level of cost, until a breakthrough model or solution is found. IT financial management is a mandatory element in order to achieve this result.

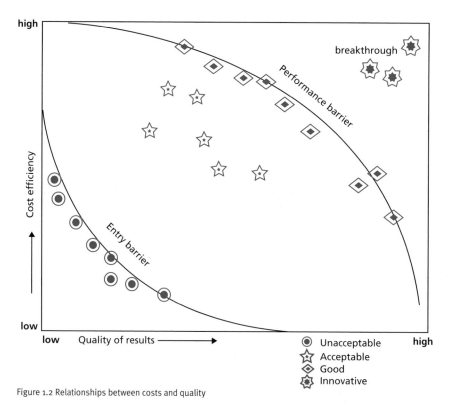

Figure 1.2 Relationships between costs and quality

This is one of the key reasons for the growing importance of IT financial management, which will be defined in more detail in the next chapter.

## 1.3    The nature of IT financial management

We can interpret IT financial management as the practice, or the function, managing the evaluation, planning, funding, controlling and charging of IT investments and costs. Financial management has always been a topic on the agenda of CIOs and it is born with IT. Historically, the IT department has often grown internally from what was previously known as "accounting", and nowadays as "the financial department. In many cases the IT department is still positioned as an element of the financial department. This is mainly due to the fact that the accounting and human resources systems (another typical organizational unit where IT department can be found) were among the first areas of automation. For this reason, in the 60s and early 70s, the IT people and resources were mainly allocated to the financial department. Later, as IT capabilities were improving and accounting systems were getting more mature, the focus moved towards automation of other parts of the business organization, but the IT department often stayed with the financial department.

Financial management has evolved too. Initially, the term was used for the function providing management accounting services to the whole organization. This was often known as the administration, or the administration and control department. Later, in the 80s, the role of this function has evolved, together with the concept of "value creation". Globalization and competition have leveraged the importance of strategic decisions and of planning and control. The administration department turned into an administration, finance and control department with new responsibilities such as the monitoring of the value of the organization, the evaluation of investment decisions from an economic/financial point of view, and the timely funding of resources to support the company's initiatives and projects. In parallel, the new function has been generally placed under direct responsibility of the CEO and often renamed into the administration, control and financial department or, more simply, the financial department (finance).

Like all other departments, IT too has been influenced by financial management, adopting the scope, rules and procedures defined by the financial department. Activities like investment management, budgeting, accounting and charging, which we will discuss in detail in this book, have grown in the financial management department and have been forced upon the other departments of the organizations. The scope, the structure, and the level of granularity of the output of the financial management activities were initially designed for the overall management of the organization. For example, the company budget was structured for each company function, including IT.

Additional rules, originating from the IT department, are often used to further detail the IT budget. This is generally done to better support the planning and controlling objectives of the IT department without overloading the central financial system with detailed information. For example, the IT budget is often structured per technology platform or function, such as windows vs. UNIX, or operations vs. application management. These additional details are then managed outside of the financial system.

So, on one side, the IT department needs to respect and apply the company rules regarding financial matters, and on the other side the day-by-day management of IT investments and costs may lead to specific views, rules and activities to be managed. Therefore, outside of the traditional domain of control of the financial management department, several financial topics are often managed by IT, with a consistent but different and specific approach requiring a mix of IT and financial skills.

One example area is project management, as many projects are dealing with IT. General rules are normally provided by the IT financial department, e.g. how to classify and manage project costs, or how to determine Return On Investment. Nevertheless the level of granularity required by the common financial policies for projects may be insufficient to provide full control of project costs. For example, there can be the need for a more granular view of cost types, or the need to manage resource activities by means of timesheets. Therefore the IT department may decide to manage financial topics with a different approach, but respecting and interfacing with the overall rules and financial practices of the company.

Another great example is the evolution of IT service management (ITSM). One of the main goals of the modern IT department is to supply IT services, aligned to the needs of the business, with agreed characteristics, levels of quality and at optimal costs. This "service orientation" is a tremendous shift in the IT perspective, driving a change of the point of view of many traditional activities. The benefits of this shift are relevant for financial management, as it has made the efforts of the IT department and the cost of IT services much more transparent and comprehensible for the business.

Although this may all seem to be straightforward and simple, it is often not the case. Defining a budget per IT service is absolutely different from and more difficult than budgeting for organizational functions. Furthermore, the financial department and the overall financial management activities may not be ready to address this important change. This is often becoming painfully clear in ISO/IEC 20000 initiatives recommending the definition of a budget and the accounting of costs per service. The traditional financial department and the designed company financial management policies, procedures and systems, may not be ready to deal with this shift. For example, financial management systems may not be ready to address the services as a required dimension in budgeting and accounting activities.

"IT financial management" with the service perspective in mind is core to this book, and will be perceived throughout the book as "financial management for IT services". This perspective is quite different from the traditional one, but it is becoming more and more important, with the growing acceptance of ITSM best practices, such as ITIL, or standards like ISO/IEC 20000.

Until now we have discussed the reason for the importance of IT financial management and we have seen that IT financial management may be entirely but more often partially part of financial management, although related, in terms of discipline as well as in terms of organization. All this applies to a context where IT is a department of a company that has some other kind of business as its core activity. When the company is an IT service provider in the open market, the difference between financial management and IT financial management fades away. This book will regularly address both perspectives.

# 1.4   IT financial management and the evolution of ITIL

ITIL is long established. The first version was created in the UK during 1986-1992 by a government agency, called CCTA – which later became part of the Office of Government Commerce (OGC). Version one consisted of over forty booklets, based to some extent on previous documented IBM Technical Labs ISMA manuals and other IT related sources. In that first ITIL edition, cost management aspects of IT financial management were addressed in the book "Cost Management for ICT Services", published in 1990.

The second version of ITIL emerged in 2000-2006. It reduced the number of main books to seven. Two of those were most read and provided the major material for ITIL certification: 'Service Delivery' and 'Service Support'. In ITIL version two, ITSM is largely defined as eleven practices and a function, with a chapter of 40-50 pages of generic description for each. In this second edition, IT financial management was addressed as one of the core practices of the 'Service Delivery book'.

ITIL version three has an emphasis on the service lifecycle. There are five books, Service Strategy, Service Design, Service Transition, Service Operation, and Continual Service Improvement. In essence, version three covers the whole suite of version two, including the previously neglected books. Each of these five books covers approximately three hundred pages (with some 100,000 – 150,000 words in each). In this third ITIL version, IT financial management is a topic of the 'Service Strategy' book, but the way it is addressed is quite complex and in some cases contradictory. On one side, ITIL V3 slightly modifies the nature of IT financial management compared to previous edition, now being "the function and processes responsible for managing an IT service provider's budgeting, accounting and charging requirements". In ITIL Service Strategy, IT financial management is seen as a strategic tool, enabling operational visibility, insight and superior decision making and positioned as part of a service economics paragraph. That paragraph also covers other items like Return On Investment (which is a technique, generally considered to be part of IT financial management), service portfolio management (a strategic practice supported by IT financial management), service portfolio management methods (describing a practice and tool to manage the service portfolio) and demand management (another important practice supported by IT financial management). Compared to version two, ITIL version three better explores and explains the reasons and mechanisms why IT financial management is relevant and supports the business. But version three lacks practical guidance and a clear description of processes and responsibilities.

The ITIL documentation is aimed at being a general recommendation as to Good Practice. So there is a need to consider such matters and that is usually achieved by reference to domain experts. These in turn attend conferences and read papers to keep up-to-date. This is achieved largely thanks to the work of professional organizations such as, in the domain of financial management, the Institute of Management Accountants (IMA) or the American Institute of Certified Public Accountants (AICPA) for the US. Similar associations are present in all the countries and they generally have a long tradition and history, although they are not specifically dedicated to IT topics. More recently, associations with specific interest for IT financial management have been founded, such as the IT Financial Management Association (ITFMA).

ITIL version three has increased the number of ITSM practices from ten to as much as twenty-six, although the exact figure is under debate. In ITIL version three the ten ITIL practices of version two now have additional practices to cater for areas such as business relationship management, event management, and knowledge management, but also more detailed practices like service validation & testing, service portfolio management, access management and service reporting. Version two had one related function, the service desk. Version three presents several additional related functions, e.g. application management, technical management, and IT operations management.

This distinction between process, sub-processes, (groups of) activities and functions, as presented in ITIL version three, appears to be not entirely consistent within the ITIL definitions and acronyms. Applying ITIL's own definition of process to the sections that are labeled 'process' in version three also reveals that most of these sections are not described in terms of the process definition at all, and this is particularly true for IT financial management. So the word practice would be much more in line with ITIL's recognition as a set of Good or Best Practices.

*In this book we'll show how IT financial management can be perceived in an organizational context, and how it relates to process and function dimensions. For practical reasons we'll use the term IT financial management practice to indicate all activities involved with IT financial management.*

## 1.5    Parameters influencing IT financial management

ITIL talks of People, Process and Products (i.e. services, technology, tools) as the key interrelated entities concerned with the establishment of an effective ITSM practice regime. Complementary books and ISO/IEC 20000 tend to expand this to the four P's speaking of People, Process, Products and Partners (i.e. suppliers, manufacturers, vendors). This book extends the alliteration by adding Price. This arises because another characteristic of a description like ITIL is that it describes a perfect environment with the solution being applied across the board to all services and all configuration items thus ensuring total cover. In the real world such an approach requires too many staff and it costs too much. In the light of the money available, the team available and the likely benefits, a budget is established within which the practice has to live. So effort has to be focused and inevitably a categorization of services is introduced to identify those that are 'mission critical', 'key', 'production' and 'other' (or something alike). Then, for the mission critical services, the entire solution is applied in full, with less rigorous interpretation of all the related activities applied as the priority of the service decreases.

However, when considering financial management from an IT services perspective, the scope is restricted. In ITIL version 2 and ISO/IEC 20000, the final goal is to budget and account for the costs of service provision (charging is out of scope in ISO/IEC 20000). Some specific objectives are clearly distinguishable.

The objectives for **budgeting** are to:
- predict the money required to run IT services
- ensure that actual spend can be compared with predicted spend
- reduce the risk of overspending or underspending
- ensure that revenues are available to cover predicted spend (where charging is in place)

The objectives for **accounting** are to:
- account for the money spent
- account for revenues
- calculate the cost of providing IT services
- perform cost-benefit or return-on-investment analyses
- identify the cost of changes

Finally, the objectives for **charging** are to:
- recover the costs of the IT services
- operate the IT organization as a business unit (making profit) if required
- influence user and customer behavior

Another specific goal of financial management for IT services in ITIL (version 2) is to assist management decisions on IT investment by providing detailed business cases for changes to IT services.

ITIL version 3 describes the IT organization as similar to a market-facing company, further developing the concept of the business unit that was introduced in version 2. The IT organization should develop IT services that can create value for its customers. From this perspective, financial management aims to support the IT organization with data and analysis in order to define strategies, in terms of a service portfolio, and control their results. Service valuation becomes an important objective: the determination of the total cost of delivering an IT service and the total value to the business that uses the service.

The goals and objectives described above can be shown as an evolutionary path for IT financial management (Figure 2.1).

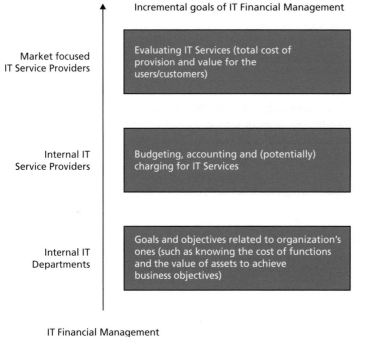

Figure 2.1 Incremental goals and maturity of IT financial management

## 2.3   IT financial management maturity levels

With the evolutionary path described in Figure 2.1 in mind, it is important to understand each of the evolutionary steps. These steps, or scenarios, will be used frequently in this book to enable a better understanding of the relevance and the context of the main topics discussed here. We will examine each of the scenarios in turn.

### 2.3.1   Scenario 1: IT financial management for internal IT departments

As we have seen earlier, there are different degrees of maturity in providing IT services. The first level is an IT department acting as an internal function and providing applications and infrastructures to the business. At this level of maturity, the IT department has probably not yet defined a Service Catalog and it communicates with the business in terms of applications, management of IT systems and evolutionary IT projects. The budget is generally structured around the IT organization (functions) and the activities/projects that it manages. The IT department is involved in the financial department's activities with objectives, roles and schedules defined by financial or corporate management. The core financial topics are the evaluation of new investments in IT, the determination of actual costs versus budget and financial plans. Charging mechanisms of the department's cost are rarely defined. Where a charging mechanism is in place, it is unlikely to be driven by the consumption of services.

Typical activities where IT is involved at this level are:
- **Financial planning** – The activity of predicting and controlling the spending of money to achieve business objectives in the medium/long term (for example a three-year horizon). This includes IT investments and operating costs, so the IT department participates by preparing its forecast based on the business (or industrial) development plan; the level of detail of data is medium to low.
- **Budgeting** – The activity of predicting and controlling the spending of money throughout the budgetary period (usually one year) to achieve business objectives; it also includes IT investments and operating costs. The IT department participates by preparing its forecast; the level of detail of data is medium to high. The budget forecast fits with the financial plan (see previous activity) for the corresponding budgetary year. One or more reviews of the budget may be necessary or planned during the budgetary period to check and identify the need for significant changes.
- **Accounting** – The activity enabling the organization to account for the amount of money and the way it is spent; this is done by means of ledgers, usually defined by the financial department. The IT department normally contributes but does not lead the activity; for example, recording of financial documents (such as passive invoices) is usually performed by the financial department's personnel, although some activities can be executed by the IT department (for example issuing requests for purchase). Accounting is strictly related to passive cycle activities (see glossary), such as procurement and order management.
- **Managing deviations** – Analyzing balance data and comparing with the budget may identify significant deviations that need to be dealt with. Analysis may be performed by the central financial department or simply coordinated by it and executed by the IT department.
- **Evaluating investments** – The activity of estimating all costs associated with an investment and comparing them with the revenues and/or savings in order to determine its economic benefit; the rules for evaluation are established by the financial department but the actual evaluation is typically executed by the IT department.

The financial department usually performs other financial activities, such as preparing balance sheets and profit and loss accounts, handling depreciation, evaluating assets, allocating and apportioning money to other departments as well as charging departments or companies for the use of IT. At this level, we generally speak of IT costs and their allocation and/or apportioning to business units and/or other departments of the organization, primarily based on the general financial structure of the business.

### 2.3.2 Scenario 2: IT financial management for internal IT service providers

At this level of maturity the IT department identified and adopted the service management approach and philosophy, even if it still provides services to a captive market, typically for a specific company or a group of related companies. This is generally because the IT department needs to provide better support to the business or simply to improve the quality of IT and optimize the costs by adopting well proven best practices and approaches. It has identified the services supplied and determined how to handle financial management information at this level, with the aim of charging for IT services, whether actually or notionally. For example, the IT department can detail the budget and can also account for each service; it may also have the ability to identify impacts on the service budget based on changes. The IT department's approach may be compatible with the practice and the general accounting structure of the company, but this is unlikely. More often, it is necessary to merge the traditional financial view (based on the analysis of the costs of departments, functions, products or other relevant core business information) with the new service oriented view.

The service oriented approach and/or processes of IT financial management may not fit the general IT financial approach and/or processes. There could be several reasons for this. IT services are not elements of core business; the central financial department might not have a mature ITSM culture; or there might be constraints within the central supporting financial management system. At this level of maturity, it is often necessary to build a dedicated IT financial management system, which will support specific needs as the IT department starts to think of itself as a company within the company, selling its products/services and managing them from a financial point of view too. This way of thinking may also lead to specialized skills and to an organizational function within IT, responsible for managing financial matters. The need to work with the centrally managed financial processes will continue, as described in the earlier level of maturity, and financial data has to be reconciled between the central system and processes and those of the IT department.

This is probably the most difficult level of maturity to manage because different financial cultures, needs and objectives will coexist in the same company. Many of the financial activities have the same title as those of the previous level but their content and approach is significantly different:
- **Financial planning** – This activity is the same as the previous level. Service orientation may influence how financial information is collected, but the structure of the financial plan will probably continue to follow the corporate approach and rules.
- **Budgeting** – There will usually be two activities. One will be similar to that of the previous level, with the aim of feeding data into the organization's global budget. A second activity may be present, with the objective to budget for the specific costs of the IT services; this will interface closely with the first activity. Budgeting by service may be significantly more complex than budgeting by function. This activity will also be performed autonomously, with restricted scope, each time a new IT service is designed and implemented or significantly changed. The traditional budget by function, needed for the organization's overview, may be derived from the IT services budget. In a mature environment, the financial department has very flexible and sophisticated supporting systems. It would be able to support the specifics of the IT department; a new combined procedure might be set in place.
- **Accounting** – this activity is very similar to the one of the previous level of maturity. Here the main issue is to record data only once, being able to feed both sets of financial views and details – by function and by service.
- **Forecasting** – a specific objective of IT service management is to check for deviations between the budget and the current costs of IT services. This can be done in two ways. The first is to have a budget disaggregated for each accounting period (for example monthly) and to compare the corresponding balance; the second is to forecast periodically for the entire costs and revenues of the IT services for the whole budgeted period and to compare them with the corresponding total budget. The forecasting activity supports this second approach and can be run periodically (e.g. each month or each quarter). Significant deviations are communicated to the budget review, which is a distinct activity. Forecasting activities may be found among the organization's financial management practices but periodic budgeting checks and reviews

are a more frequent practice. IT service management practices and standards (e.g. ISO/IEC 20000) have explicit requirements to forecast for the cost of providing IT services.

- **Managing deviations** – Deviations from budget may be identified from the forecasting activity or from the budgeting activity of new or changed specific IT services; these deviations will need to be managed. There may be a review of the budget or authorization of extra expenditure, keeping the initial budget unchanged. Significant deviations for specific IT services do not necessarily lead to relevant deviations from the overall IT budget and, therefore, from the organization's overall budget.

- **Charging** – A mature IT service oriented organization has good control of IT service costs and consumption. This is the prelude to charging IT services, which is useful in influencing users' behavior. But in a captive market, typical at this level, there can still be the need for transferring IT costs in line with corporate policies and rules (e.g. the turnover of the business units). In an international context, the principles and motivation for charging may be derived from laws and regulations dealing with the transfer of profits among organizations and, ultimately, taxation. Charging is strongly influenced by corporate strategies.

- **Evaluating investments** – This activity is the same as in Scenario 1. Methods and rules to evaluate IT investments are usually defined by the central financial department and also used by the IT department.

### 2.3.3 Scenario 3: IT financial management for market IT service providers

This is the context of an IT service provider competing in the market. Provision of IT services is the core business of the business unit or the stand-alone organization. Some initial customers may be found among companies belonging to the same group or stockholders (shareholders) but the target mission is, sooner or later, to compete in the market. In this context, there should be no difference between financial management and IT financial management. This is not entirely true as an internal IT department will probably still exist in the IT service provider; this internal department will probably act as seen in earlier levels of maturity (for example as in Scenario 1). However, with the term IT financial management we will not refer to the possible financial management of the IT internal function but to the financial management of the whole service provider. With this meaning in mind we can start to examine the activities at this level of maturity:

- **Financial planning** – The activity of predicting and controlling the spending of money to achieve the business objectives in the medium/long term (for example a three-year horizon); the level of detail of data is medium to low. The activity involves the whole organization; it is owned by top management and run with the support of the (IT) financial department.

- **Budgeting** – The activity of predicting and controlling the spending of money to achieve the business objectives for the budgetary period (usually one year). The budget forecast must fit the financial plan (see previous activity) for the corresponding budgetary year. One or more reviews of the budget may be performed during the budgetary period to check and identify the need for significant changes. The budget is normally defined at product/service level, as supplied to final customers. The activity involves the whole organization and it is normally the responsibility of the (IT) financial department.

- **Accounting** – The activity that enables the organization to account for the way money is spent; this is done by means of ledgers. The (IT) financial department leads the activity and plays an important role in related activities (e.g. recording documents such as passive invoices).

- **Forecasting** – Organizations in the open market often manage budget by period (e.g. monthly). This is driven by the need for a more precise management of financial matters to ensure that the required resources are available to run the business. Deviations may be identified by simply comparing budget with actual spend; a forecast activity may not be necessary, especially if reviews of budget are planned.
- **Managing deviations** – Control of actual spend against budget or budgeting for new or changed specific IT services may cause deviations from plans. These identified deviations have to be managed. There may be a review of the initial budget or authorization of extra expenditure, keeping the budget unchanged.
- **Charging** – An IT service provider playing in the market has to define tariffs and to charge for the consumption of services. Many different charging models can be applied. This is a critical activity where the main roles are usually played by the marketing and sales functions, together with the (IT) financial department.
- **Evaluating investments** – Methods and rules to evaluate IT investments are normally defined by the (IT) financial department and used by others.

The scenarios described above will be referred to throughout this book. Specific topics can be inherent to one or more of these scenarios; we will also refer to the scenarios to explain the possible differences or implementations.

## 2.4 Scope

We have learned from the section above that the meaning and scope of IT financial management greatly depends on context. In Scenario 1, IT financial management for internal IT departments, the scope is part of the wider financial management, in terms of activities, but also of items to deal with (e.g. only costs related to IT). In Scenario 2, IT financial management for internal IT service providers, the scope may be wider compared to the previous scenario. The IT department may be autonomous and decide to build a specific set of functions and a more detailed view (for example, by IT service) of financially relevant data. Finally, in Scenario 3, IT financial management for market IT service provider, the scope of IT financial management is interpreted as equivalent to financial management.

In this book, we will frequently focus on Scenarios 2 and 3, for example for activities. In Scenario 1 IT is generally viewed as one of the company's many internal departments, and its specific needs may be ignored by top management. Organization, activities, etc. may be very different from company to company and far from a common IT service management best practice.

Our attention will be dedicated to those aspects of financial management that are specific to IT and their relationships with the company's cross-departmental activities. For example, we will not focus on the financial planning activity crossing the entire organization; but we will explore its interfaces with IT specific practices; or we will examine IT specific activities within it.

Figure 2.2 graphically represents the activities and the scenarios in this book. Other perspectives are not ignored here but better guidance is found for them in other publications.

| Activities ⬇  Scenarios ⬆  ☑ In scope | Internal IT departments | Internal IT service providers | IT market service providers |
|---|---|---|---|
| Financial Planning | | | ✓ |
| Budgeting (and reviews) | | ✓ | ✓ |
| Accounting | | ✓ | ✓ |
| Forecasting | | ✓ | ✓ |
| Managing deviations | | ✓ | ✓ |
| Charging | | ✓ | ✓ |
| Evaluating investments | | ✓ | ✓ |

Figure 2.2 Scope of the book

## 2.5 Specific elements of IT financial management

There are different specifics of IT financial management when compared to other service management practices, such as incident management or capacity management.

First, financial management is a common discipline applied to other departments in the organization; it is characterized by a shared culture, vocabulary and often by common activities and supporting tools. It inherits constraints and/or interfaces, which are clearly identified when addressing activities or structural changes. For example, there is the definition of which costs should be managed as capital expenses and which are operational expenses. This is normally part of the organization's general accounting policies and approach, in compliance with external regulations, such as General Accepted Accounting Procedures (GAAP), which are followed by all departments. Another example relates to the timing of budgeting, often dictated by the organization's timetable with input/output relationships among the activities of the different functions or departments (e.g. business initiatives, such as the building of a new plant, which would need to be known before defining the budget for IT services).

Another important specific is that IT financial management practices, as we will see later, are closely interfaced and related to other practices, especially those belonging to the passive cycle (activities starting from the identification of a need for buying something and concluding with the payment for the goods/services purchased). A decision about the detail of the accounting level may influence the complexity in other areas of the organization, such as the purchasing department or administration. For instance, if we decide to manage costs by service, orders to suppliers would probably be split accordingly, which might lead to a significant increment of the number of items to be recorded in orders and invoices. This decision could finally lead to higher costs for the purchasing activities. In this case, there has to be a careful evaluation of the benefits and the decision shared with all involved parties, as others (typically the purchasing department and/or the corporate financial department) may be strongly affected by it.

Because of these inter-relationships with other practices, another specific is also related to the tool supporting the IT financial management practices. With other IT service management practices the supporting tools are quite independent from other departments in the organization, although very much integrated in the service management domain. In the case of IT financial management, supporting tools are often those managing the overall organization's financial practices or, if independent, they are closely integrated with them. Whether to adopt and adapt the existing tools or to interface new specific tools is a key decision to be taken.

# 3 Perspectives and benefits of IT financial management

## 3.1 Perspectives and benefits of IT financial management

IT financial management generates benefits according to the scenarios described in the previous chapter. The different perspectives typical of each scenario are the key to understanding them and to understanding the points of view of the different roles involved in IT service management practices: customers, users, the financial department and IT staff. Before starting the analysis of perspectives and points of view, it is useful to explain the difference between 'customer' and 'user'. Customers of IT services are the decision makers, who are responsible for the acquisition of services and paying for them. Users are those actually receiving and using IT services. In some cases users and customers may correspond but this is not always the case.

### 3.1.1 Scenario 1, internal IT departments

In Scenario 1, IT financial management is part of corporate financial management. IT is one of the many departments providing services to the business unit(s). In some cases, the importance of this support may be extremely relevant but sometimes IT is not perceived as adding value to the business and it is often considered simply as a cost center necessary to run the business. In this scenario customers (e.g. a business unit) cannot choose and think of IT to be an unavoidable cost, based on general criteria such as the number of users, number of workstations, bandwidth usage, etc. and not always linked to the use and/or quality of IT services. IT financial management is generally not designed to help with understanding of the contribution (value added) of IT to the business. In many cases, at least in small to medium organizations, it is not designed at all, in the sense that it is entirely part of corporate financial management and therefore targeted to corporate aims.

The benefits of (IT) financial management in this context are described and ranked in Figure 3.1 according to the probability of experiencing them. This probability depends on the processes implemented and on the culture and maturity achieved by the organization. At this level of maturity, the most common positive effect experienced is financial compliance, which is the ability to assess whether actual raising of funds and spending comply with the budget mandate, which in turn complies with the overall corporate plans.

Financial compliance is ensured by the management of budgeting and accounting activities and by the fact that these activities are governed by the financial management department. Another relevant benefit experienced is the ability to demonstrate how money is spent: knowledge of costs. This is derived from the accounting management activity.

Besides these two common benefits, organizations may also be able to evaluate investments correctly and therefore optimize them. This depends mainly on the maturity of the organization, as there is not always adequate culture and good practices in place to systematically calculate the advantages of projects (see also section 6.5.15 for further information on how returns can be

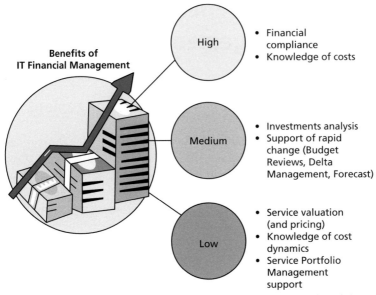

**Benefits of
IT Financial Management**

High
- Financial compliance
- Knowledge of costs

Medium
- Investments analysis
- Support of rapid change (Budget Reviews, Delta Management, Forecast)

Low
- Service valuation (and pricing)
- Knowledge of cost dynamics
- Service Portfolio Management support

Figure 3.1 Benefits of IT financial management for Scenario 1, ranked according to the probability of experiencing them

calculated). This benefit arises when an investment evaluation activity is well defined, interfaced with project management and working properly.

Another set of activities may support flexibility in the face of change and reduce the risks related to business change. These activities are budget review, forecasting and management of deltas (deviations) between forecasts and budgets. In Scenario 1, budget review is commonly in place while it is less usual to find forecasting activities. Management of deltas is probably an existing activity but it might not be optimally triggered because of several reasons: the periodic forecast activity is not run or is run with insufficient frequency, reliability of budget articulation by period is insufficient or there is no articulation at all for comparisons with actual values.

*In Scenario 1, IT financial management for internal IT departments, the benefit of IT financial management that is most often experienced is the ability to determine and assess compliance of spending according to budget and to demonstrate how money is spent. Some organizations may also experience improved decision making, deriving from financial evaluation of investments and changes.*

### 3.1.2  Scenario 2, internal IT service providers

In Scenario 2, IT financial management for internal IT service providers, we assume that IT has changed its approach: it will no longer consider itself as a cost center and it will no longer be viewed as a cost center by the rest of the organization but as a 'service center' where money spent clearly returns value to the customers' business. To obtain and maintain this reputation, the core focus of the IT organization shifts and concentrates on value creation. The support of IT financial management is needed to evaluate the creation of value and to compare it with the cost of creating it. This is usually done by means of IT services, the core object of all these evaluations. In medium-sized organizations and, especially, in large organizations the effort and requirement to support this perspective will lead to IT financial management as an independent function, probably still strongly interfaced to corporate financial management or perhaps still a subset of the corporate function.

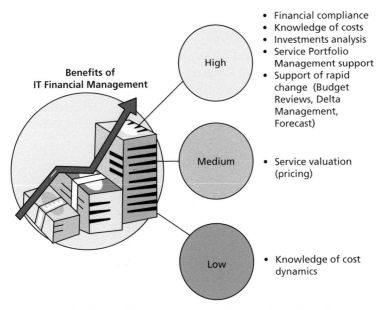

Figure 3.2 Benefits of IT financial management for Scenario 2, ranked according to the probability of experiencing them

Figure 3.2 illustrates the increasingly experienced relevance and benefits of IT financial management in this scenario. It is not only about the range of activities covered, which is a wider scope than in Scenario 1, but also the structure and detail of information. IT financial management starts to manage the costs and (probably) revenues of IT services, ideally by individual service, instead of those of IT globally or by department. The traditional benefits of IT financial management remain: financial compliance and knowledge of costs.

The challenge of providing value to customers by means of services emphasizes the need for support and, therefore, the benefits of IT financial management. Investment analysis becomes fundamental to support decisions, for example whether new or changed services will provide value to customers. Service portfolio management is supported too, to make it easier to identify and concentrate efforts on services that provide greater value to customers. Finally, supplementing controlled flexibility with forecasts and delta management activities contributes to the assurance that value is constantly maintained in situations of environmental and business changes.

In this scenario, another relevant benefit may derive from service valuation, if charging is applied and prices are calculated on the basis of value provided by the service. This is intuitive but not all the organizations in Scenario 2 are charging for services; very few of them use value as the basis for charging, because it is difficult to determine.

*In Scenario 2, IT financial management for internal IT service providers, the focus of IT shifts to the value of services for customers. Benefits deriving from IT financial management increase proportionally to its contribution to value creation, control and charging. Traditional benefits still remain: assurance of compliance and knowledge of costs.*

### 3.1.3   Scenario 3, market IT service providers

In Scenario 3, IT financial management for market IT service providers, IT financial management merges the role of financial management in non IT organizations with its role as in Scenario 2. Its core business is IT, so financial management manages all aspects of Scenario 2 and other activities, such as fund raising, taxation, etc. In this scenario, it becomes more difficult to classify the relevance of benefits of IT financial management as done before, because of its pervasive and central role. All the following are relevant benefits, as described in Figure 3.3:

- financial compliance
- knowledge of costs
- investment analysis
- support of service portfolio management
- support of rapid change (budget reviews, delta management, forecast)
- service valuation (and pricing)

**Benefits of
IT Financial Management**

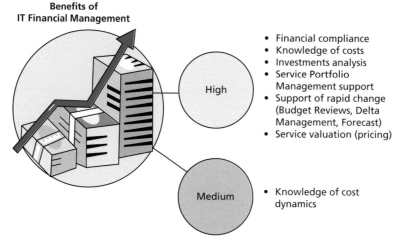

- Financial compliance
- Knowledge of costs
- Investments analysis
- Service Portfolio Management support
- Support of rapid change (Budget Reviews, Delta Management, Forecast)
- Service valuation (pricing)

- Knowledge of cost dynamics

Figure 3.3 Benefits of IT financial management for Scenario 3= ranked according to the probability of experiencing them

Compared with Scenario 2, determination of the value and price of the IT services supplied becomes increasingly important, together with developing extensive knowledge and control of costs. This means better understanding of cost dynamics – for example, what happens, from a financial point of view, if the number of servers or users increases? IT financial management, besides the traditional benefits related to compliance and investment analysis, contributes greatly to strategy definition for the provision of services and to some operational tasks typical of marketing and/or pre-sales, such as price definition. This enables better business decisions and optimal decision making for services, which ultimately contributes to the organization's competitiveness and survival.

In this scenario, financial management also deals with activities not detailed in this book, such as management of capital structure, distribution of profits to shareholders, tactical financing (such as how to fund required resources), taxation and management of the relationship with banks. These activities bring additional relevant benefits.

### 3.1.4   Stakeholders' perspectives and benefits

In this section we discuss the points of view of some important stakeholders of IT financial management and the benefits for them. The identified stakeholders are: customers, users, IT staff and management. The difference between customers and users has already been described. It is now useful to understand what we mean by management: we will refer to the top management of the organization which includes some representation from the IT department (primarily the Chief Information Officer – CIO).

**Customers**

Customers are always well identified in Scenario 2 and 3; but in Scenario 1 they may not be clearly targeted. In Scenario 1, IT financial management might not be perceived yet as an independent function and set of activities but as part of overall corporate financial management, so we do not discuss this scenario further here. Instead, we will concentrate on those where IT financial management is perceived by the customers. In Scenario 2 and 3, IT financial management will be mainly seen as the function (and the set of activities) responsible for charging for IT services. To be effective, formal agreements should be managed by service level management; new requests, as well as budget, should be managed by demand management activities, which should interface with IT financial management. The direct benefit, for the customer, is to establish a clear interface to gather and discuss information about charges. The indirect benefit is that charges are determined on the basis of deeper knowledge of costs and cost dynamics; thus there is better knowledge to isolate the costs relating to a specific customer and to charge only for those costs. An obvious additional advantage is that charges may be made transparent: more comprehensible and easier to understand. This is likely to improve relationships between customers and IT over time. However, all this is not necessarily true for Scenario 3, where market dynamics and providers' strategies will determine actual charges and relationships with service providers also depend on the competition.

**Users**

Users are influenced by IT financial management, especially by means of charging. The price will influence the consumption of IT services. For example, if a department is charged more when using applications within specific working hours, it will probably make an effort to avoid the higher charges by keeping within the agreed level of consumption. The main benefit of IT financial management, from the users' perspective, is having a function (and practices) that provides information on consumption and the costs of using IT services. However, attention to costs can lead to inappropriate behavior, for example sharing of accounts, which must be monitored and detected as soon as possible because of the risk of associated problems such as security issues.

**IT department and staff**

The IT department is greatly dependent on financial management; the benefits for its staff are all those identified in section 3.1.1, 3.1.2 and 3.1.3, depending on the specific scenario. IT financial management ensures that costs are budgeted and controlled to comply with corporate objectives and targets, as well as those of the IT department. IT financial management also provides vital information on the most advantageous investments and helps to optimize costs continuously. Knowledge about costs is also fundamental to correct pricing and any decision about changed or new services. IT departments should experience the full range of benefits deriving from IT financial management, depending on the scenario relevant to their circumstances.

## Management

In Scenario 3 there is no difference between IT and the business and the whole set of benefits described in section 3.1.3 should be experienced by management. The role of IT financial management is vital because the survival of the organization depends on it. Correct financial planning, budgeting and pricing will contribute to the key decisions of management, which will affect the fortunes of the organization.

In Scenario 2 and, especially, Scenario 1 a key benefit of IT financial management for management is its contribution to compliance and alignment with corporate objectives. As for all other departments or business units, IT financial management will ensure that IT investments and other IT costs are defined and controlled in line with corporate objectives and targets and that financial policies are actually followed.

Another important benefit may be experienced by management, especially in Scenario 2. If the costs of IT services are defined on the basis of a relevant quota of their direct components, this should lead to improved transparency and better relationships with customers. Because of transparency, the real cost of services is visible and better understood. This transparency facilitates benchmarking with other market IT service providers, leading to optimized sourcing and/or charging decisions for specific IT services too. Transparency and evidence of an increasing component of direct costs in IT services (e.g. hardware, software, labor costs) helps to reduce disputes with customers. However, there is a negative side-effect of transparency: if the IT organization's performance is poor, the business might look for more convenient alternatives (e.g. outsourcing services) if free to do so.

Independent of the scenarios, support of greater flexibility is an important benefit for management. IT financial management can provide quick answers about IT matters and frequent questions related to business decisions, such as: how much will IT services cost if we are going to open a new office or plant? What are the IT costs to be considered if we add a specific number of new users deriving from an acquisition?

## 3.2   Costs of IT financial management

There will be initial and ongoing costs associated with any implementation and execution of activities. For IT financial management, the initial costs to be considered are:
- staff and consultancy to design and implement organizational and process changes
- staff and consultancy to design and implement automation, including interfaces with external processes, functions, and related supporting tools
- procurement of infrastructure (e.g. hardware, middleware, bandwidth) and of supporting tools (applications for IT financial management)

- recruitment and training of resources to run the target activities
- accommodation, utilities and travel expenses to manage the change
- project management
- costs of defining the baseline (e.g. assessing the initial situation), which may be run as a project itself with all related costs (e.g. internal effort, external consultancy, etc.)

Ongoing costs are:
- staff to execute activities (internal or external)
- materials, consumables
- services (external, such as consultancy, and internal)
- maintenance fees for infrastructure and supporting tools
- costs of maintaining knowledge and skills (training)
- costs of continual improvement

Section 3.2.1 details the costs listed above.

### 3.2.1   Initial set-up costs

By initial set-up costs, we mean all those related to the set-up of IT financial management in one of the target scenarios described. Few organizations will be starting from scratch and some of the activities will already exist. However, management will often consider that the current level of support of IT financial management is not sufficient and decide to run a new project to improve the situation. The objectives of the project will include one or more of the following: implementing new practices, significantly changing existing practices, improving the level of automation. We will describe how to implement IT financial management in detail in Chapter 6. Here we will concentrate only on possible costs associated with the project.

Design, implementation and set-up of the target organization and practices will require internal commitment and staff; very often, external consultancy will also be required. Internal staff will be involved in running day-to-day activities; their available time may be not sufficient, if the target situation is considerably different from the starting point. In addition, external support is often a key enabler in breaking down barriers in strongly entrenched environments, where a long history of operating practices exists; external resources are seen as independent and are listened to more often. External resources may also be valuable when making the transition from one of the previously described scenarios to another. Internal knowledge and perspective may be not adequate and the support of experienced external resources is recommended to avoid errors and shorten implementation. External support is also useful to set the baseline, one of the important steps of continual service improvement, which is recommended before starting activities. This is often done by means of assessment techniques and benchmarks; the help of external experts, used with these approaches, may greatly facilitate the task.

An often underestimated cost of the design phase is related to the retrieval and preparation of data to test and set up changed or new cost models (see section 6.5.8 for further details about cost models) and cost apportioning models (see section 6.5.10 for further details about cost apportioning models). Testing, usually performed before final automation, is strongly recommended to verify the validity and the results of target models before their adoption. Retrieving information and performing apportioning (in order to test) without adequate supporting tools (automation) is a time intensive task. The cost of the task depends on the level of detail of models, which also drives the cost of related activities. For example, if we need more data because the aim is to analyze costs of services per activity, such as incident or change management, this will lead to increased detail of information to be gathered and managed during the test period and later on.

External support will probably be significant in the case of a new tool to be introduced to automate IT financial management practices too. Competencies and resources will be needed in order to prepare analysis, customize or implement the tool, install and setup the new solution. This is not the only cost associated with automation, as new infrastructure (such as servers) and license fees of software may be required. Another cost element to be included is the cost of interfacing critical processes and related supporting tools, such as asset management and all the monitoring systems used to gather information needed to calculate costs and/or apportion them. The cost of automation is usually significant as only small organizations can support effective IT financial management efficiently without tools. Fortunately, some important tools for automation such as the accounting systems (further discussed in section 6.5.5), are often already present and operating.

As we will see (Chapter 5), new practices will probably require changes to existing roles or new roles to be introduced; changes in the organization (e.g. new functions or departments) have to be expected too. This may require skill inventories to search for matching profiles; when good matches with internal resources cannot be found, there will be a need for recruitment. Nearly always, costs for training are also expected.

Where the change is large enough to justify using a project-based approach, additional categories of costs will need to be considered – for example, the use of offices and utilities for the project teams, travel expenses for presentations, coordination meetings and communications. Coordinating and managing the project is another element of cost to be considered. In many cases, project management will be mandatory and specific roles will have to be set up (typically project manager, project management office) which, again, will require internal staff and/or recruitment of external resources and/or acquisition of external services.

Initial set-up costs should be calculated to identify all the resources needed until all the targeted changes are implemented and signed off by the IT financial management practice owner.

### 3.2.2  Ongoing costs

Ongoing costs are those related to the day-to-day execution of IT financial management practices, to support other departments or external functions (e.g. accounting, controlling, legal department, government authorities) and to perform small changes for continual improvements. Major changes and their associated costs should be managed as described for initial set-up costs – that is, by means of specific projects.

The most obvious ongoing cost is related to the internal or external staff needed to run processes. While some relevant roles, discussed in Chapter 5, are usually internal and full-time or allocated for a considerable amount of time so that related costs are easy to identify (e.g. IT financial manager), many others spend just a small proportion of their time to run IT financial management practices and it may be difficult to determine their associated costs. The cost of external staff, in this phase, is often associated with professionals or consulting organizations with expertise on financial matters to provide information about compliance issues and the evolution of regulatory aspects.

The cost of running IT financial management practices is influenced by the level of detail of data to be managed and the level of automation. This has been highlighted in section 3.2.1 earlier. For example, if detailed information is required on how the time of IT service management staff is spent, the introduction and management of meticulous time management (based on timesheets) will lead to greater effort. Another example is the passive cycle (see glossary), including orders and invoices registration. A higher level of detail and direct allocation of costs to IT services will require a higher number of records to be managed. For example, if a large contract with a supplier for server management exists, orders and invoices could be detailed at different levels: customer, service, service/activity. Managing information by service would lead to higher effort (e.g. internal requests for purchase, orders, and invoices recorded with details by service) if compared to managing information traditionally (e.g. by function).

A higher level of detail is not necessarily a positive thing. It becomes useful only if this leads to valuable information and reporting that is requested and used to control or make decisions. Otherwise, it just add costs; an optimal balance needs to be found.

The costs of materials and consumables are directly related to the relevance of paper support in the organization and the number of reports and analyses produced. This can range from a small amount, in paperless contexts, to substantial costs, in large organizations with a traditional paper oriented approach.

Supporting tools, infrastructure (e.g. servers) and facilities need to be maintained and updated to remain effective. This is frequent, especially for solutions supporting IT financial management, and it does not only imply maintenance fees for dedicated hardware and software. Competencies and staff are needed to update the configuration of tools or even to customize them to support required changes (e.g. new functionalities, reporting, adaptation to regulatory constraints, interfaces, etc.). This maintenance service might be supplied by the IT department, by external staff or both, according to available competencies. It is wise to carefully budget for these costs too.

Changes in turnover, changes of business context and regulatory constraints (such as rules to manage depreciation or accruals or rules to design reporting, such as profit and loss statements) mean that there is a constant need for updating and adjusting the knowledge of resources involved in the practices. There will need to be a budget for training costs.

Finally, as we have already anticipated and we will explain further in Chapter 7, there is a continual need for improving practices and this applies to IT financial management too. The IT department should adopt and perform one of the numerous available approaches for improvement, such as the Deming Cycle (Plan-Do-Check-Act) and should be prepared to fund the costs associated to set up and run it (again staff, external services, tools, etc.). These costs should be budgeted as this effort is often not compatible with day-to-day routine and because, usually, specific tools or implementations are needed, for example to monitor performances of the practices. In the Plan-Do-Check-Act approach there is an ongoing component of costs (to support monitoring and analysis) and also an ad hoc component, depending on the actions to be implemented to improve practices. Each action identified will typically have the same cost components previously described in section 3.2.1 (initial setup costs) and should be managed through a change management process, assessing and managing the impact and relationships with all the other service management processes.

## 3.3   More quantifiable benefits or costs?

We have discussed, in section 3.1, the high potential of benefits driven by IT financial management and the associated costs for its implementation and execution (section 3.2). Some questions arise: are the benefits quantifiable and can the costs be justified? Is it possible to evaluate trade-offs before starting implementation and, if so, how?

First, running IT financial management practices is not always an option. To ensure the minimal required level of control of costs and revenues in line with corporate financial policies, many organizations will implement IT financial management. In particular, budgeting and accounting activities are often mandatory: annual budget, budget reviews, periodic and annual closures (these activities will be described in detail in Chapter 4). For organizations charging customers for IT services other practices will be mandatory too: in particular, customer charging and, in some cases, pricing.

Costs associated with the execution of the activities listed above, at a basic level (sufficient to comply with corporate financial policies), will need to be budgeted and managed. There may be no need for cost justification as management requires it to be done. The questions arise for other practices and when a higher level of sophistication is required. There will be a point at which the cost cannot be justified: a level of sophistication where the cost of improving (e.g. the level of detail of costs managed) is too high compared to the potential incremental benefits deriving from the proposed improvements.

Chapter 7 deals with Key Performance Indicators (KPIs) for IT financial management practices. Improvement of performance, in terms of both efficiency and effectiveness of the practices, is often the underlying rationale to justify investments in IT financial management. Section 7.3 describes KPIs to measure improvements in practice; some of these KPIs are related to costs. In addition, Table 3.1 shows the relationships between benefits, their impacts and related savings/earnings. Measuring is not an easy task but a correlation between investments and their final positive expected effects, in terms of improvements, should be identified and proved. Investments in IT financial management should be managed in the same way as any other investment using the practices and techniques to evaluate and select them as described in this book (see section 4.1.3 for practices and section 6.5.15 for techniques). This means that expected benefits should be compared with costs and investments checked for available resources. If the acceptance criteria (considering the associated risks and their costs) are met, improvements can be approved; otherwise further analysis is needed and justification should be investigated further or the project discarded. There may be situations where available resources and organizational capacities do not

| Benefits | Impacts | Savings or earnings |
|---|---|---|
| **Ability, frequency and precision of forecasts** | – Correct and timely fund raising | – Reduced payments of interest<br>– Reduction in wasted effort due to aborted or delayed initiatives (e.g. for unavailable funds) |
| **Ability to understand appropriate and remunerative IT services** | – Customer satisfaction<br>– Higher price of services and/ or demand | – Higher sales prices or sales volumes leading to higher margins<br>– Reduced ongoing costs |
| **Knowledge of cost dynamics and investment analysis** | – Improved and efficient decision making | – Cost reduction leading to lower prices or higher margins<br>– Reduction in wasted effort due to aborted or delayed initiatives (e.g. for unavailable funds)<br>– Reduction of decision-making costs (e.g. time spent by managers) |
| **Support of rapid change** | – Shorter time to market<br>– Customer satisfaction | – Higher volumes of activity leading to better use of resources and/or increment of revenues and margins |
| **Optimization of IT financial management practices** | – Improved organization and processes (efficiency and effectiveness) | – Cost reduction<br>– Increased productivity of involved staff |
| **Improved compliance** | – Improved contribution to corporate objectives and optimized use of corporate resources<br>– Reduction of errors | – Reduction in wasted effort due to aborted or delayed initiatives (e.g. for unavailable funds)<br>– Reduced ongoing costs<br>– Reduced costs of error recovery |

Table 3.1 Benefits, impacts and related saving/earnings of IT financial management

allow to proceed with a specific investment, even if it takes considerable benefits. In such a case, investment should be postponed and reviewed when resources and capacities will be available.

In Chapter 6, we will discuss in detail how to implement IT financial management; an incremental approach will emerge as an appropriate alternative. From an investment perspective this means that effort may be distributed over time. It should be easier to justify smaller investments, which are also compatible with the existence of an ongoing budget for process improvement, as described in section 3.2.2. However, it is important to check that this money spent is delivering the expected tangible results. It is essential to continue comparing saving/earnings with costs; justification should be found regardless of the roadmap chosen (initial relevant investment vs. incremental improvements).

# 4 Description of financial management activities

In this chapter we will focus on IT financial management activities, some of which have been briefly introduced earlier. The objectives are:

- To give an overall picture of the IT financial management activities and their internal and external interfaces (especially those that interface with other IT service management practices).
- To describe the most relevant activities in detail.

Figure 4.1 shows the IT financial management activities that we will analyze further in this chapter. Each scenario previously described may have a different combination of activities with some specific features. In this chapter we will concentrate on Scenario 2. Organizations in Scenario 1 will probably be without some of the activities described, such as pricing and charging. Organizations in Scenario 3 will have additional activities not described in Figure 4.1 These activities are related to the organization's financial management in decisions about capital structure, distribution of profits to shareholders, tactical financing (such as how to fund required resources), taxation and management of the relationship with banks. These are very technical subjects, which are managed by the financial management department in Scenarios 1 and 2 (in Scenario 3, there is probably no separation between IT financial management and financial management). Information about these topics is widely available in literature as it is part of the body of knowledge required for financial staff; it is not typical of IT financial management. These specialist topics and related activities will not be discussed further in this book.

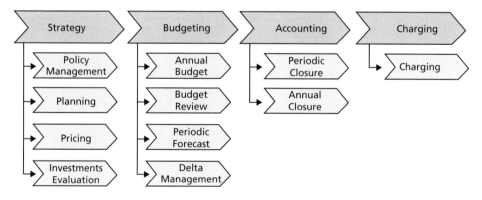

Figure 4.1 IT financial management activities

A question is raised when looking at Figure 4.1: where are the activities that are generally considered part of accounting activities, such as recording invoices? These activities are generally part of what we have called the passive cycle – that is, the set of activities managing all steps needed to handle purchases, from order issue to suppliers' payment – and/or corporate accounting activities. These activities have not been considered part of IT financial management core activities but interfaces with them are clearly fundamental. Recording and accounting invoices, for example, is generally managed by the accounting or purchasing departments for all goods and services purchased by the organization, including IT.

In the next sections we will introduce and describe each of the activities with a standard approach. For each activity we will supply detailed objectives, a short description, a detailed activity flow and a description of it.

The IT financial management activities are closely interrelated; Figure 4.2 shows the main interfaces between them. The content of each interface will be better understood when describing each activity. Figure 4.2 also shows the external entry points or activation triggers deriving from practices or events not included in the IT financial management domain that is described in Figure 4.1. These triggers can be identified easily in the detailed description of practices, in particular in their event-process-chain.

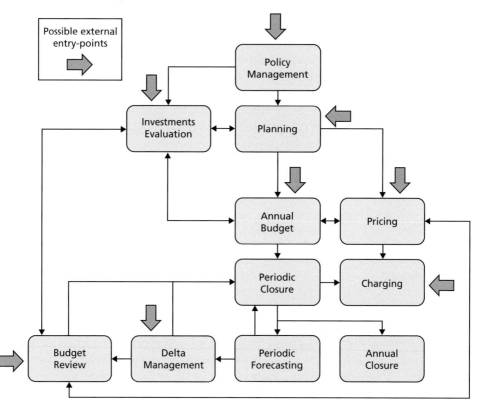

Figure 4.2 Relationship between IT financial management activities

To detail the activities we will use the Event-Process-Chain (EPC) model, which legend for interpretation is available in Figure 4.3. This model is widely used in business process management and supported by most commercial tools for process design. We have used the IDS-Scheer notation used in EPCs to describe activity schemas in this book.

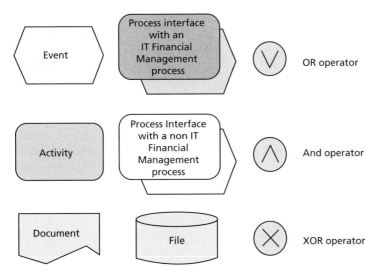

Figure 4.3 Legend to interpret activity schemas

## 4.1 Strategy

Under this label we have grouped four activities that have a long term impact and a high-level decision maker. These activities are: policy management, (financial) planning, pricing and investment evaluation management.

### 4.1.1 Policy management

**Objectives**
The objective of policy management is to define and maintain a set of policies to manage IT financial management. Policies should define the objectives to be met and should provide clear guidelines to manage and perform IT financial management.

**Short description**
The activity aimed at managing the IT financial management policies is a very simple one. Policies are defined, distributed and updated (this includes withdrawing and replacing old policy) when necessary. The need for policies may be an organization's decision or may derive from external requirements, such as Sarbanes-Oxley (SOX) or Basel II. In Scenario 1 policies, when existing, are generally defined by the financial department and IT simply acquires and implements them.

The content of policies depends on the scenario adopted by the organization and on each organization's maturity and objectives. ISO/IEC 20000 sets some requirements about this topic, which are suitable for organizations following Scenarios 2 and 3. According to ISO/IEC 20000, IT financial policies define clear guidelines and practices for:
- budgeting and accounting for all components including IT assets, shared resources, overheads, externally supplied services, people, insurance and licenses

- apportioning indirect costs and allocating direct costs to services
- effective control and authorization

Policies should also define the level of detail to which budgeting and accounting are performed, in particular the cost types to be accounted, rules to apportion overheads, level of detail about the customer's business, rules governing the handling of variances against budgets and links to service level management. For example, policies would need to define how to deal with relevant variances of costs compared to budget which might over-stretch resources and related impacts on service levels; this could imply involvement of the service level manager and technical staff to evaluate impacts and approve them.

### Activity details

Figure 4.4 describes the policy management activity. The initial step is the definition of policies for the first time. To define the policy, relevant inputs are the more generally applicable policies, for example accounting principles and/or financial management policies. Once defined, policy must be approved. Approval levels depend on the scenario and on organizations' corporate arrangements, but it is important that both IT and financial managers agree on it and, in every case, that management is involved.

After the approval step, the policy is implemented, communicated and activated. Finally the policy is checked for conformity and deviations are managed. Usually non-compliance is related to cultural aspects of the organization: behavior that needs to change. Corrective actions will have to be identified and applied to achieve the desired behavior. In some cases, deviations may be caused by erroneous or unsuitable policies that need to be improved.

We have described, in practice, the application of the Deming cycle (Plan-Do-Check- Act) to the management of policies. Organizations applying ISO/IEC 20000 are naturally implementing this cycle as part of the requirements of the standard. It is important that in any scenario and regardless of ISO/IEC 20000 commitments, an IT financial management policy is defined, applied and improved.

### 4.1.2  Planning

### Objectives

The objective of planning is to predict and control the spending of money to achieve the business objective in the medium/long term. The business objectives are defined in the strategic business plan.

### Short description

The IT financial planning activity is part of the overall strategic business planning practice of an organization. Timing is defined by this activity, which normally covers a three to five year horizon. The strategic business planning activity is executed before budgeting; it is an important input to budgeting. This enables the budget to be aligned with strategic planning figures. An IT financial plan, articulated per year, is the output of the activity. The plan is part of the overall financial plan, which is part of the strategic business plan. Figure 4.5 shows this hierarchy, typical of Scenario 1 and often of Scenario 2. In Scenario 3, the IT financial plan corresponds to the organization's overall financial plan.

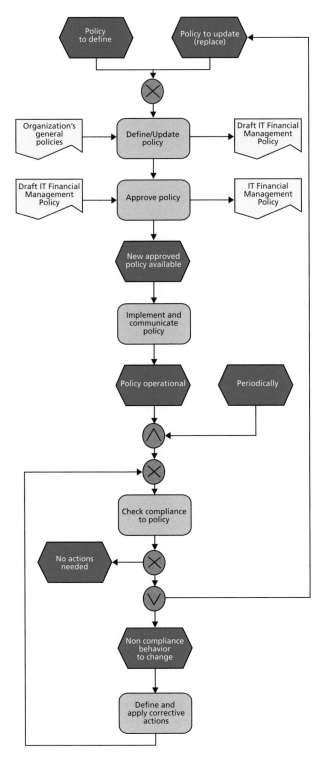

Figure 4.4 The IT financial policy management activity

Figure 4.5 IT financial plan as part of the overall strategic business plan

## Activity details

Figure 4.6 shows a simplified business strategic planning practice. There are several triggers. Some organizations simply manage business cycles and perform their strategic business planning before each cycle. Often the activities are executed when opportunities or threats face the organization. Strategic business planning is also recommended in start-ups or when new businesses are launched.

The first step of the activity aims at defining the mission and objectives of the business for the target planning horizon (e.g. three to five years). These will be the key inputs for the plan. Environmental scanning is the second step where information is gathered from the business environment in order to achieve a sustainable competitive advantage. It can be a complex activity and describing it is out of the scope of this book (more details on how to scan, e.g. understanding the customer and opportunities, can be found in ITIL V3 Service Strategy book, section 4.1).

After these first steps, the business strategy is formulated. This activity will have, as an input, all the information gathered from the previous steps and it will produce the strategic business plan. The contents of this plan may vary considerably depending on the size of the organization and the objectives stated. A financial section will always be present (often as a separate financial plan).

The financial plan typically contains, for the planning horizon, the following sections with figures and comments:
- a financial summary
- the figures about the investments needed to perform all initiatives and run the business in line with the decisions contained in the strategic business plan
- high-level profit and loss and balance sheet statements for each year of the planning horizon
- cash flow projections needed to execute the plan
- funding requirements (the presence of this section depends on the scenario; it is typical for Scenario 3 where IT financial management corresponds to IT financial management; in Scenario 2, where charging is applied, it should be clear which services and customers are generating revenues, either actually or notionally, and how much)
- conclusions

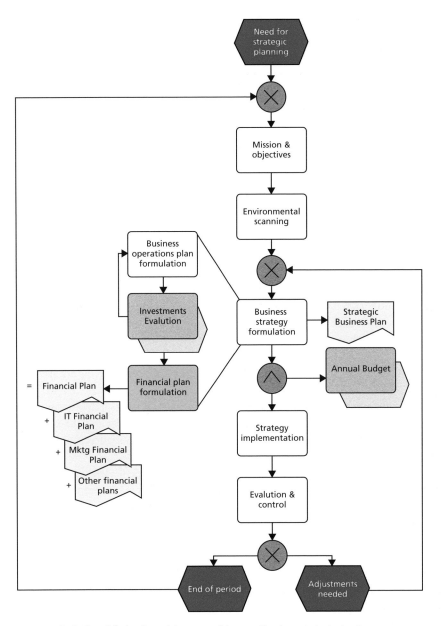

Figure 4.6 The (IT financial) planning activity as part of the overall business strategic planning

This information is vital, together with detailed objectives to be implemented, in order to check the progress of the plan over time. In Figure 4.6 we set out some steps of business strategy formulation and highlight those related to financial aspects with a green background.

The core activities are determination of the value and resources needed for each initiative and definition of the financial plan. The financial plan is usually built starting from business assumptions and plans (marketing, operational). The construction is often bottom-up: each business unit and department is required to formulate its financial plan to perform all its activities required by the corporate business plan. The IT financial plan is one of these plans; it is consolidated with others to produce the overall financial plan. Often, the production of the IT financial plan is similar to the budgeting activity but the level of detail is lower. In smaller organizations, this activity can be entirely executed by the CIO. In larger organizations it is often a bottom-up exercise where each IT function or department receives inputs (such as operational plans of business units) and determines the financial initiatives and related figures needed to support them. The main differences between the budgeting and the planning activity are the degree of uncertainty about timing and initiatives in the plan, which leads to:

- less detailed figures
- year or semester as the reference period for operations (in budgets the time frames considered are shorter, such as months).

The activity in Figure 4.6 does not include other important aspects of planning: iterations and approvals. Iterations are necessary because when the plans of each department or business unit are consolidated they need to be checked for consistency, feasibility (based on overall available resources) and historical performance (results achieved in previous years). If any of these aspects requires it, further cycles are necessary to achieve the required changes. Approval may be a very complex activity, depending on the size and culture (delegation vs. centralization) of the organization. Each level of consolidation of the plan normally requires at least one level of authorization. Business strategy formulation includes all this complexity and produces all the plans (the strategic business plan, which includes all the other plans shown in Figure 4.5).

After formulation and approval, the plan is executed. The financial plan will become one of the main sources for formulation of budgets. The figures in the budgets, more detailed than those of the financial long-term plan, should be consistent at each defined aggregation level.

The execution of the plan is controlled either by management or by dedicated boards. Often, control is included in other financial practices, where actual figures are compared with budgets and with those forecasted in the long-term financial plan. This happens at least at the end of a period of the long-term plan, typically a year. The annual closure activity is appropriate for this purpose.

Some strategic business plans are rolling plans: at the end of each period, a new strategic business plan is formulated starting from the previous year and covering one more year ahead. In such a case, the strategic business plan may be substantially updated (this is described by the end of period branch in Figure 4.6). This is not done often, because performing the whole planning activity is an intensive effort. When business plans are not managed on a rolling basis, there may be events triggering the execution of the activity, for example when relevant deviations are determined during the evaluation and control step or when major events occur in the business environment.

### 4.1.3   Investment evaluation

#### Objectives
The objective of investment evaluation is to determine the suitability of investing money to implement an initiative (e.g. an IT project). This is performed by comparing costs with the benefits expected from implementing the initiative.

#### Short description
The evaluation activity is invoked by many other functions when an investment decision has to be taken. Used correctly, the activity leads to better choices and, therefore, to superior performance. The business context should always encourage policy makers and managers to question and justify investment decisions with a coherent and consistent approach.

The purchase of IT equipment and software is among the most important investment decisions that organizations must take and IT investments contribute to the overall business as long as IT strategy supports the overall business strategy. It is crucial that such decisions are properly included in the organization's strategic planning (see 4.1.2) and budgeting (see 4.2).

The evaluation activity is based on the following steps:
1. Acquire information.
2. Perform evaluation.
3. Analyze results and prepare a final report and recommendations.

Investments are frequently linked to each other and every organization's resources are limited, so not all of them can be approved even if each is profitable. The selection of investments is often managed through a specific activity, project portfolio management, which is part of strategic business planning. Investment decisions are generally included in business strategic plans and approved with them.

It is a good practice to prioritize all investments and approve them according to available funds. Discarded investments may be evaluated again, if not obsolete, when conditions change or in the future (e.g. a new budget cycle).

#### Activity details
Figure 4.7 describes the investment evaluation activity. When an investment evaluation has to be done, the first step is to acquire the necessary information to perform the appraisal. IT financial policies are a vital input because they should include the technique(s) to be used (e.g. Return On Investment (ROI), Internal Rate of Return (IRR) or others as described in 6.5.15) and the basic assumptions to be made (for example how to define the discount rate to be used or the number of years characterizing the life of the investment to be considered). This mandatory information is completed with the specific data of the investment: detailed description, its purpose, amounts needed and occurrence time, expected savings and occurrence time, other benefits, etc. When all the required data have been gathered, all assumptions are documented and the evaluation scenario is built, which should be approved by the requesters of the evaluation.

When the scenario document is ready, evaluation can be performed using the required techniques (for further details about these, see 6.5.15). In practice, this means running a simulation and determining some indexes used to rank investments. The results are passed to the final step where they are compared with target figures. Those not generating the expected results will not be recommended, from a financial point of view. For example, this may happen if ROI is negative or below a target positive value (e.g. 10 percent). This does not automatically mean that the investment will be rejected, as it may be mandatory because of regulatory constraints or may bring relevant intangible benefits. The final report, the evaluation report, summarizes all information managed throughout the activity (scenarios, calculations) and includes the final comments and recommendations based on financial analysis. In some cases, projects may be linked, as some may be pre-requisites. These correlations should be clearly identified and described and an overall evaluation of related projects should be performed.

The results are passed to the requesters, who make their final choice based on the financial evaluation and all other relevant aspects to be considered.

### 4.1.4 Pricing

**Objectives**
The objective of pricing is to determine the selling price of the IT services supplied.

**Short description**
There can be completely different activities depending on the approach defined for charging and pricing (for further details see 6.5.1 for charging and 6.5.11 for pricing considerations). We simplify them in two categories: an approach based on transfer price and an approach based on market price. A charging/pricing policy (e.g. recovering costs and having a simple pricing system), often included in financial policies (discussed in 4.1.1), should have been defined previously in both cases.

**Transfer price approach**
There are normally no specific activities for this approach. All decisions are generally predefined in policies – for example, the pricing model (cost or cost plus, see 6.5.11), and transfer prices are simply determined and applied as part of the accounting activities (periodic or annual closures).

**Market price approach**
In the market price approach (see figure 4.8), the activity exists of three steps, triggered by events or periodically launched:
• evaluate pricing position
• consider pricing strategies
• set prices

Pricing is strictly related to the business strategy. The strategic business plan (see 4.1.2) is a fundamental input where the position of the organization and its products/services in the market is set. This approach is typical of organizations in Scenario 3.

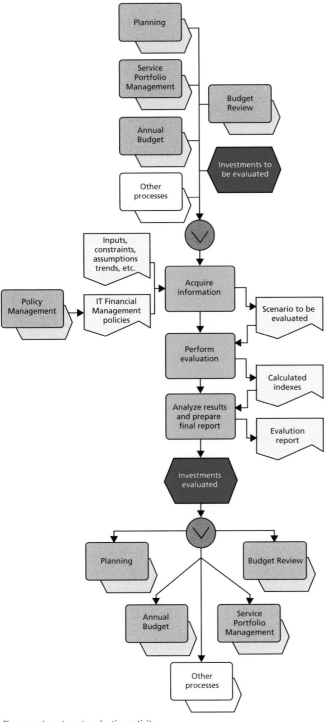

Figure 4.7 Investment evaluation activity

## Activity details (market price approach)

Pricing, when a market price approach is chosen, is usually considered as a marketing activity instead of a financial activity. There is plenty of literature about how to set prices for products and/or services, so in this book we will discuss the topic briefly.

The activity may be activated by many triggers: scheduled periodical reviews of price lists, customers' requests, market analysis, the need to add new or significantly updated services, competition.

The first step to be performed is checking and understanding the current price position for the services whose prices are to be reviewed. Several inputs are needed to execute this task: information about competitors' prices, trends and feedback about sales, information about the costs of providing the services, information about customers' opinions and requests, etc. The output of the task is a document representing the starting situation. It should appear evident which pricing position is achieved in comparison with competitors: lower prices, higher prices, parity. The positioning may vary depending on the services supplied. The price ranges to identify when a position is achieved should also be defined and profitability should be checked against the achieved position (high prices should also be accompanied by appropriate profits, for example).

After initial analysis, the achieved position is compared with the target position, deriving from the business and marketing strategy. During this task, the target position for each service is confirmed or modified, thus providing a fundamental input to define their target prices.

Target price positioning of services is then passed to the last step of the activity, which is determining the final price list. Accurate simulation is performed in order to adjust the final price, analyzing impact on sales and probably on business results. There will be some iterations until the optimal configuration is identified and approved. The price list of services is updated and communicated. In some cases, the price of services may be included in the Service Catalog, which is also updated.

The main role of financial management in this activity, which is generally performed by marketing, is to provide information about the costs of services and to support simulation of business impact.

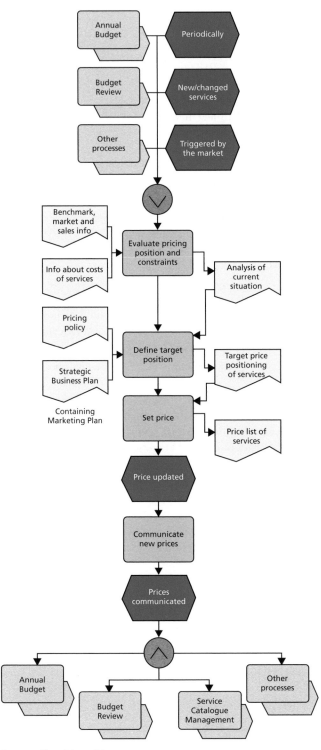

Figure 4.8 The pricing activity

## 4.2   Budgeting

We have grouped several activities together dealing with budget: annual budget, budget review, periodic forecast and delta management. The first activity is aimed at creating a new budget, and is typically run every year. The second is aimed at reviewing the defined budget when needed. Forecast is the activity for estimating the costs and revenues to the end of financial year and delta management is the activity that deals with all identified deviations from the budget. Altogether, these are the core activities of IT financial management together with accounting practices.

### 4.2.1   Annual budget

**Objectives**
Budgeting, in our context, is the activity ensuring that the correct financial budget is defined for the provision of IT services. It is also the means of delegating control and monitoring performance against predefined targets. Budgeting of IT services should be integrated with the overall corporate budgeting and with financial management policies and practices.

**Short description**
In Scenarios 1 and 2, all organizations have a periodic (e.g. annual[1]) round of negotiations between the business departments and the IT organization covering expenditure/revenue plans and agreed investment programs, which sets the budget for IT. In Scenario 3, the budget of IT services is the budget of the business.

The first phase of the budgeting activity is preparation or set-up. All assumptions, external information and constraints, internal from the IT organization and external, are gathered. In medium to large IT organizations, the budget is split among cost centers, which may correspond to organizational departments or functions. This is typical of Scenario 1, while in Scenarios 2 and 3, they may correspond to IT services. The owners of cost centers are generally also the owners of the corresponding allocated budget. They are asked to prepare an estimation of the costs and revenues, if any, for the budget year based on the communicated assumptions and constraints.

The individual owners' budgets are later consolidated and processed (for example to calculate accruals or depreciation or to determine apportioning), often using software tools. Budget reporting is the final output of this step. It is checked for integrity, consistency and compliance with inputs, e.g. financial policies and constraints. When all the checks are positive, the budget is passed to the approval activity. Here, management (Board, CTO, CIO, CFO and CEO, depending on the organization's structure and culture) will verify and approve the budget. This may also include a presentation to the business/customers' representatives; definitive approval is generally given by the individual responsible for the overall corporate budget (in Scenario 1 and 2).

**Activity details**
For organizations performing the planning activity, this last activity is generally executed before budgeting and normally includes its planning horizon. All assumptions and outputs of the planning activity are therefore passed to budgeting.

---

[1]   The budget year often coincides with the fiscal year, which often corresponds to the calendar year. This is not the case for all organizations and sometimes the budget year is a 12 months period different from the calendar year.

The structure of the budget follows the reporting structure (see 6.5.13 for details about reporting) which also depends on the cost and cost apportioning models. The budget is used to set targets and check the progress of costs and revenues; its structure should be aligned to these models, although the level of detail of the budget is probably not the highest possible. For the same reason budget is typically split by financial reporting period. The steps of the activity are described in Figure 4.9

In Scenarios 1 and 2, the annual budget is activated by the overall corporate budgeting activity. This activity produces corporate assumptions, objectives and targets, which are passed to IT budgeting.

An initial activity, generally performed by IT management, transforms these inputs into specific objectives and targets for IT. Assumptions on expected variations, such as inflation and costs trends are provided. In parallel, dedicated support staff (e.g. controllers) prepare all the required support information (for example, the budget for the previous year, actual costs for the previous year, current year actual costs and forecasts if available) and load them into the tool supporting the budgeting activity. Timescales for the activity and schedules are also defined and, when everything is ready, a preliminary budgeting meeting is held with management and the owners of the budget (those accountable for forecasting and approving expenses or revenues for specific assigned domains).

Each budget owner will then start to prepare their estimation for the part of costs and revenues that they manage. To perform this task, they will need to gather all relevant information needed in addition to those initially supplied:
• given objectives for the budget
• plans for the next years (see the planning activity, 4.1.2)
• portfolio of projects and their status (costs, achievements, etc.)
• portfolio of services and their status (costs such those of support contracts or previous year purchases, service levels, etc.)
• capacity plan
• price list of services
• requests from customers
• all existing constraints from IT financial management policies, communicated objectives and targets.

It may be necessary to review price lists before starting budgeting, by using the pricing activity (this step is not described in the activity reported in Figure 4.9).

The information gathered should clearly set out:
• limits on capital expenditure
• limits on operational expenditure
• agreed workload and set of services to be delivered
• projects to be included (e.g. to enhance functionality)
• the drivers to apportion indirect costs
• the drivers to estimate charges to customers.

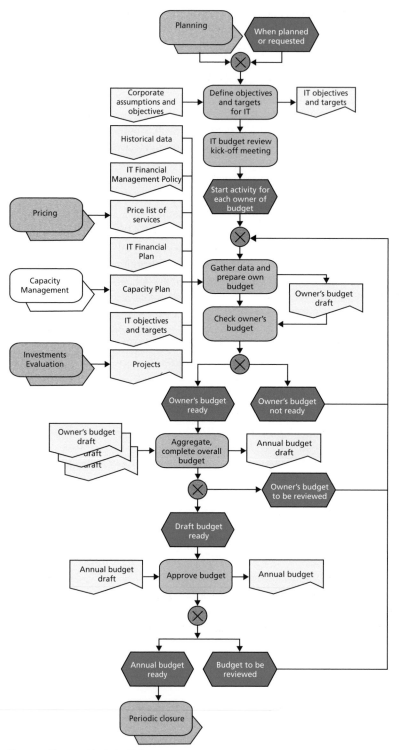

Figure 4.9 The annual budget activity

When all the required information is available, the domain owner prepares the budget proposal for the domain(s) (e.g. functions, cost centers or IT services). This is the most critical step of the activity. If the IT organization is large and the budget for the individual domain is relevant, this step can be executed by means of a specific sub-process, normally involving several resources and managed bottom-up. For example, it is common to check budgets line by line against the previous year's spend. Budgets are typically split by financial reporting periods and are often influenced by a mixture of known events and predictions. Records should be kept, as this evidence about spend can be easily be supported when budgets are under pressure. For the same reason, a good practice is to categorize costs according to their level of certainty (e.g. license costs or renewal of multi-year contracts vs. purchasing of new hardware) and their source (internal or IT or external projects). Sometimes different budget scenarios may be prepared, corresponding to different assumptions deriving from the business or generated internally from IT. In some organizations, contingencies are also clearly identified and evaluated; to some extent this depends also on the approach to budget review (see next activity) as if this activity is performed at suitable time intervals, the necessity for contingencies is reduced. In any case, a bad practice to avoid is inflation of costs, which makes budgets unreliable. When this behavior is perceived, top management may decide to cut budget proposals, which could affect budgets that were correctly estimated, thus leading finally to unrealistic and insufficient budgets.

When revenues are budgeted, e.g. for organizations in Scenario 3, this is normally managed separately and often by specific functions, e.g. sales. Some revenues may be linked to specific costs needed to provide services and it is important to trace these relationships. This will help to avoid mistakes such as reducing costs while keeping revenues unchanged.

These steps may be supported by a single budgeting tool (if one is available) or they may be managed by each owner with different approaches (often by mails and spreadsheets). The assistance of (IT) financial controllers is very important in this phase: they provide support on which costs to consider, when opting for operational or capital expenditure, how to interpret constraints, how to use the supporting tools, etc. They also check schedules and provide help if there are delays. When the owner has prepared the budget proposal, an assigned (IT) financial controller usually performs a final general check for compliance. If any problem is found, a request for amendments is sent to the IT budget owner.

When all the owners' budget proposals are ready, the first draft of the budget is assembled. In medium to large organizations this is generally performed by support staff from the IT or financial department (e.g. IT financial controllers). The time required to accomplish the task depends on many factors:
• the complexity and feasibility of constraints (e.g. target values for costs)
• requirements and complexity of accruals
• requirements and complexity of depreciation
• requirements and complexity of apportioning indirect costs
• quantity of data and number of owners
• features of the tool supporting budgeting

At this stage, budgets are normally reported back to their owners to evaluate their profit and loss statements. Again, this may lead to some iterations and adjustments.

When the aggregated budget is ready, it is passed to the approval step. This phase is dependent on the size, the culture and managerial approach of each organization. Approval of the IT department is normally not the final authorization step, which is usually achieved within the corporate budgeting activity. Again, this may generate new iterations as reviews of the overall budget may affect IT as well.

It will not be possible to estimate all the costs and revenues accurately at budget time. This is because:
• the business needs will change over time (e.g. projects)
• tariffs and costs may vary because of external factors out of the organization's control (e.g. inflation)
• some costs may depend on the profile of usage and workload may vary because of external factors (for example driven by business needs again)

These uncertainties add to those deriving from human competence and time constraints. To avoid unwelcome surprises at the end of the period, IT budget owners tend to keep safety margins (normally by over-budgeting costs) to accommodate possible future changes. This is a further reason to recommend periodical control of the situation, by verifying actual costs against forecasts and by reviewing the budget at programmed intervals.

We have described above what is known as 'bottom-up' budgeting, which is still the traditional and most used approach. One of the major advantages of bottom-up budgeting is that the budget can be quite accurate for individual services and projects, as long as no activities and tasks have been forgotten. Bottom-up budgeting usually involves many people, which can be a benefit in terms of company morale and involvement.

However, bottom-up budgeting may lead those who are responsible for services and projects to ask for more funding than will actually be needed. This is done to ensure that enough money is allocated for each task to be accomplished, since most people assume that they will not be given all the money that they request. This situation can lead to a waste of money and also a situation of distrust between various members of projects and different managers. Another problem of bottom-up budgeting is that it may be difficult to actually draw up a complete and thorough list of every activity and task.

Top-down budgeting works in the opposite direction from bottom-up budgeting. Top-down budgeting begins by estimating the costs of higher-level activities and tasks, and then those estimates will constrain the estimates for the costs of lower level activities and tasks. The entire activity of arriving at a budget will begin with upper-level management and an overall estimate of the entire services and projects. Then the overall budget is divided among the first level of activities of Services and tasks of projects and so on. This continues until funding has been given to all of the activities and tasks necessary for a service and project.

It is important that those managers who are responsible for determining the overall budget have enough experience to determine an initial budget that is adequate and accurate overall. If not, there may be insufficient funding or waste.

What we have described is also known as 'baseline' budget, as we have assumed that, to prepare estimates, the previous year's data were used. The 'zero-based' budgeting approach, on the contrary, compels organizations to think from scratch. Proponents insist that preparers who start from scratch in developing their budgets will be more likely to base them on assumptions that are current and relevant. Many budget items change from year to year. By re-considering each item in the budget, the preparer is more likely to account for the effects of extraordinary or non-recurring items than if the calculations were based upon only a cursory review of historical data.

Despite its advantages, there are major disadvantages to 'zero-based' methods. The most obvious disadvantage is the amount of time and complexity involved in the activity. Without the benefit of historical or budgeted data to base their assumptions upon, preparers may be forced to justify routine operations; they may spend inordinate amounts of time essentially recreating the effects of cyclical trends in the business's operations.

Some businesses have very predictable operations that vary little over time. It is not efficient or effective for a preparer to spend a great deal of effort developing data that could be obtained quickly and accurately by extrapolating historical data (this is often the case for IT services). 'Baseline' budgeting offers the preparer the advantage of building upon the organization's existing base of knowledge about its operations. Preparers are often able to analyze historical data and extrapolate cyclical or seasonal trends quickly. For many organizations, this method is reliable and saves valuable time.

Managers who are considering implementing or revising budget activities should consider several factors before selecting either a 'baseline' or 'zero-based' approach:
- availability and relevance of historical information
- the organization's cyclical or seasonal trends
- the likelihood of extraordinary or non-recurring budget items
- preparers' experience in developing budgets
- the amount of research and analysis necessary to develop quality information.

## 4.2.2 Budget review

### Objectives
The objective of budget review is to check and review a previously defined and agreed budget and to set a new budget, which will replace the previous and will become 'current', used to verify and track progress of costs and revenues.

### Short description
There are many reasons why a budget may become obsolete. Budget review activity may be scheduled periodically (once or more in a year, typically when aligned with shareholders reporting) or launched at any time, in case of major variations between actual and budgeted values, re-organizations, mergers or outsourcing. Rules for budget reviews should be defined in IT financial policies.

The budget review activity is very similar to the initial annual budget activity. A set-up phase, where updated targets and objectives are defined, is followed by the gathering of required information. The time to perform a budget review is generally shorter than the time required for initial budget definition.

Older budgets should not be lost and, for this purpose, a good practice is to use versioning. This will allow for later retrieval and use for comparisons.

### Activity details

Budget review is described in Figure 4.10 and looks very similar to the annual budget activity, reported in Figure 4.9. We will avoid a complete activity description, concentrating instead on the main differences.

The first difference is about the activation of the activity. Budget review is frequently a planned activity and it is usual to have at least an intermediate review during the year; in some cases, reviews can be even more frequent. Budget review can also be triggered by the delta management activity (see 4.2.4 for further details on this activity). This activity can show relevant deltas, which may challenge the reliability of the initially estimated budget. In such a case, authorizing deltas and leaving the budget unchanged may be not the desired approach; a more formal and complete review of the budget (which will replace the older one) may be requested.

The output is the reviewed budget. The time needed to execute this activity is generally shorter than the time needed for an annual budget. The latter should take from one to two months (although in some organizations this time could be longer and, in any case, linked to the corporate budgeting timing). The review should probably be contained within weeks or a month. This is because, practically, only part of the budget will be changed where opportunities (e.g. savings) or negative surprises arise.

Other differences between the initial and the budget review activity involve the preliminary and approval steps, which may be less formal for the latter.

### 4.2.3  Periodic forecasting

### Objectives

Periodic forecasting is aimed at defining the costs and revenues from a certain instant, e.g. when forecast is required, to the end of a period, for example the budget year. Forecast, together with balance, is typically used to be compared with budget.

### Short description

Forecasting means, at a certain instant, to predict the results that will be achieved at the end of a period. For example, in our context, this may mean to estimate expected results at the end of the year (by means of preparing a set of reports, e.g. profit and loss) each month. These estimations may be compared with budget in order to identify deviations as soon as possible, providing valuable information to act to minimize or eliminate them.

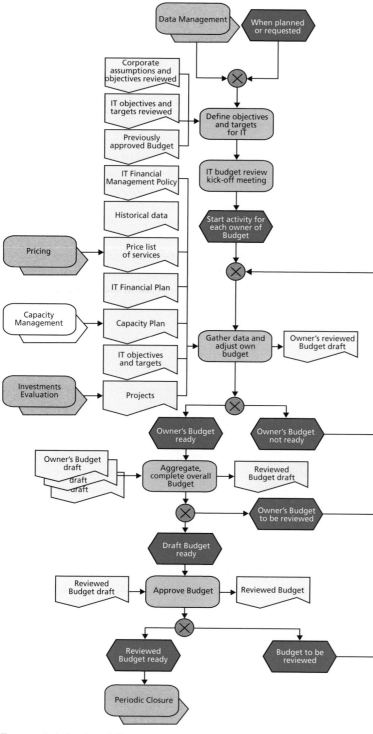

Figure 4.10 Budget review activity

To prepare forecast figures, some major inputs are needed: target when available (budget is assumed), actual figures and any known information that will affect achievements (e.g. tax rate changes, new projects etc.). The budget is provided by either annual budget or budget review activities while the actual figures are provided by the periodic closure activities. When the required information is available, work can begin on estimations. Together with budgeting, forecast can be built bottom-up by IT budget owners. When aggregated and checked, forecast data are ready to be used to identify and manage deltas and for reporting. The delta management activities will deal with any deltas that are identified.

Forecasting is based on available knowledge and it is generally performed under time constraints. This means that its results are not exact information; their reliability increases while approaching the end of the estimated period and when more time is available to perform it, which allows higher accuracy and completeness in all the steps of the activity.

The activities described here are typical of organizations in Scenario 2. IT organizations in Scenario 1 do not often use forecasting, unless this activity is required by financial policies. They often prefer to run a budget review activity periodically (at least once a year). Organizations in Scenario 3 need a detailed and precise budget per period (typically per month), which is not common for organizations in Scenario 1 and 2. This reliable budget can be compared periodically (e.g. each month) with actual spend to identify deltas (input to delta management activity). Again, a forecast may not be necessary in this case and can be replaced by budget reviews.

### Activity details

It makes sense to execute a forecast when new relevant inputs are available. This happens typically after each periodic closure that supplies fresh actual data. Some organizations may decide to run periodic forecasts after each periodic closure execution. But, as the activity is not effortless, others may decide to execute the activity depending on the dynamics of figures and/or periodically at programmed points in time. For example, it may happen that forecast are prepared only each quarter. This will generally depend on financial policies but a shorter frequency may also be decided by IT for specific needs, for example if relevant projects are in progress or new significant services have recently been delivered.

When the periodic closure activity is completed, IT budget owners may start gathering necessary data and information and preparing their forecasts. The forecast is the quantity (costs, revenues but also efforts) needed to the end of a period (budget year in our context), assuming an initial balance at the beginning of the forecasted period (for example for a calendar annual budget period, if the balance is 10,000,00 euros at the end of March, the forecast to the end of December may be 50,000,00 euros, so that the total expected cost is 60.000,00 euros, which may be compared with the budgeted cost). If necessary, for example when new services are added during the forecasted period, the pricing activity may be invoked before starting the activity, to define selling prices. This step is not reported in Figure 4.11.

The result of the forecast should be checked for completeness and compliance with constraints and policies; this can generally be done with the help of the (IT) financial controller(s). As remarked for budgeting, this step may imply a bottom-up collection of information from several resources for each budget domain. IT budget owners will be responsible for this activity. Once they have completed their forecast, the data can be assembled. This normally requires apportioning of indirect costs and determination of depreciation and accruals. It is usually the (IT) financial controllers' task to execute this step. Later, a full forecast is available and it can be used for comparison with the budget, which is again done by the IT budget owners. Financial or IT financial policies should define the tolerances for deviations between balance plus forecasts and budgeted figures. It is common to define upper limits but lower limits should be defined as well, because under spending should be taken under control so that saved funds can be removed or switched to other investments. The reasons for any differences should be recorded and, if deltas are greater than the allowed tolerance, the delta management activity is executed. This is a decision activity and it may take time to define how to manage deltas. For this reason, it may be decided to prepare and distribute reporting before the results of delta management are known. Reporting will contain the budget, balance and forecast information; it will provide evidence of the amounts (deltas) submitted to the delta management activity and therefore under evaluation and approval. The next periodic forecast activity will be performed after the next periodic closure.

### 4.2.4  Delta management

#### Objectives
The objective of delta management is to make a decision on deltas between forecasted (balance at a date plus estimations to the end of budget period), or actual costs, versus budgeted costs and revenues at the time they are determined.

#### Short description
Forecasted and/or actual amounts deviating from budget and defined tolerances (upper and lower, generally defined in policies) should be analyzed and authorized by management. This can be done by means of the delta management activity. This activity analyzes all deviations previously determined and passed to it by other activities. Deltas may be relevant and may require review of the entire budget or they may be localized in specific budget domains (e.g. an IT service).

#### Activity details
Requests for authorization of variances from budget may be detected from different activities: periodic closures (actual against budget), periodic forecast (balance plus forecast against budget), change management process or from the demand management activity too. It is preferable to detect them as soon as possible, which means that the preferred order is demand management, periodic forecast, change management and, finally, periodic closures.

There are many reasons for changes and deviations. High-level reasons have been discussed within the description of budgeting activities. In more detail, the reasons may be:
- changes in the level of customer activity or number of users
- changes in the size and/or type of customers' business
- unexpected costs (for example major disaster or wrong project evaluation)
- changes in technology or suppliers' behavior and/or strategy
- the introduction of efficiencies or inefficiencies into processes (e.g. service improvement)
- poor identification of costs during periodic budget (and budget review) activities
- over simplified allocation of total budget to the accrual periods (for example using the rule 1/12th)
- unexpected changes in external costs (e.g. inflation)

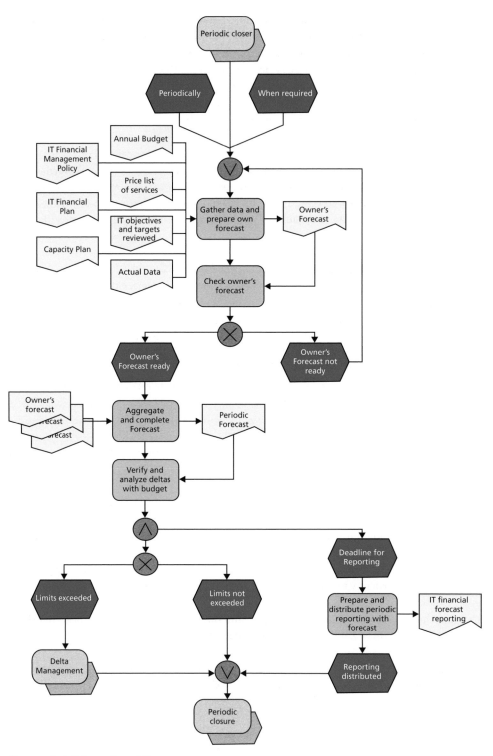

Figure 4.11 Periodic forecasting activity

Figure 4.12 shows delta management in detail. Independently from their origin, deviations should first be analyzed and the cause of the deviation identified. This can be done by IT budget owners with the support of (IT) financial controller(s). Once the causes of deviations have been documented and recorded and mitigation actions identified, they can be passed to the adequate authorization level, which is dependent on the organization's size and culture but also on the value of delta required. There should be tolerances for a single specific authorization and tolerances for the IT budget owner's cumulative extra budget requests. These tolerances should be identified in the financial or IT financial policies.

If the deviation is inherent to many domains of the budget or is a significant absolute amount, policies may state that a complete review of the budget is necessary. This would activate the budget review activity and it should happen, for example, when changes of quantities and/or of costs and/or of revenues lead to substantial changes of standard tariffs used to allocate/apportion and/or charge for services.

If this is not required, the specific deviations should be dealt with. Authorization may be delegated or not but, in every case, results are given back to requesters, either IT budget owners for internally generated deltas (e.g. from periodic closure or periodic forecast) or requesting customers for externally generated deltas. In reporting, the authorized amounts should not affect the initial budget and they should be given as evidence for authorized extra or limited budgets. In forecasts they should be added to the budget with the aim of checking deltas correctly in the future. Deltas that have not been authorized must be still dealt with; for example, project plans and/or schedule of changes could be reviewed. These activities are not described in the delta management activity, as they are considered as included in external processes (e.g. change management).

Demand for extra resource (which incurs cost) is often because of attempts to resolve poor service or because of additional work to complete budgeted tasks where the estimates are now shown to be inaccurate. Customers usually expect IT to manage this without additional cost although there may be no IT budget available. The likely effect is overstretching of resource, which affects all service levels; hence service level management must be involved in any decisions to provide chargeable service in excess of agreed budgets. For organizations in Scenario 3, funding of extra costs should be borne by customers when the reason for the cost is their changes in demand and by the service provider when the costs are related to their responsibilities. The same principle should apply transparently to organizations in Scenarios 1 and 2. In these cases, customers should always be informed about the consequences of overstretching resources when the service provider has no additional resources and has to keep within budget, either when the service provider is responsible for the deltas or when customers do not want to pay more.

When a delta involves minor costs it should be dealt with as well. Funds can be removed and either transferred to other areas requiring more, or simply removed. Additional funds may be available from management of positive deltas, generated by lower costs or more revenues than forecasted. Positive deltas can be managed as described here, although they do not generally require any authorization. They can be dealt with in two ways: if relevant, they can trigger a budget review, otherwise they should be recorded to facilitate the reuse of resources as explained above and avoid raising the same delta again.

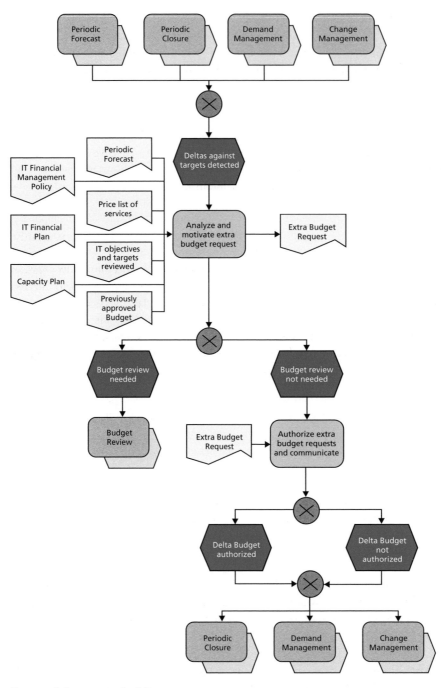

Figure 4.12 Delta management activity

# 4.3   Accounting

Under this label we have grouped two activities dealing with the determination of actual costs and revenues for IT at different points in time: periodic closure and annual closure.

## 4.3.1   Periodic closure

### Objectives
The objective of the periodic closure activity is to provide accurate and reliable information and reports (e.g. profit and loss statement) about actual costs and revenues of a closed period of the financial year or budget year (for example a specific month).

### Short description
The activity is run periodically, typically monthly. A fundamental input is information recorded by all of the organization's activities, such as the passive cycle, which are outside the scope of this book. When the information is updated and the time has come for closure, the activity performs the periodic operations (e.g. calculation of accruals, depreciations and apportioning of indirect costs) and prepares and distributes reporting. If the period is the last of the budget year, the annual closure activity will be run instead. If customers are to be charged, the charging activity will be typically activated after the periodic closure, which determines actual quantities and costs. However, in some cases charging may be independent (for example, when it is based on agreed tariffs with customers, independent from accounted costs).

### Activity details
The periodic closure activity is detailed in Figure 4.13. Several inputs have been represented, as the activity may occur after annual budget, budget review, delta management, periodic forecast and, of course, periodic closure itself (when none of the previous activities is executed from period to period).

A continuous input to the activity is determined by all the organization's operational activities, such as the passive cycle or activities such as billing. These activities are out of scope for this book but they are very important, as financial records are largely entered automatically by performing these activities. For example, when issuing a passive order, records about amounts and other details, depending on the accounting systems, are generally automatically entered in financial ledgers at the same time. Although financial records can be entered manually in ledgers, it is not efficient and therefore not recommended. Modern accounting departments manage only a few manual data entries, and recording data for financial purposes generally occurs automatically when performing business transactions.

The maximum quantity of data, referring to the period up to close, should be available before the activity is started. This normally takes some time, so a time-lag needs to be defined between the end date of the period and the start of the activity. Even with this time-lag, it is usually impossible to have all the information about the period registered; it is often necessary to manage accruals.

The first step of the activity consists of verifying whether minimal data to perform the closure activity are actually available. The amount of effort necessary for this step is dependent on the level of automation of the supporting financial management systems and the level of maturity (and performance) of the activities feeding into the periodic closure, such as the passive cycle or activities like billing. If all basic information (for example orders) is recorded and the system is able to calculate accruals automatically (goods/services received but not invoiced, accrued charges that can be calculated on the basis of the orders, or goods/services delivered but not invoiced, accrued income that can be calculated on the basis of orders), there will be no need to verify documents. Conversely, if activities have to be performed manually this will take time and effort.

If, after the above step is completed, charging is expected, the activity should be performed to include related revenues in the final reporting. This generally happens for IT organizations in Scenario 3 and sometimes for those in Scenario 2. If charging depends on actual costs, then the charging activity will be activated by the periodic closure, as shown in Figure 4.13. In every case, even if the charging activity is independent from actual costs (e.g. fixed charges are agreed), it is necessary to wait for its completion (posting of charges or invoices to the ledger) before continuing the activities of the periodic closure activity.

When all data have been recorded and information is available, the core activities of periodic closure can be executed: the calculation of accruals, reversal of prior period accruals, capitalizing, amortizations, depreciations and apportioning (of indirect costs to the analysis criteria, for example cost centers or IT services). In some organizations, accruals, capitalizing, amortizations and depreciations may be determined by different staff than those who do the apportioning. Knowing about the data and what is associated with it is an important aspect for the quality of results and, therefore, the assistance of a specialized financial controller or a dedicated IT financial controller may be helpful.

When the closure operations are completed, periodic reporting can be produced and distributed, if online access is not supported. This usually implies the production of a profit and loss statement and balance sheet for the whole IT department and for the supported views of costs (for example, by cost centers or IT services).

The periodic closure activity is repeated for all the periods of the annual budget. When the last period arrives, the annual closure activity is activated after its conclusion. If the period is not the last, IT financial management activities may continue with either periodic forecast (if scheduled for the closed period) or with the next periodic closure.

## 4.3.2  Annual closure

### Objectives
The objective of the annual closure activity is to provide agreed reports (e.g. profit and loss statements) for the closed budget year.

### Short description
The first step of the activity consists of checking the completeness and accuracy of information for the whole financial/budget period up to close. After these controls have been performed, the annual closure operations are executed and reporting is produced and distributed.

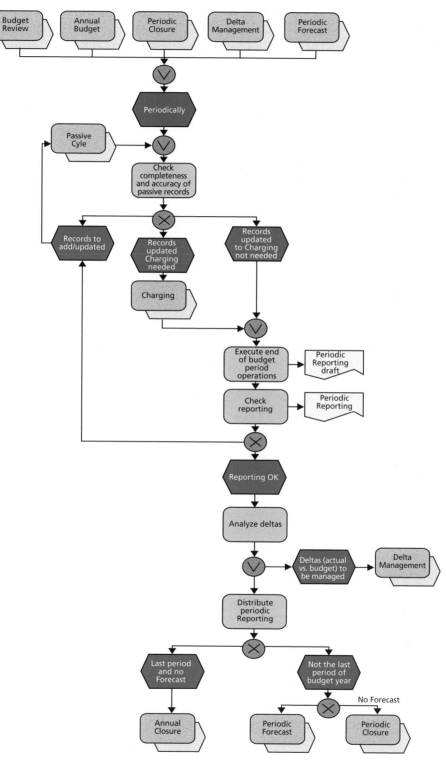

Figure 4.13 Periodic closure activity

**Activity details**

In some organizations, this activity is executed together (integrated) with the periodic closure activity for the last period of the budget year. In this book, we have described when this activity is performed separately and after the last periodic closure (generally some weeks or months later). In such cases, the entry point is the periodic closure activity, as no forecast will be performed after the last reporting period of the budget. Separating the two activities enables immediate, although incomplete, information (see accruals) and reporting (from the periodic closure) when the last period is achieved. It also enables full and reliable reporting (with minimized accruals) when all information about the closed budget year is available (for example, data about suppliers, such as invoices, may take some weeks to arrive).

Another reason to manage periodic and annual closures separately is that management may decide to make permitted changes to the profit and loss statement before definitively closing it; this typically requires some time to be done. After these changes are performed, accruals, depreciation and apportioning of indirect costs can be determined again and updated agreed reports produced about the budget year (e.g. profit and loss statements).

When the reporting is checked and correct, data about the budget year period are finally frozen.

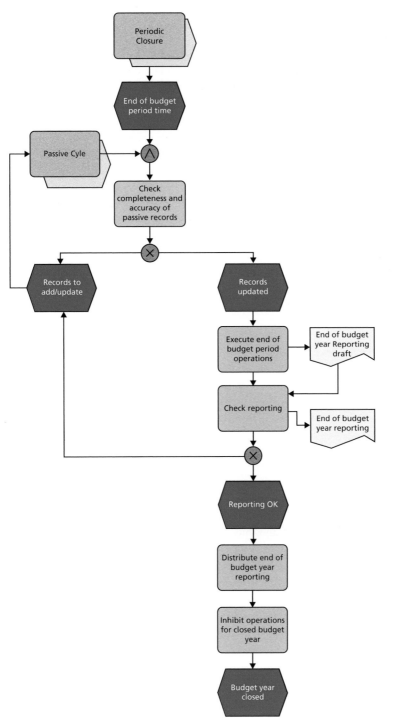

Figure 4.14 Annual closure activity

# 4.4  Charging

## 4.4.1  Charging

### Objectives
The objective of charging is to charge customers according to agreed terms and conditions.

### Short description
The agreed terms and conditions for charging greatly influence the activity. Activation of this activity is linked to the periodic closure if the conditions depend on actual costs. If not, activation is generally scheduled periodically (e.g. at the end of each month) or linked to agreements with customers. The outputs and documentation produced by the activity depends on the type of charging (transfer price mechanism, notional charging or market price with invoices). The core activity described here involves the production of charging documentation and records to support it. Other activities that follow may include receipts and credit management. These are normally part of IT financial management only for organizations in Scenario 3 (for these organizations IT financial management is the same as financial management); they are out of the scope of this book.

### Activity details
Charging is activated based on the agreed schedules with the customers. Schedules may be synchronized so that an individual monthly charging cycle takes place. This is frequent for organizations in Scenario 2. In Scenario 3, charging may occur several times in a month, depending on the number of customers, the type of services and the agreements in place. For organizations charging on the basis of actual costs, the periodic closure activity will produce the required input.

When data for charging is not provided by the periodic closure activity, it has to be gathered. This is the first step of the activity where all required information, such as workloads, quantity for the charging drivers and unit tariff, are retrieved. This may be done by a billing function or department with the help of IT service management staff if required (for example, the capacity manager may report on the capacity used and thus determines the quantities to be charged).

When all data are collected, the charging activity can be executed. This may be supported by automatic billing tools that calculate the bills, starting from data entered about agreements, workloads and charging drivers. This is strongly recommended for organizations in Scenario 3, where the outputs of the activity are real invoices. If customers are captive, as in Scenario 1 and often Scenario 2, and a notional charging or transfer price mechanism is applied, the calculation might still be performed manually. The size of the organization, number of customers and/or services will greatly influence the level of automation independently from the scenario.

When all charging documentation (pro forma invoices, invoices, resources driving charging usage summaries and details, lists of charged goods and expenses, etc.) is ready, it is checked. This can be done by verifying whether the values of drivers are realistic, for example based on previous consumptions, and if changed tariffs have been agreed by means of checking contracts; when charging is based on deliverables, documentation certifying acceptance can be controlled.

If no problems are encountered the charging documentation is sent to customers. If a transfer price mechanism is adopted, some accounting records to provide evidence of the charged amounts will be entered. Invoices issued manually will be recorded in accounting books as well. If a supporting tool is adopted, all registrations will normally occur automatically. If errors are detected, remedial actions are taken, preferably before sending the charging documentation or notices to customers.

During the charging activity, abnormal charging profiles may be detected. Where too much revenue is generated the cause must be identified, justified or corrected. Unless absolutely necessary the charges must not be altered. Some of the reasons for generating excessive revenue include:
- the workload has been higher than forecasted and flexible *charging* has resulted in increased charges although sufficient capacity was available without the IT organization incurring additional costs
- customers are having to buy more IT resources because of inefficient services
- incorrect figures have been used or other errors have been made.

Where a poor service is the difficulty, the underlying causes must be addressed. When workload growth is a problem, forecasts must be revised and it may become necessary to make a case to procure additional resources.

When necessary, a strategy to deal with unplanned high charges should be defined. This may include holding back excess charges in a special account to phase and release them in several subsequent periods when charges are lower than expected (applicable for Scenarios 1 and 2 and Scenario 3, if agreed with customers), or agreeing at a senior level not to charge (applicable for all scenarios).

If lower revenues than expected are generated, possible causes include:
- running insufficient work (perhaps the forecasts of workload were too high)
- incorrect figures have been used or other errors have been made.

Once again, it may be necessary to revise forecasts. Where running *costs* are the problem, the IT service organization will have to examine the possibility of making economies.

Another trigger for the activity is requests for reimbursements to customers, for example to correct charging errors. These requests are processed and may determine the need to issue credit notes. Charging not only includes the management of the customer's debits but their credits as well.

We make a final comment about service level agreements and Service Catalogs. Although prices may be included in these items, we have preferred to use the price list as the source of prices for the charging activity. This is because prices are not always included and because often the billing system is not integrated with them and a price list is managed separately.

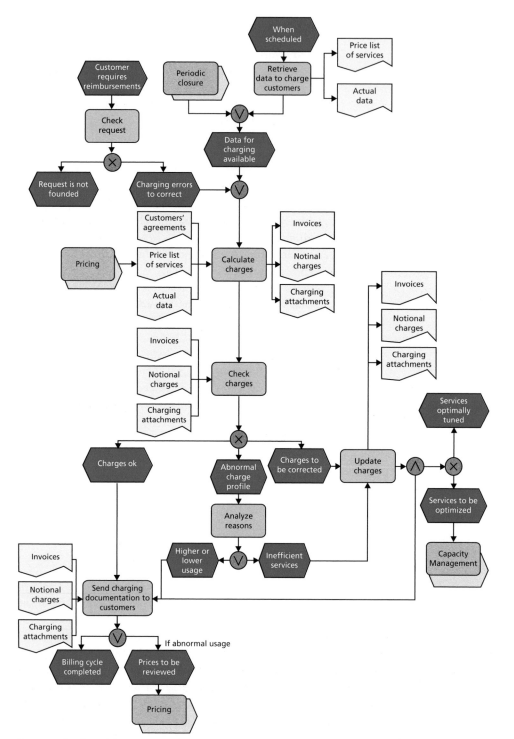

Figure 4.15 Charging activity

## 4.5   Relationships with other functions, processes and practices

IT financial management has a set of relationships with other important processes and practices of IT service management. Some aspects of these relationships have been explored when examining each activity of IT financial management in the previous sections of this chapter. We will now examine them in more detail, from the viewpoint of the external interfaced processes and practices.

### 4.5.1   Demand management
Demand management is a critical aspect of service management and is linked to IT financial management. This happens because a tight coupling exists between demand and capacity (see Figure 4.16), which means that peaks of requests cannot always be managed without impacts on service quality. Tariffs generally affect demand, as higher costs should reduce demand. This effect may be used to control demand by means of techniques such as differential charging, which encourages customers to use services at less busy times. Demand management should pass information back to IT financial management about the results achieved when such techniques and, more generally, control of demand patterns is achieved by making use of IT financial management.

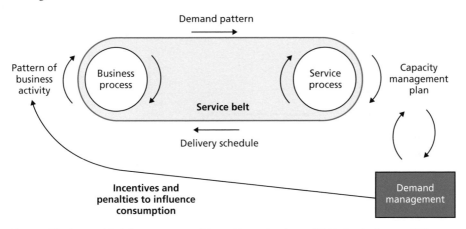

Figure 4.16 Business activity influences patterns of demand for services (source ITIL V3, Service Strategy, OGC)

### 4.5.2   Risk management
Risk management, according to the definition provided by the UK Office of Government Commerce's Management of Risk (M_o_R) methodology, is 'the task of ensuring that organization makes cost effective use of risk processes'. Risk management covers a wide range of topics, including business continuity management, security, program/project management and operational service management, which covers IT services too. Risk management uses many techniques to identify, evaluate, plan, control and monitor risks. Some of these techniques may interact with IT financial management, in particular with the investment evaluation activity, to evaluate the impacts of risks, the costs of mitigation actions, the costs and benefits of projects and/or programs related to risk management.

### 4.5.3 Supplier management

According to ITIL V3, the supplier management practice (see Figure 4.17) has the goal of managing suppliers and the services they supply. This clearly includes contracts and the financial aspects related to them.

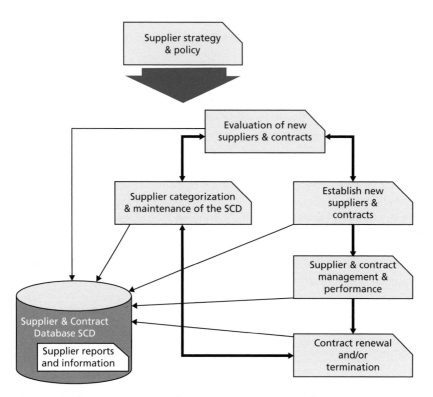

Figure 4.17 Supplier management practice (source ITIL V3, Service Design, OGC)

IT financial management provides information to supplier management to evaluate the performance of suppliers from a financial viewpoint (costs of services supplied). From the opposite viewpoint, IT financial management provides adequate funds to finance supplier management requirements and contracts and advice/guidance on purchase and procurement matters.

### 4.5.4 Incident management and request fulfilment

The goal of incident management is to return normal IT services for customers as quickly as possible (or agreed) after an incident, minimizing impacts. Categorization of incidents is a fundamental step of incident management to achieve its objectives and financial impact is one of the relevant aspects to be evaluated to fulfil it. IT financial management should provide easy-to-use guidelines and information to incident management to evaluate and use the financial impact for incident categorization. For example, the cost of loss of an IT service per time unit is very useful.

For a long time, request fulfilment has been considered part of the incident management process, according to ITIL V2, but it has become an independent practice in the next release of the framework. Service requests, a generic description for many types of demands, may vary greatly. Some of them, e.g. a password reset request, are repetitive and are generally included in the Service Catalog. When charging is performed, these service requests may be priced, in line with the IT financial management pricing activity. As discussed previously, pricing usually influences demand.

### 4.5.5 Access management
The goal of access management is to provide rights for users to be able to use IT service(s). Addition or removal of a user changes the demand pattern and, according to policies, may lead to changes in charging. It is therefore important that access management provides IT financial management with updated information about active users on services when this is a driver for charging.

### 4.5.6 Problem management
The primary objective of problem management is to prevent incidents from happening, by taking away the root causes of incidents, or by taking away risks for incidents to happen, thus contributing to minimizing their adverse impact on the business. The problem management process goes through several steps and uses several techniques to achieve its objective. A key question is whether the cost of definitively fixing a problem is justified by the savings derived from avoiding incidents related to it. IT financial management assists in assessing the impact of proposed resolutions or workarounds as well as in evaluating the financial impact of incidents related to problems.

From the opposite viewpoint, problem management provides IT financial management with the cost of resolving and preventing problems, which is used as an input to many IT financial management activities (planning, budgeting and forecasting).

### 4.5.7 Change management
According to ITIL V3, the objective of the change management process is to ensure that changes are recorded and then evaluated, authorized, prioritized, planned, tested, implemented, documented and reviewed in a controlled manner. Among the recommended aspects to be evaluated, we also find the assessment of:
- costs to implement the change
- changes to the running costs of service management activities due to its implementation
- inclusion of costs in the existing budget

Technically, it is incorrect to say that there is a process interface between change management and IT financial management, in the sense that the change management process already includes the assessment step that performs financial evaluation. As IT financial management is considered to be a function (or department), the relationship is the same as between any other department and process: financial roles (such as IT financial controllers) should be involved in the assessment step to perform or support it and the IT financial manager should be involved in service definition activities that result in calculating the budget for the transformation.

For organizations in Scenario 3, funding of changes should be carried out by customers when derived from their requests and by the service provider when due to its responsibilities. The same principle should apply transparently to organizations in Scenarios 1 and 2. However, in these cases customers should always be informed about the consequences of overstretching resources when a service provider authorizes changes and has no additional resources to cover their implementation costs.

### 4.5.8  Service Catalog management

The Service Catalog may include the prices of services. In order to do so the pricing activity, part of the IT financial management practice, should pass information about them. From the opposite perspective, the Service Catalog management practice passes the Service Catalog to the pricing activity.

### 4.5.9  Service level management

There is a relationship between investments and costs in services and a sustainable level of services. Generally, to improve service levels higher costs may be necessary. IT financial management provides advice and guidance to service level management to negotiate service levels.

Whether previously evaluated or not, changes to service levels should be managed through the change management process which assesses them for all aspects, including any impact on financial aspects.

In practice, demand for extra resources (which incurs cost) is not always driven by changes to improve service levels. Often, it is due to attempts to resolve problems or due to additional work needed to complete budgeted tasks, where the estimates are shown to be inaccurate. *Customers* usually expect IT services to manage this without additional cost, although there may be no IT budget available. The likely effect is an overstretching of resources, which affects all service levels. If such a situation occurs, any decision about costs (such as not funding required changes) should involve service level management to appraise and manage all effects. A challenge for IT service management is to overcome this situation, minimizing the cases where extra resources are needed to resolve problems.

For organizations in Scenario 3, there may be agreed penalties related to missed achievement of service levels. Such a clause would affect the revenues of the organization and is an input from service level management to the charging activity of IT financial management.

### 4.5.10 Capacity management

Capacity management is a function responsible for ensuring that IT resources are planned and scheduled to provide a consistent level of service that is matched to the current and future needs of the business, as agreed and documented in Service Level Agreements (SLAs) and Operational Level Agreements (OLAs). In conjunction with the business and its plans, capacity management provides a capacity plan that outlines the IT resources and funding needed to support the business plan, together with a cost justification for that expenditure.

The capacity plan is a fundamental input of the planning and budget activities; it is also important for delivering reviews and all periodic forecasts. It contains scenarios for different predictions of business demand, taking into account availability plans and costed options to deliver the agreed service level targets. While preparing it, financial management roles (e.g. IT financial controllers) should be involved as capacity plans are a significant source of costs to be tracked. Their involvement typically invokes the investment evaluation activity to ascertain cost justification of options and feeding all requested information for the purpose of controlling costs and savings associated with capacity plans. Another relationship between capacity management and IT financial management occurs with ongoing *changes* to the capacity plan: the changes should be reported to financial management for inclusion in forecasts and reviewed budget. Again, this may generally be done through the change management process, as modifications of the capacity plan may be addressed through formal changes when not periodically planned.

## 4.5.11 Asset management

### Introduction to asset management

According to ITIL V3, asset management is the practice 'responsible for tracking and reporting the value and ownership of financial assets throughout their lifecycle. Asset management is part of an overall service asset and configuration management process'. In ITIL V3 the asset management practice is described together with configuration management, as a configuration item may be an asset. From deeper analysis, it is clear that ITIL describes mainly configuration management; no specific processes or practices are described in detail to manage assets from the financial perspective.

Configuration items may correspond to asset items but this is not always true. Effectively, one of the main problems to face is the possible existing difference between assets in the accounting system and configuration items. Let us consider, for example, some servers that have been bought, each made of several components (central unit, disks, monitor, keyboard, operative system, virus protection software, etc.). The minimal and mandatory objective of financial management is to record and keep updated the value of goods in order to reflect that value correctly in reporting (e.g. balance sheets).

Purchase, stock and book values are often the only attributes managed and as a consequence the essential detailed information is lost. This is a case where 'finance' is concerned with meeting its information need for external reporting, as opposed to accommodating information requirements to fulfil business needs.

Stock and related value of goods can be managed with different approaches in financial management, such as by type or by detail. This is generally a matter of Management Accounting Systems (MAS) (see also section 6.5.5 for further details on MAS) when considering IT (except for Scenario 3 and, less frequently, for Scenario 2). In practice, in Scenario 1 and probably 2, financial management (and General Accounting Systems – GAS) does not deal with stock for IT related items (stock is managed only for items sold by the business).

Managing stock value by type means categorizing goods, for example monitors, and tracking existing quantities and values in stock. The value of each category of items is therefore managed as an average.

The approach above described raises several issues:

- it is not possible to track each item as no specific records are available
- the value of each type of item is an average and does not necessarily reflect the possible value of each item (a server costing 20,000 euros could be grouped together with servers costing just a few thousand)
- inventories may be difficult to perform (for example if the count of items does not correspond to the expected quantity, there is little or no information to understand what and where to find missing items)
- tracking is impossible to perform (labeling would be possible but it is generally not performed when adopting this approach)

Nevertheless, managing assets' value by type is still very much used, especially for intangible assets, such as software, which are very difficult to identify and/or 'label'. Assets that are physical items, such as servers, personal computers, routers, printers, scanners, PDAs, are frequently considered as a single and specific asset, with extensive information recorded about them (such as identifier, original cost, purchase order, location, supplier, etc.) in addition to value. If this is done, many of the disadvantages previously described are resolved. Unfortunately, managing by item adds relevant costs:

- initial recording and subsequent management of information (e.g. labeling) in line with asset management activities
- costs associated with the asset management tool (which may not align with the accounting system)
- probably, dedicated staff to run the activities (consider the initial recording and labeling or inventory management in large organizations)

To reduce the number of items and, therefore, the associated management cost, a mixed approach may be used: intangible assets and low value physical assets (e.g. mice) may be managed by quantity; and high value physical assets, by item. It is appropriate to set the threshold that distinguishes between low and high value items by policies (e.g. 500 euros). This value is sometimes established by governing law and regulations.

IT stock and related value is generally not frequently managed in Scenario 1; it is managed by a specific IT oriented Management Accounting System in Scenario 2 and is managed by a General Accounting System and probably Management Accounting System in Scenario 3. Regardless of scenarios, attention should be paid to controlling and justifying the costs associated with asset management through policies giving guidance on the methods and level of detail required in managing stock.

Managing (accounting) book value of goods requires a calculation of depreciation, which is performed in line with fiscal regulations and the accounting model. Depreciation is calculated on the basis of purchase invoices; the calculation is performed by the General Accounting System (see also section 6.5.5 for further details on General Accounting Systems), even when a stock of assets is not physically and logically managed. Depreciation should be considered in the calculation of ROI (see section 6.5.15) and in evaluation of the total cost of ownership (TCO).

.

Another important aspect to be understood is that, even when assets are managed by item, a configuration item may not necessarily correspond to an asset item and vice versa. Consider the following example: a personal computer has been bought and, from an Asset Management point of view, one item has been identified (the whole personal computer corresponding to the item present in the invoice). This is enough to track and report the value and ownership of financial assets, which is the aim of asset management. However, from a configuration management point of view, this would probably be not enough. The goals of configuration management, according to ITIL V3, are different and wider:

• supporting the business and customers' control objectives and requirements
• supporting efficient and effective service management processes by providing accurate configuration information to enable people to make decisions at the right time, e.g. to authorize changes and releases or resolve incidents and problems faster
• minimizing the number of quality and compliance issues caused by improper configuration of services and assets
• optimizing the service assets, IT configurations, capabilities and resources

To support these objectives, configuration management would analyze the personal computer and create several configuration items with specific attributes and relationships, e.g. central unit or cabinet, operating system, virus protection software, specific software installed. This situation is described graphically in Figure 4.18.

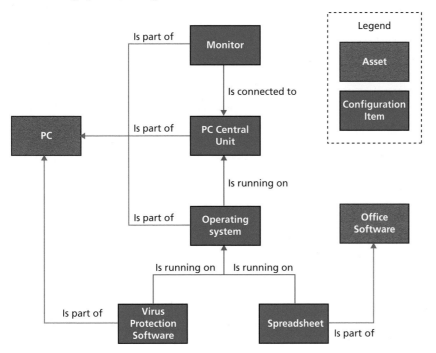

Figure 4.18 Example of relationships between asset and configuration items

Although it is typical that an asset is composed of several configuration items, the opposite relationship is also possible. For example, racks may be expensive physical goods and, therefore assets; nevertheless, they might not be managed as configuration items but simply as an attribute (e.g. location) of other configuration items (e.g. servers).

Another example to explain the possible differences between assets and configuration items is becoming very common with the introduction of virtualization of machines. On one physical asset, the server, many virtual servers (configuration items) may be defined and, on top of them, many software instances (possible assets) may run.

Finally, we have learned that asset management can be either an independent practice or, preferably, integrated with configuration management and that many-to-many relationships or correspondences may exist between asset items and configuration items.

Another aspect to be considered is the possible implications of the term 'financial assets' in the ITIL V3 definition of asset management referenced earlier. From a mere financial perspective, a financial asset on the balance sheet represents assets net of depreciation. The majority of organizations continue to use useful and efficient assets after they have been fully depreciated; this is because the depreciation timeframe often does not coincide with the duration of the lifecycle of the asset). These assets may remain on the floor (e.g. print server) generating real economic value, but would not show up on the balance sheet as an asset. Their salvage or market value may also be deemed to be zero thus complying with regulations on adjusting for market value, but they still deliver value to the organization. Since they are deployed, they must also remain as a registered configuration item and should only be removed from the configuration management system through a change when they actually stop being used.

## Software asset management
Traditionally, software assets are often managed with a lower level of detail than physical assets. This does not mean that they have a smaller economic value. On the contrary, the most relevant result and therefore asset of IT efforts for organizations is often software. Unfortunately, software is not always easy to identify and label. For example, all computers and, more generally, all hardware items are characterized by a serial number, but for software the best known identifier is probably the license key for packages, while for custom applications there is practically none. Furthermore, even a license key (the best identifier) is not always a unique identifier. For example, it may be possible (and often it is appropriate) to install software on different computers using the same license key. Although licenses may be not a good identifier of configuration items, they typically are the organizations' assets and therefore need to be managed accordingly. They are often a source of costs related to maintenance fees, which should be considered in financial management activities (e.g. budgeting and accounting) even when their book value is zero.

ISO/IEC 19770-1:2006 has been developed to enable organizations to prove that they are performing software asset management (SAM) to a level that is sufficient to satisfy corporate governance requirements and ensure effective support for overall IT service management. Good practice in software asset management should result in several benefits, and certifiable good practice should allow management and other organizations to be confident and rely on the adequacy of these practices. Through certification, the expected benefits are achieved with a high degree of certitude. software asset management should, for example, facilitate the management of business risks, cost control and thus enable the achievement of competitive advantage.

## Asset management activities and interfaces with IT financial management

Figure 4.19 describes the framework of practices constituting ISO/IEC 19770-1:2006.

| Organizational Management Processes for SAM | | | |
|---|---|---|---|
| **4.2 Control Environment for SAM** | | | |
| Corporate Governance Process for SAM | Roles and Responsibilities for SAM | Policies Processes and Procedures for SAM | Competence in SAM |
| **4.3 Planning and Implementation Processes for SAM** | | | |
| Planning for SAM | Implementation of SAM | Monitoring and Review of SAM | Continual Improvement of SAM |

| Core SAM Processes | | | |
|---|---|---|---|
| **4.4 Inventory Processes for SAM** | | | |
| Software Asset Indentification | Software Asset Inventory Management | Software Asset Control | |
| **4.5 Verification and Compliance Processes for SAM** | | | |
| Software Asset Record Verification | Software Licensing Compliance | Software Asset Security Compliances | Conformance Verification for SAM |
| **4.6 Operations Management Processes and Interfaces for SAM** | | | |
| Relationship and Contract Management for SAM | Financial Management SAM | Service Level Management for SAM | Security Management for SAM |

| Primary Process Interfaces for SAM | | | |
|---|---|---|---|
| **4.7 Life Cycle Process Interfaces for SAM** | | | |
| Change Management Process | Software Development Process | Software Development Process | Problem Management Process |
| Acquisition Process | Software Release Management Process | Incident Management Process | Retirement Process |

Figure 4.19 Software asset management practices according to ISO/IEC 19770-1

Among operations management processes and interfaces for software asset management, we can identify financial management for software asset management as a specific practice related to IT financial management. The objective of the financial management for software asset management activity is budgeting, accounting and charging for software and related assets, and ensuring that relevant financial information is readily available for financial reporting, tax planning and calculations such as total cost of ownership and Return On Investment. Financial management for software asset management does not cover charging.

Through implementing software asset management practices, organizations should develop formal budgets for the acquisition of software assets, account for actual acquisition against budget, provide documented information about the value of assets (including historical cost and depreciation), review at least quarterly actual expenditure against budget with documented conclusions and defined actions.

In addition to ISO/IEC 19770-1, OGC SAM is a relevant practice. Once again, in OGC SAM, financial management is one of the core asset management activities, and it includes:

- ensuring the preparation of reliable financial information for all software assets, including during their procurement, operation (e.g. regular depreciation) and subsequent retirement and disposal
- the collection of cost/benefit information related to the use of software assets, to allow the calculation of Total Cost of Ownership (TCO) and ROI
- proper consideration of accounting and tax treatments

What has been seen for software assets may easily be extended to non-software assets. The architecture of ISO/IEC 19770-1 (see Figure 4.19) and the processes of OGC SAM are suitable, with adaptations, to be used for non-software assets as well. The relationships described above, between software asset management and financial management, can be extended to asset management and financial management too.

## Conclusions

Specific practices and activities, dedicated to the financial management of assets, will be present in organizations where asset management is evolved and mature. These should interface with the IT financial management practices and activities described in this book in both directions, e.g. acquiring inputs for budgeting and/or charging and providing outputs for accounting. Finally, policies for asset management and IT financial management should be logical and consistent.

IT asset management is an important discipline whose relevance is growing with the value of IT assets (hardware and, especially, software). Budgeting and accounting are the key financial management areas where IT asset management may define specific approaches, activities and methods. IT asset management may be implemented as integrated with configuration management, although this does not mean that there will be a complete correspondence between configuration and asset items.

In practice, there may be different situations, depending on the organization:

a. no specific IT asset management responsibilities and activities are present; some activities related to asset management are performed within other IT financial management activities (budgeting, accounting, etc.)
b. IT asset management responsibilities and activities are defined, interfaced and harmonized with those of IT financial management
c. IT asset management and configuration management activities and responsibilities are defined and integrated; these responsibilities and activities are interfaced and harmonized with those of IT financial management.

Case a. is typical of organizations in Scenario 1 while situations b. and c. are found in Scenarios 2 and 3.

## 4.6    IT financial management and the service lifecycle

IT financial management activities are part of the wider family of IT service management processes. As discussed in the introduction, ITIL V3, the most widely known and used reference framework for IT service management, has approached service management from the lifecycle perspective. The service lifecycle is an organizational model that provides insight to:
- the way service management is structured
- the way the various lifecycle components are linked to each other
- the impact that changes in one component will have on other components and on the entire lifecycle system.

The service lifecycle approach is illustrated in Figure 4.20 and it consists of five phases:
- service strategy
- service design
- service transition
- service operation
- continual service improvement

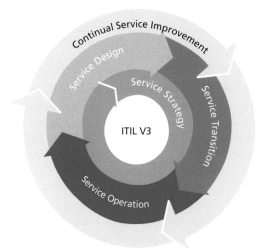

Figure 4.20 ITIL V3 Service lifecycle (source OGC, ITIL V3)

Service strategy is the axis of the service lifecycle that drives all other phases; it is the phase of policy making and setting objectives. The service design, service transition and service operation phases are guided by this strategy, focused on delivery, adjustment and change. The continual service improvement phase stands for learning and improving, and embraces all other lifecycle phases. This phase initiates improvement programs and projects, and prioritizes them based on the strategic objectives of the organization.

The key question raised is: how does the service lifecycle perspective fit with IT financial management? In the original ITIL V3 framework, this is simply resolved by arranging IT financial management in the service strategy domain and, therefore, in that book. However, this vision simplifies too much and does not explain how activities such as charging or accounting can be considered 'strategic' in the sense meant by the framework. Figure 4.21 shows a different point of view where the activities of IT financial management have been split along the different service lifecycle phases.

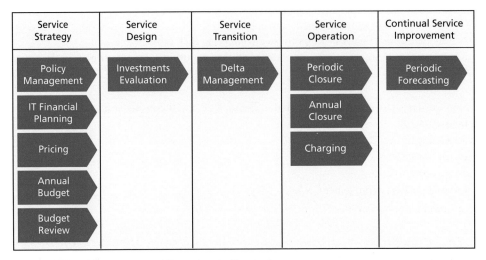

Figure 4.21 IT financial management activities and service lifecycle phases

In some cases, defining where to position activities is easy and straightforward. This is the case of the activities positioned in service strategy: policy management, IT financial planning, pricing, annual budget and budget review. Investment evaluation is invoked by activities and practices positioned in different phases, e.g. IT financial planning, capacity management, change management and problem management. The final choice has been to position it in the design phase because that is where the service is carefully evaluated for the first time, from a financial perspective too. Financial evaluation is expected to be a core activity during the identification of requirements and design of the service. Delta management is also invoked by several practices but is strongly related to the change management process. For this reason it has been placed in the service transition phase. It should be straightforward to position the activities located under service operation too: periodic closure, annual closure and charging. Conversely, periodic forecast is probably one of the most difficult to position. The decision has been to consider it part of the continual improvement phase as gathering data, processing them, analyzing and identifying trends (which are key activities for the seven-step improvement process of continual service improvement) are core activities of periodic forecast too. There is much of continual service improvement in periodic forecast.

The positioning chosen for the IT financial management activities into the service lifecycle phases may be questioned, but it is clear that activities cannot be simply considered part of a single phase, and are distributed among them instead.

# 5 Roles of IT financial management

## 5.1 Overview of roles

The roles of IT financial management depend on the scenarios we have described in Chapter 2. First, we will analyze each of them to understand the main roles involved and possibly their positioning in organizations. Later, we will discuss some of the roles identified in dedicated sections.

We will try to show where responsibilities lie by means of RACI charts. RACI is an acronym for the four main roles of:
- **responsible** – the person responsible for getting the job done
- **accountable** – the person responsible for achieving the target result (only one person can be accountable for each task)
- **consulted** – the person who is consulted and whose opinion is sought
- **informed** – the person who is kept up-to-date on progress.

The RACI charts presented later in this chapter should not be interpreted as the unique solution for organizational issues. They have been defined through thinking about generic scenarios and situations, but every organization will face a different and specific one. The charts have to be considered as useful and common examples of how responsibilities may be split among activity actors, and therefore they can be useful for designing and implementing an adapted set of roles and positions.

## 5.2 Roles for Scenario 1: IT financial management for internal IT departments

In this scenario, the IT department is one among the many departments participating in the financial activities of the organization. Its actual organization depends on many factors; among them, the size of the organization is a very relevant one. In our example, we will refer to a small to medium organization, where IT has not defined specific roles for financial management. Figure 5.1 describes the main roles involved in this scenario and their responsibilities for IT financial management practices and topics. So, for example, the row of the RACI about the planning activity reports responsibilities related to the domain of IT and not of the whole organization.

The main roles identified in this scenario are the Chief Information Officer (CIO or IT Manager), the financial controller, the IT budget owner and the budget requester. The CIO participates in the definition of the financial management activities related to IT but in the RACI we have set the Chief Financial Officer (CFO) as accountable for final design. The CFO has to guarantee the overall coherence of financial management practices and systems. The CIO plays also an important role for the definition of policies for IT financial management but, again, the CFO is the final accountable role as coherence and overall perspective is the most relevant aspect of this scenario. For IT investments and budget, the CIO is accountable and he/she plays an active role in the related activities (at least to give final approval but also to coordinate activities). Financial controllers (probably belonging to the financial department) play an important supporting role. They can be more than one, depending on the organization's size, and they are typically allocated several responsibilities:

- implementing and monitoring internal controls
- collecting, checking, preparing and distributing information (for example historical data) required to execute activities
- ad hoc consulting, to the benefit of actors of the activities (for example about the rules to be followed to prepare budget or business cases)
- executing operational tasks (such as launching batch processes or reporting)
- performing analysis of results

| IT related processes | CEO | CFO | Business Executive | CIO | Financial Controller | IT Budget Owner | Budget Requester |
|---|---|---|---|---|---|---|---|
| Definition of processes | I | A/R | C | R | C | C | I |
| **Strategy** | | | | | | | |
| Policy Management | C | A/R | I | R | I | I | I |
| Planning | C | R | C | A/R | R | C | I |
| Investments evaluation | I | C | C | A/R | R | R | C |
| Pricing | | | | | | | |
| **Budgeting** | | | | | | | |
| Annual Budget | C | C | C | A/R | R | R | C |
| Budget Review | C | C | C | A/R | R | R | C |
| Period Forecast | I | I | C | A/R | R | R | C |
| Delta Management | C | C | C | A/R | R | R | C |
| **Accounting** | | | | | | | |
| Periodic Closure | I | A | C | R | R | I | I |
| Annual Closure | I | A | C | R | R | I | I |
| **Charging** | | | | | | | |
| Customer Charging | | | | | | | |
| Claims Management | | | | | | | |

Figure 5.1 Roles and RACI chart for Scenario 1

## 5.3 Roles for Scenario 2: IT financial management for internal IT providers

In this scenario, the IT department has specific needs and objectives for financial management. In this domain it acts with more autonomy, performs a larger number of activities and it probably also appoints specific roles to deal with financial topics. This is especially true for large organizations with relevant IT departments. Figure 5.2 shows the main roles involved in this scenario and their responsibilities for IT financial management practices and topics.

| IT related processes | CEO | CFO | Business Executive | CIO | IT Financial Manager | IT Financial Controller | IT Budget Owner | Budget Requester |
|---|---|---|---|---|---|---|---|---|
| Definition of processes | I | C | C | C | A/R | C | C | I |
| **Strategy** | | | | | | | | |
| Policy Management | I | C | I | C | A/R | I | I | I |
| Planning | C | R | C | A/R | R | R | C | I |
| Investments evaluation | I | C | C | A/R | R | R | R | C |
| Pricing | C | C | C | A/R | R | R | | |
| **Budgeting** | | | | | | | | |
| Annual Budget | C | C | C | A/R | R | R | R | C |
| Budget Review | C | C | C | A/R | R | R | R | C |
| Period Forecast | I | I | C | R | A/R | R | R | C |
| Delta Management | C | C | C | A/R | R | R | R | C |
| **Accounting** | | | | | | | | |
| Periodic Closure | I | R | I | I | A/R | R | I | I |
| Annual Closure | I | R | I | I | A/R | R | I | I |
| **Charging** | | | | | | | | |
| Customer Charging | | | I | I | A/R | R | | |
| Claims Management | I | I | C | C | A/R | R | | |

Figure 5.2 Roles and RACI chart for Scenario 2

The IT financial manager is a new central role. He/she has the responsibility to define the specific activities of IT financial management. This is done by consulting with all the relevant stakeholders of the activities, among which there will certainly be the CFO and CIO. In this scenario, policies are probably specific for IT financial management. They are defined by the IT Financial Manager, interacting with the CIO/CFO. The IT Financial Manager will probably also be responsible for the periodic closures for IT. This task is always performed in strict conjunction with the financial department's staff and finally with the CFO. In some organizations, coordination of closures may be managed by the financial department, cooperating with the IT Financial Manager. The CIO will still remain the final accountable role for IT figures: planning data, budgets of IT. He/she will manage deltas from budgets. However, to determine the responsibilities and performed activities precisely, the organization's internal system of delegations plays a fundamental role. Deltas within certain limits will usually be authorized by the owner of the IT budget (typically someone delegated by the CIO) while important deviations will probably require the authorization of CFOs, when not CEOs.

The role played by the financial controller in Scenario 1 will be performed by the IT financial controller in large IT organizations. The controller will execute a large number of the activities needed to execute IT financial management activities. In Figure 5.2 this is true for customer charging and claims management as well. This is an appropriate option when notional charging is the choice (see also section 6.5.1 for further information about charging perspectives). However, when a significant number of customers is actually billed, then a dedicated billing department, belonging to the IT or financial department) will probably be a better option.

## 5.4 Roles for Scenario 3: IT financial management for market IT providers

In this scenario, IT services are the core business and IT financial management is the organization's financial management. The scope of activities goes beyond those described in Chapter 4 and embraces responsibilities for fund raising, payments, taxation, the organization's balance statements, etc., which are not shown in Figure 5.3. For these reasons, we have also deleted the label 'IT' in front of many roles.

| Financial Management processes (partial list) | CEO | CFO | Business Executive | Financial Controller | Billing Manager | Budget Owner | Budget Requester |
|---|---|---|---|---|---|---|---|
| Definition of processes | I | A/R | C | C | C | C | I |
| **Strategy** | | | | | | | |
| Policy Management | C | A/R | I | I | I | I | I |
| Planning | A/R | R | R | R | I | C | I |
| Investments evaluation | I | R | A/R | R | I | R | C |
| Pricing | I | C | A/R | C | C | | |
| **Budgeting** | | | | | | | |
| Annual Budget | A/R | R | R | R | I | R | C |
| Budget Review | A/R | R | R | R | I | R | C |
| Period Forecast | R | A/R | R | R | R | R | C |
| Delta Management | A/R | R | R | R | I | R | C |
| **Accounting** | | | | | | | |
| Periodic Closure | I | A/R | C | R | C | I | I |
| Annual Closure | I | A/R | C | R | C | I | I |
| **Charging** | | | | | | | |
| Customer Charging | I | I | C | C | A/R | I | |
| Claims Management | I | I | C | C | A/R | I | |

Figure 5.3 Roles and RACI chart for Scenario 3

Exploring all possible allocations of responsibilities in a financial department goes far beyond the scope of this book. Nevertheless, the simplified RACI of figure 5.3 shows a possible option, where a more relevant business role appears.

## 5.5 Details of roles

In the previous sections, an overall view of IT financial management roles has been given, focusing on the whole picture and the relationships existing among them (RACI charts). In the following sections, we will enter into a role-centric perspective, where some of the roles previously identified will be analyzed in detail. We have chosen those roles that are more strictly related and key to IT service management, especially in Scenario 2: IT financial manager, IT financial controller and IT budget owner.

### 5.5.1 IT financial manager

The IT financial manager is the key role of IT financial management. He/she is the owner of the activities. Some organizations have a dedicated IT finance manager, but in others the role may be played by someone from the finance department or senior IT managers, especially those with responsibility for other service management practices (service level manager and capacity manager, for example) and the head of IT. The need for a dedicated role usually arises when the culture of IT service management grows and when the specific needs of IT become clear. This is the typical situation of Scenario 2. In large organizations, a specific function will probably be created in the IT department with responsibilities for IT financial management, often including asset management (at least the financial attributes of assets). In such a case, the IT financial manager may become the head of this function.

Table 5.1 shows some of the typical advantages of positioning the IT financial manager in the IT department versus the financial department. Independently from where they are located, the IT financial manager must have an adequate level of seniority and leadership to manage all his/her responsibilities.

| IT financial manager belonging to IT department | IT financial manager belonging to financial department |
| --- | --- |
| Hierarchical relationships with IT department's staff | Relationships with financial department's staff, especially CFO |
| Knowledge of IT service management | Knowledge of financial management practices |
| Knowledge of supplied IT services | Knowledge of accounting and investment evaluation principles and techniques |
| Knowledge of service management tools | |
| Knowledge of IT specificities | Knowledge of financial management systems |

Table 5.1 Comparisons of advantages of positioning the IT financial manager in the IT department vs. financial department

Opting for the IT department usually gives the CIO better leverage and confidence that the IT financial manager is focused on the IT mission and objectives; it is normally the preferred solution.

### Key responsibilities

The key responsibilities of the role are:
- ownership of IT financial management activities, meaning:
  - designing activities involving all stakeholders
  - designing and identifying suitable tools to support all IT financial management practices

- being owner of the projects aimed at implementing or improving IT financial management activities and/or tools
- preparing and maintaining all documentation inherent to the IT financial management practices
- publicizing the activities
- defining and controlling KPIs to evaluate effectiveness and efficiency of the activities
- preparing periodic and ad hoc reporting about the performance of the activities
- preparing and maintaining a practice improvement plan (see also continual improvement, section 6.1)
- improving the effectiveness and efficiency of the activities
- reviewing any proposed enhancements to the activities
- providing input to the ongoing Service Improvement Plan
- addressing any issues with the running of the activities
- ensuring all relevant staff have the required training in the activities and are aware of their role in the activities
- ensuring that the activities, roles, responsibilities and documentation are regularly reviewed and audited
- interfacing with line management, ensuring that the activities receive the necessary staff resources
- ownership of IT financial management policies, meaning:
  - preparing of policies in cooperation with all stakeholders and, in particular, the CIO and CFO
  - communicating the policies
  - providing support about their interpretation and use
  - controlling their adoption, taking corrective actions and escalating issues to top management (in particular the CIO, CFO)
- supporting the organization's planning, budgeting, delta management and investment evaluation activities for IT aspects, meaning:
  - acquiring input and constraints from top management, in particular the CIO and CFO
  - supporting the definition of timing and deliveries
  - coordinating IT financial controllers in charge of key activities
  - monitoring the activities (timing, quality)
  - acting as the key interface between stakeholders (top management) and actors of the activities
  - providing support for executing the activities and required information (for example analysis required by service owners, service level manager, capacity manager, etc.)
  - solving or escalating issues related to the activities
- ownership of forecasting, closure, charging and claims management activities, meaning:
  - being responsible for the results and for the correct execution of the activities
  - coordinating all actors of the activities
  - providing support for the activities as meant in the previous bullet

In Scenario 1, the key responsibilities of the IT financial manager are usually taken by the CIO. In Scenario 3, they are split between the CEO and CFO of the organization or business unit, as providing IT services is the core activity.

## Recommended skills

The following is a short list of the recommended skills for an IT financial manager:

- sound numerical and financial skills
- ability to interact successfully with all levels of the customers' and organization's management
- ability to coordinate teams dedicated to activities or project tasks
- thorough approach to documentation and scheduling
- excellent communication and negotiation skills
- good presentational skills.

## Recommended knowledge

The following is a short list of the recommended competencies for an IT financial manager:

- advanced knowledge of accounting principles, methods, techniques (e.g. cost accounting) and financial reporting
- advanced knowledge of investment appraisal methods and techniques
- advanced knowledge about local -or international if necessary- country laws (legal and fiscal requirements)
- good knowledge of statistical and analytical principles and activities
- good knowledge of IT service management practices and roles
- basic knowledge of supplied IT services, characteristics and figures
- good knowledge of business process management and optimization
- good knowledge of financial and service management tools, features and functionalities
- good knowledge of project management principles, activities and methods
- good understanding of the customers' businesses and of how IT can affect the delivery of their products or services
- basic knowledge of suppliers' contract structure and management
- basic knowledge of customers' contract structure and management.

It will be difficult to find a candidate with all the required skills and competencies, at least one with the right seniority and leadership and immediately available for the role. It is common to search for the best matching choice and to start training programs to reinforce weak competencies and/or skills.

### 5.5.2 IT financial controller

The IT financial controller is another key role of IT financial management. Controllers have a supportive role to other actors in many of the activities but also carry out many specific tasks.

## Key responsibilities

The key responsibilities are:

- supporting the design of IT financial management practices
- preparing and controlling data and reports input for all other activities (for example the initial information needed to prepare a budget such as current balance or the previous year budget)
- coordinating and controlling activities of other actors of IT financial management (for example the periodic preparation of forecasts)
- supplying required information and guidance to other actors of IT financial management (for example, information on how to use accounts or cost centers or support inherent to the use of tools)

- producing and checking integrated output, meaning:
  - assembling partial results (for example putting all IT budgets together)
  - verifying completeness of input data and managing its retrieval
  - launching batch operations (e.g. for calculation of depreciation and accruals or billing) and reporting
  - checking results and managing corrections and iterations
  - performing analysis (for example variance analysis) and preparing related comments
  - distributing reports
  - activating escalations

The IT financial controller ensures that activities are correctly executed, plays a back-office role and performs many of the analysis required. A controller is a typical role of financial and accounting departments but specific competencies about IT and provided services are needed, so an IT financial controller may come from the financial department or from IT. Regardless of where they are located, an IT financial controller may be specialized in specific IT services or domains (for example applications or infrastructures) and he/she is a key support to the IT financial manager. For this reason, it may be preferable to make them report directly to the IT financial manager.

## Recommended skills
The following is a short list of the recommended skills for an IT financial controller:
- advanced numerical and financial skills
- ability to interact successfully with intermediate levels of the customers' and organization's management
- advanced capabilities to manage documentation and scheduling
- good communication and negotiation skills
- optimal presentational skills.

## Recommended knowledge
The following is a short list of the recommended competencies for an IT financial controller:
- advanced knowledge of accounting principles, methods, techniques (e.g. cost accounting) and financial reporting
- advanced knowledge of investment appraisal methods and techniques
- advanced knowledge about statistical and analytical principles and activities
- advanced knowledge of financial and service management tools, features and functionalities
- good knowledge of IT service management practices and roles
- good knowledge of assigned budget domains (IT services, projects)
- good knowledge about local -or international if necessary- country laws (legal and fiscal requirements)
- basic knowledge of project management principles, activities and methods
- basic understanding of the customers' businesses and how IT can affect the delivery of their products or services.

One of the critical aspects of this role is to correctly size the number of IT financial controllers and to find resources with ideal skills to take the role. Several seasonal factors may influence the level of activity. For example, during the planning and budgeting periods the effort is substantial while in the central part of several months of the year it may be not so intense.

### 5.5.3 IT budget owner

IT budget owner is a role common to all scenarios. The final owner of the IT consolidated budget is the CIO but it is a common practice to split the overall budget among IT managers, based on different criteria. The traditional approach to assign budgets is by domain (e.g. infrastructure or application or project). Owners of the budget have the responsibility to suggest and control it and, when authorized, to approve specific investments or costs referred to it. The right to actually approve investments and costs depends on the organization's internal system of delegations, which generally assigns responsibilities on the basis of amounts to approve. Depending on the scenario (certainly for Scenario 3), there can also be IT budget owners for revenues, whose main responsibility is typically to close and manage agreements with customers to achieve the target figures for revenues. These may be positioned in a demand management department, interfacing with captive customers, or in the sales department when the organization is facing the open market.

The IT service management approach may lead to the introduction of a less traditional assignment of budgets, the driving principle being IT services. In such a case, the service budget may be assigned to its service owner, possibly with intermediate levels of consolidation, corresponding to IT line managers. A particular characteristic of this approach is the fact that budgets by service may be generally not technologically homogeneous (for example only servers and related management activities) but collect heterogeneous components, such as servers, applications, middleware (e.g. databases). This also means that owners will need to possess more cross-skills. The definition of budget responsibility by service may co-exist with budget responsibilities defined by domain. For example, an IT budget owner of a server platform service can provide resources to an IT budget owner of an end-to-end service. In this case, they will both be responsible for their own services and budgets and there will be a negotiation between them about the usage and costs of the server platform service. The owner of the end-to-end service budget will acquire resources(actually or notionally) from the owner of the server platform service, who should be responsible for SLAs/ OLAs/ as well (treated as an internal supplier). In this case, the IT budget owner of the server platform service would probably be responsible for the internal revenues of its service, in addition to the costs to run it.

### Key responsibilities

The key responsibilities of the IT budget owner are:
- defining proposals for investments and management costs for their assigned domains to prepare financial plans and budgets
- endorsing business cases for investments and proposing their execution
- approving investments within the limits of authorized expenditure defined by budget and policies (e.g. the system of delegations)
- confirming the balance of periodic and annual closures
- forecasting the remaining costs and investments of IT services and projects according to the forecast activity and using balance information
- approving emerging or requested deltas of costs and investments within the limits of authorized expenditure defined by budget and policies (e.g. the system of delegations)

## Recommended skills

The following is a short list of the recommended skills for an IT budget owner:
- basic numerical and financial skills
- ability to interact successfully with intermediate levels of customers' and organization's management
- good communication and negotiation skills.

## Recommended knowledge

The role of the IT budget owner is aligned to the IT organization and assigned to many resources with different profiles, competencies and skills. Resources allocated to this role are often not dedicated to it but cover also other roles; their main competencies and skills will be strongly influenced by these additional roles. The following short list should therefore not be interpreted as an exhaustive list of recommended competencies for an IT budget owner but as common characteristics, which should complete the profile:
- basic knowledge of accounting principles, methods, techniques (e.g. cost accounting) and financial reporting
- basic knowledge of investment appraisal methods and techniques
- good knowledge of IT service management practices and roles
- advanced knowledge of assigned budget domains
- basic knowledge of financial and service management tools, features and functionalities
- understanding of the customers' businesses and how IT can affect the delivery of their products or services.

# 6 Planning and implementing IT financial management

Defining the approach for planning and implementing is a general question that arises in many areas of IT service management, not only in the IT financial management domain. The approach to implement capacity management, configuration management or other practices of IT service management may be effectively the same as the approach used for IT financial management at a high level (the steps, methods and techniques applied).

When it is necessary to improve some areas or aspect of an organization, the following are practices that may be very useful: business process engineering, improvement and management, project management, continuous improvement (Kaizen) and organizational change management. In section 6.1, we examine the practices that best address continual improvement (improvement by predetermined steps) (e.g. business process reengineering). In section 6.2 we describe an example of structure and phases of a project aimed at implementing an IT financial management systems, as project management is a fundamental technique supporting continual improvement. In section 6.3, we address the practices to deal with continuous improvement (Kaizen, ITIL CSI approach). Section 6.4 describes how to deal with the issues raised by organizational change. In section 6.5 we explore the key decision to be taken while designing IT financial management. Related to this chapter is section 10.4, describing additional techniques that can be used to facilitate and achieve improvements. Finally in section 6.6 we present the main challenges, possible problems and critical success factor of introducing/improving IT financial management.

## 6.1 Continual service improvement

The most widely known and used method for process improvement in the past has been business process reengineering. The business process reengineering method (BPR) is described by Hammer and Champy (2003) as 'the fundamental reconsideration and the radical redesign of organizational processes, in order to achieve drastic improvement of current performance in cost, services and speed'. Rather than organizing a company into functional specialties (such as production, accounting, marketing, etc.) and looking at the tasks that each function performs, Hammer and Champy recommend that, with this approach, it should be looking at complete processes and 'rebuilding' the company, from materials acquisition, through production, marketing and distribution. Hammer and Champy suggested a structured approach to achieve the desired change, which includes the following steps.

1. Develop the business vision and process objectives.
2. Identify the business processes to be redesigned.
3. Understand and measure the existing processes.
4. Identify IT levers.
4. Design and build a prototype of the new process.
6. Adapt the organizational structure and the governance model.

In practice a complete review of the business is not a frequent need for most organizations. More often organizations need to improve specific process areas or solve specific problems. The original approach, designed to achieve radical changes, has been often tailored and used to deal with these reduced objectives and the business process reengineering term has been misused to refer to these projects. Process engineering and process improvement, as illustrated in Figure 6.1, are more appropriate terms for this type of intervention.

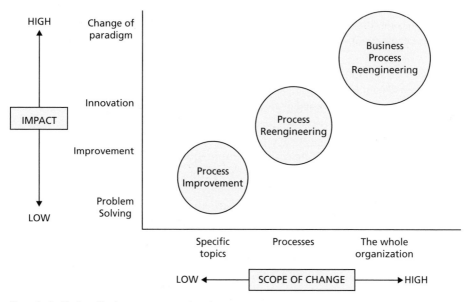

Figure 6.1 Positioning of business process reengineering

Regardless of terminology, it is important to observe that the method behind business process reengineering, process reengineering and process improvement terms has the objective of moving an organization from an initial situation (as-is status) to a target one (to-be status), both analyzed and fully described. This normally happens by means of a program or a project, depending on the scope and impact of changes to be achieved, which may affect processes, tools, roles, responsibilities and partners. The assumptions supporting this approach are:
• change is a phased transition between one stable status to another
• change is a rational process
• change can be analyzed and planned
• change can be managed.

This method can be applied to IT financial management. Relevant changes, which may be considered business process reengineering projects, could be (for example) moving from Scenario 1 or 2 to Scenario 3. Examples of process engineering projects could be introducing or reviewing the charging activity, or introducing a management accounting system to manage the full cost of IT Services. Finally, an example of process improvement could be the reduction of the time needed to prepare financial statements. A complete example of a project aimed at changing the existing financial system is described in section 6.2.

As the only constant thing in life is change, there is no static status that can be optimal forever. In addition, in the real world, many process improvement or reengineering projects have failed to release the desired benefits at the desired costs, at least at the first attempt. There has been early recognition of the need for a continual and iterative approach to attain full implementation and optimization of processes. Business process improvement or business process management are terms used to refer to practices that have addressed these issues by introducing the concept of process lifecycle management, where optimization is a core part of their model. This concept and approach is also present in IT service management culture and practice. Figure 6.2 describes the implementing/improvement cycle that is suggested by both ITIL version 2 and version 3 frameworks. By means of iterative cycles, processes can be implemented/improved using this approach.

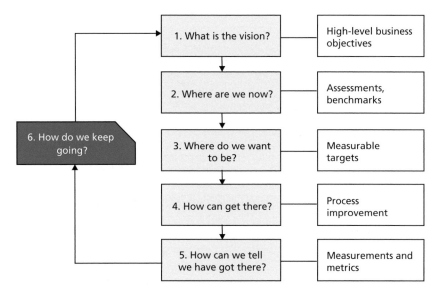

Figure 6.2 Implementation/improvement cycle (source OGC)

Maturity frameworks, such as the one described in section 10.1 and applicable to IT service management processes, provide excellent support for the improvement cycle. Organizational maturity refers to an organization's ability to perform. Maturity frameworks define the evolutionary levels that an organization passes through as it becomes more competent and optimized. An initial assessment, as described in section 10.4.1, will position the organization in the maturity frameworks and help it to understand its capabilities (this means accomplishing step two of Figure 6.2). This can be used to define the next step of improvement (this means accomplishing step three of Figure 6.2), which is often a step of maturity ahead of the initial assessed level.

Maturity frameworks can be general, as the one described in section 10.1, which can be applied to IT financial management as well, but these give limited guidance for specific activities. Other examples of specific maturity frameworks for IT financial management may be derived from COBIT (see section 10.3 for more information about the COBIT framework). Specific maturity frameworks are clearly preferable to drive the improvement of activities.

Table 6.1 describes the maturity levels that are part of the CobiT 'DS6 Identify and Allocate Costs' objective that is applicable to the accounting practice described in section 4.3 of this book.

| |
|---|
| **0 Non-existent** when<br>There is a complete lack of any recognizable process for identifying and allocating costs for information services provided. The organization does not even recognize that there is an issue to be addressed for cost accounting, and there is no communication about the issue. |
| **2 Repeatable but Intuitive** when<br>There is overall awareness of the need to identify and allocate costs. Cost allocation is based on informal or rudimentary cost assumptions, e.g., hardware costs, and there is virtually no linking to value drivers. Cost allocation processes are repeatable. There is no formal training or communication on standard cost identification and allocation procedures. Responsibility for the collection or allocation of costs is not assigned. |
| **3 Defined** when<br>There is a defined and documented information services cost model. A process for relating IT costs to the services provided to users is defined. An appropriate level of awareness exists about the costs attributable to information services. The business is provided with rudimentary information on costs. |
| **4 Managed and Measurable** when<br>Information services cost management responsibilities and accountabilities are defined and fully understood at all levels and are supported by formal training. Direct and indirect costs are identified and reported in a timely and automated manner to management, business process owners and users. Generally, there is cost monitoring and evaluation, and actions are taken if cost deviations are detected. Information services cost reporting is linked to business objectives and SLAs and is monitored by business process owners. A finance function reviews the reasonableness of the cost allocation process. An automated cost accounting system exists, but is focused on the information services function rather than on business processes. Goals and metrics are agreed to for cost measurement but are inconsistently measured. |
| **5 Optimized** when<br>Costs of services provided are identified, captured, summarized and reported to management, business process owners and users.<br>Costs are identified as chargeable items and could support a chargeback system that appropriately bills users for services provided, based on use. Cost details support SLAs. The monitoring and evaluation of costs of services are used to optimize the cost of IT resources. Cost figures obtained are used to verify benefit realization in the organization's budgeting process. Information services cost reporting provides early warning of changing business requirements through intelligent reporting systems. A variable cost model is used, derived from volumes processed for each service provided. Cost management is refined to a level of industry practice, based on the result of continuous improvement and benchmarking with other organizations. Cost optimization is an ongoing process. Management reviews goals and metrics as part of a continuous improvement process in redesigning cost measurement systems. |

Table 6.1 CobiT maturity levels for cost accounting practice (Source CobiT 4.1, ISACA)

Table 6.2 describes the maturity levels that are part of the CobiT 'PO5 Manage the IT Investment' objective and are applicable to the investments evaluation and budgeting practice described in sections 4.1.3 and 4.2 of this book.

| |
|---|
| **0 Non-existent** when<br>There is no awareness of the importance of IT investment selection and budgeting. There is no tracking or monitoring of IT investments and expenditures. |
| **1 Initial/Ad Hoc** when<br>The organization recognizes the need for managing the IT investment, but this need is communicated inconsistently. Allocation of responsibility for IT investment selection and budget development is done on an ad hoc basis. Isolated implementations of IT investment selection and budgeting occur, with informal documentation. IT investments are justified on an ad hoc basis. Reactive and operationally focused budgeting decisions occur. |
| **2 Repeatable but Intuitive** when<br>There is an implicit understanding of the need for IT investment selection and budgeting. The need for a selection and budgeting process is communicated. Compliance is dependent on the initiative of individuals in the organization. There is an emergence of common techniques to develop components of the IT budget. Reactive and tactical budgeting decisions occur. |
| **3 Defined** when<br>Policies and processes for investment and budgeting are defined, documented and communicated, and cover key business and technology issues. The IT budget is aligned with the strategic IT and business plans. The budgeting and IT investment selection processes are formalised, documented and communicated. Formal training is emerging but is still based primarily on individual initiatives. Formal approval of IT investment selections and budgets is taking place. IT staff members have the expertise and skills necessary to develop the IT budget and recommend appropriate IT investments. |
| **4 Managed and Measurable** when<br>Responsibility and accountability for investment selection and budgeting are assigned to a specific individual. Budget variances are identified and resolved. Formal costing analysis is performed, covering direct and indirect costs of existing operations, as well as proposed investments, considering all costs over a total life cycle. A proactive and standardized process for budgeting is used. The impact of shifting in development and operating costs from hardware and software to systems integration and IT human resources is recognized in the investment plans. Benefits and returns are calculated in financial and non-financial terms. |
| **5 Optimized** when<br>Industry good practices are used to benchmark costs and identify approaches to increase the effectiveness of investments. Analysis of technological developments is used in the investment selection and budgeting process. The investment management process is continuously improved based on lessons learned from the analysis of actual investment performance. Investment decisions incorporate price/performance improvement trends. Funding alternatives are formally investigated and evaluated within the context of the organization's existing capital structure, using formal evaluation methods. There is proactive identification of variances. An analysis of the long-term cost and benefits of the total life cycle is incorporated in the investment decisions. |

Table 6.2 CobiT maturity levels for budgeting and investment evaluation practices (Source CobiT 4.1, ISACA)

## 6.2 An example of an improvement project

IT financial management can be very complex to implement. The general approach has been illustrated in section 6.1. where it has been remarked that project management is an invaluable technique to support the achievement of a desired target status for IT financial management. In this section, we provide more information on how to successfully structure and manage a project by means of an example.

We will assume that the initial IT financial management system is largely inadequate or non- existent and, therefore, that the design and implementation efforts are relevant and that management of a project using a framework such as PRINCE2 is appropriate.

## 6.2.1  Starting up the project

The first phase of the PRINCE2 methodology starts with a project mandate. The project mandate could be derived from the definition of the target situation, see 6.1.3 'where do we want to be'. The mandate can be a formal or informal document but this is not important as this initiation phase will clarify the mandate. The aim of this phase is to design the project management organization and to define a project brief, an initial document where the key aspects of the project are initially defined: its purpose, background, objectives, scope, exclusions and interfaces to other projects/ areas, deliverables, constraints, assumptions, preliminary risk assessment, customers and their expectations, acceptance criteria, an outline of the plan with timing, and budget.

For project organization, the following roles should be appointed:
- a project board
- a senior executive
- a project manager
- a project management team

The composition of the project board depends on the scenario (see 2.3). For example referring to Scenario 2, IT financial management for internal IT service providers, the project board members could be:
- the director of IT
- a senior manager in the financial department
- one or more of the customers of IT services
- a representative of IT services management

The senior executive is chosen from the members of the project board and he/she is the ultimate decision maker. Again, the choice will depend on the scenario. In our case, Scenario 2, the director of IT is a suitable choice as project executive.

The project manager assumes day-to-day responsibility of the project throughout all its stages (see below). He/she takes directions from the project board and applies project management practices and techniques. This means, for example, planning and checking the delivered products, defining and controlling (project) budget.

A complex project is usually performed by several resources, organized in teams, responsible for delivering the project products (deliverables) assigned to them. A team manager may be appointed to co-ordinate a group of resources in charge of the implementation of assigned products. In smaller projects, the leadership of teams can be taken directly by the project manager.

For very large and complex projects, the project board may also decide to assign project assurance activities, but not responsibility, to external or internal resources.
For the project team, and especially the project manager, it is vital that members have a fundamental appreciation of both the organization's business and of the IT services to enable them to understand the options available to management. They must also understand the principles of IT accounting.

The project board makes all the relevant decisions, such as approving the start and closure of each project stage, providing ad hoc direction such as in the case of issues, approving exception plans that are proposed in the case of deviations of the project beyond agreed tolerance inherent to budget, timing, quality, etc.

According to PRINCE2, it is appropriate to split a relevant project into stages, the first one being the start-up phase, which we have just described. Figure 6.3 illustrates the possible stages of the project and some, although not all, inputs and outputs for each stage.

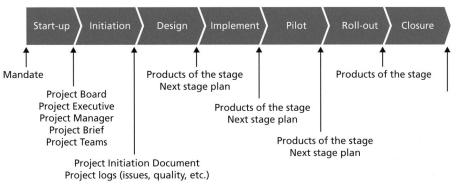

Figure 6.3 Possible stages of an IT financial management project

## 6.2.2  Project initiation

In PRINCE2 this stage is known as Initiating a Project (IP). The main objective of this stage is to produce a document (Project Initiation Document, or PID) to be approved by the project board, along with a next stage plan. The document clearly defines the why, who, when and how of the project. This is produced in addition to the next stage plan and together they are submitted to the board for a decision on whether to authorize the project and proceed with the next stage of work. During this stage, the business case and the risks of the projects are carefully defined and analyzed. After this stage has been executed, the following aspects will have been clarified and approved:

- scope
- objectives
- defined method and approach to achieve the objectives
- expected deliverables
- exclusions and constraints
- costs (project and ongoing)
- expected benefits
- risks
- timescale
- breakdown into stages
- details for next stage to authorize
- project organization and responsibilities
- project management information (such as plans, tolerances, controls, etc.)

When we refer to IT financial management projects, important guidelines for subsequent phases will be provided in this stage. The higher the level of guidance, the lower will be the risks later. Some aspects that should be clarified are, for example:

- the initial scenario and situation
- the target scenario, situation and the expected benefits
- the approach to get there
- specific guidelines such as:
  - charging perspective
  - organization, roles and responsibilities for IT financial management
  - architecture of IT services and scope to be considered
  - practices to be improved and interfaces to the rest of the organization
  - accounting systems to be used and implementation approach and effort
  - if (and possibly which) cost apportioning model to be used
  - pricing strategy
  - financial cycles
  - dimensions and periods to be managed (if not mandatory)
  - reports and variables to be considered in analysis
  - investment appraisal techniques to be used
  - regulations to be compliant with

This does not mean that the design phase occurs at this stage. It is important here to understand the main alternatives for each design topic and, when possible, to define the chosen one or to identify those to be considered in the next steps. For example, for the accounting system, the approach could state the use and improvement of the existing Management Accounting System as the most appropriate alternative to support the target desired situation. This should imply the involvement of the administrator of such a system as a member of the project team. If alternatives, such as implementing a new Management Accounting System, were considered, this should be described at this stage, as well as when the final decision is expected and the definition of risks (possibly quantified) related to choosing one or the other.

For the reasons above, completing the first stages of the project (start-up and initiation) will require a detailed comprehension of the as-is situation from many points of view (people, process and technology).

Obtaining the complete picture, setting objectives and understanding the costs, benefits and risks will be time consuming. It is reasonable to expect that this initial phase will take one to three months, depending on the size and complexity of the IT organization and the availability of data. Sometimes, required information and guidelines can be provided by a previously executed feasibility study, which may have been launched before the start-up phase of the current project. The availability of such a study will shorten the first phases of the project, depending on the scope, level of detail, quality and age of collected data and results.

At this stage, setting up a cost awareness campaign in the organization before project initiation has significant benefits in reducing any resistance to new practices and in helping customers and users to gain a fuller understanding of how they can affect costs. Short presentations should be given about how to identify costs and why costs must be controlled. The presentation must cover plans for cost recovery and the timescale over which it is intended to recover the identified costs.

If it is the policy of the organization to profit from IT, or indeed to plough back profit into IT, then some information about how the profits are to be used is also appropriate.

## 6.2.3  Design stage

After the approval of the project by the project board, activities can quickly start. Design is typically the first phase where details about all aspects of IT financial management will be defined according to guidelines deriving from previous stages and further analysis. Products that are delivered in this stage are reported in Table 6.3 and they refer to the design topics described in 6.5. The products are typically documents.

| Product | Content |
| --- | --- |
| Organization, roles and responsibilities for IT financial management | This includes the job descriptions for each role and its positioning in the organizational structure (sometimes a new organizational structure is required and therefore defined and illustrated); it also includes the skills and competencies required for each. |
| Skill inventory and resource plan | This includes the mapping of required skills and competencies for each role with those of candidates and a detailed plan to fill the gaps. |
| Service Catalog structure update | The Service Catalog is generally an input, but the IT financial management project will probably add information to it (for example drivers and cost units for the apportioning of costs to other services). |
| Practices and procedures design | This product contains the detailed design of practices and of procedures. It also includes the definition of cycles (6.5.12) for each. |
| Systems requirements | This contains the detailed requirements to be implemented to support the target IT financial management scenario and practices. This concerns the accounting systems and all other interfaced systems. |
| Accounting, cost models and depreciation management | This product contains the detailed models to be implemented for IT (accounting model, principles and rules for accounting, and cost mode, which type of costs to manage and description of how to do for each[1]). If depreciation is managed, it will also contain the required rules[2]. Finally this document includes all changes needed to the chart of accounts |
| Cost apportioning model | The chosen cost apportioning model is developed in detail. This means identifying apportioning drivers and rules for each type of service and requires, as input, the Service Catalog. |
| Pricing model | The pricing approach (transfer price vs. service tariffs) should have been decided as an input guideline. Here, the specific pricing rules are defined and detailed[3]. |

---

[1]  An example is the cost of personnel. The design document could establish that three profiles of employees are defined and that, for each, a standard unit cost is determined on the basis of the total annual costs divided per the number of resources of each category. The document could continue by establishing that the actual cost of services is determined using the standard cost multiplied working time deriving from a timesheet.

[2]  For example, the depreciation rule for hardware could be a straight line method with fixed percentage in three years (See section 6.2.7).

[3]  For example, a pricing rule might define that the price of a service is defined as the budget cost of the service divided by the forecasted quantity of its usage uplifted by 30 percent.

| Product | Content |
|---|---|
| Reporting and analysis | This contains the design of each report (6.5.13) and also the requirements for the filtering criteria that can be used to launch them. |
| Investment appraisal methods | This contains the detailed explanation of the investment appraisal methods with some examples of how to use them and references to the tools supporting them. |
| Performance indicators | This product contains the identification and description of the main performance indicators used to evaluate the results of IT financial management. |
| Approach to roll-out | This includes the definition of the approach to introduce the new IT financial management environment, by means of a roll-out plan and, possibly, a pilot. |

Table 6.3 Possible products of the design stage

There are some important considerations to be made about the products of Table 6.3. First, many of them are related to each other and therefore they have to be synchronized and/or cross-referenced. Alternatively they can be combined together in a single document (product). For example, reporting is strictly related to the cost model as cost categories appearing in reports can only be those supported by it.

Secondly, there can be reciprocal influence and impacts between IT financial management and other practices in the organization. For example, the passive cycle is strictly related to the accounting activities. When deciding which type of costs to manage, in particular as direct costs, it is important to understand if they are easily identifiable without affecting the passive cycle (management of orders and passive invoices).

## 6.2.4 Implementation stage

This phase can start only when the products of the previous stage have been accepted and the project board has approved the corresponding next stage plan. The objective of this stage is to implement the designed IT financial management environment. This implies delivering several products, not all of them being documents. Table 6.4 briefly illustrates the typical products to be delivered.

Another important product of this stage, not reported in Table 6.4, may be simulation. Simulations refer in particular to the behavior of the designed cost and apportioning models. They are used to anticipate and evaluate the use of the new rules and methods and, sometimes, they can be applied to previous periods. Simulation enables comparison of the new results (such as budget or profit and loss statements) with to the previous results for the same period. As it can be difficult to perform simulation, because of the lack of information (such as usage of services) and the necessity to find it, it can be limited in scope. Depending on the cost objects chosen, simulation can be limited to some customers or IT services.

The time necessary to implement IT accounting and charging depends on the tools and information already available; it can take six or more months, even with good tools and information readily available.

| Product | Content |
|---|---|
| Service Catalog content update | The content of the Service Catalog, redesigned in the previous stage, is updated to reflect the new or changed information. |
| Systems specifications | This intermediate product has the requirements as input. Requirements are turned into detailed technical specifications of what has to be done to implement all the affected systems (e.g. General Accounting System). |
| Implemented systems | Changes to the existing systems, such as the Management Accounting System, or new systems are implemented according to the specifications. An accurate test of the changed systems must be performed with detailed reporting of the results, which must pass the acceptance criteria previously defined. For more information, please refer to ITIL V3 Service Validation and Testing practice. |
| Training material | For each role defined this product contains the training material about practices, methods, and tools to be used. |
| Updated accounting manuals and accounting documentation[4] | Existing accounting manuals and documentation should be updated to align with the changes introduced by IT financial management. If not yet existing, an accounting manual should be introduced. Another typical document is the accounting policy. |
| Updated data | New or updated charts of accounts, apportioning rules, etc. |

Table 6.4 Possible products of the implementation stage

## 6.2.5  Pilot stage

If the implementation of the IT financial management involves important changes such as charging the customers or accounting per service, it is recommended to start with a pilot scheme. The pilot may be characterized by a reduction in scope (for example a limited subset of customers or services and/or a limited subset of activities, for example charging excluded) or a partial introduction of the new concepts (for example notional instead of real charging). Driving a pilot enables the project team to check the quality of design and implementation and the reaction of all the parties involved in the activities, especially the customers. This is a very important aspect but running a pilot may be not easy.

The typical timing to start a pilot is the beginning of a new financial period (but any time is theoretically possible). The new budget for the services in scope may be defined according to the new logics; later accounting and, eventually, charging activities will be activated. A first problem that may occur is that the accounting systems and the organization may be not able to manage two different approaches, the one previous and the one subsequent to the project. In such a case the decision to be taken is not easy, either managing and duplicating information on the two

---

4   It is not advisable to attempt to implement a system without proper and complete documentation. It is important to cover:
   - how and when IT management and customer management will be informed of costs
   - how IT accounting data is to be collected
   - how the charging system works and what pricing structures are to be used
   - how budgets are monitored between bills
   - how accounts are to be settled
   - who is responsible for policing the IT accounting system and producing reports, bills, and so on
   - how and when auditing takes place
   - what contingency option(s) are in place
   - how errors in billing will be handled
   - what change control is applied to the IT accounting system.

   The analysis and design deliverables should be retained as detailed support documents.

different systems or managing different scopes with each system (for example, pilot services with the new one, others with the older). The advantages of the first approach are that integrated and consolidated data are immediately available with no effort and that returning to the previous situation simply means stopping the pilot, with little or no effect on customers. The trade-off is the effort of running duplicated systems and probably activities (also depending on scope and on possible interfaces that can be built).

On the other hand, managing two different systems for different scopes has the advantage of limiting the impact of the test in terms of effort but has the disadvantage that building integrated and consolidated views of financial data is time consuming, when not impossible, and that the organization will apply different behaviors for different scopes (which may lead to errors and confusion). In addition, while the first approach can be easily activated during the financial year (as nothing is replaced), the second one is much more simple to start at the beginning of a new financial year (this also means that it will last for the whole year).

The two approaches can be also combined in a two-stage approach to the pilot: the first stage, during the financial year for a limited time frame, duplicates activities for a small scope; the second stage, at the beginning of a new financial year, runs the new approach for the whole IT services or a subset of them.

If affected, customers should be notified at the earliest possible stage about events that are likely to cause changes to their bills. It is important that customers are aware of any likely alterations.

## 6.2.6 Roll-out stage

The experience and results of the pilot, if executed, gives important feedback to fine-tune the IT financial management project and complete the roll-out. Again, this stage starts after detailed planning and authorization from the project board.

A typical approach to introduce a new IT financial management system is a 'big-bang' (start of new activities for all the services together) at the beginning of a new financial year. This is quite a risky approach and, if charging is introduced for the first time, it is at least recommended to start for a period with notional charging. An alternative approach, starting with some IT services only and expanding them gradually, is possible. Because of the considerable additional effort of data consolidation and possible confusion deriving from the use of more than one accounting system at the same time, the time frame of a progressive roll-out should be kept as short as possible.

## 6.2.7 Closure stage

Every project should come to a controlled close. In PRINCE2, this activity is to ensure that closure happens and covers the work carried out by the project manager to bring the project to a planned close (or bring to a premature closure if necessary). The work required during this activity is to provide the project board with sufficient information to obtain their confirmation that the project should close. Closing the project does not mean that IT financial management will stop evolving and that no further improvements will be needed. On the contrary, the final feedback from the project including pending issues or risks, work required, lessons learned, will be passed to service management and, if existing, to continual service improvement, as discussed in 6.1.6. In particular, the IT financial manager role will take responsibility for the evolution and improvement of the activities.

From the project viewpoint, this stage will assess whether the objectives stated in the Project Initiation Document have been achieved and all expected products have been handed over and accepted. With the closure of the project, the specifically assigned resources are released and activities are left to be run autonomously in line with the service management practices, in particular with IT financial management, and related responsibilities.

# 6.3   Continuous improvement

### 6.3.1   Drivers for continuous improvement
The need for continual justifiable improvement has been already introduced and briefly discussed in this book. In section 6.1 0the implementing/improvement cycle has been described, focusing attention on the initial or major improvements (those typically managed as projects) of IT financial management. In this section we focus instead on smaller and continuous improvements.

The reasons for continuous improvements lie in lack of optimization and the need for changes. If the context never changed, it could be theoretically possible to reach an optimized target situation where no further enhancements are required. After a certain number of enhancements any further improvement would be demonstrated as not cost effective. For example, a cost model has been developed by service, so that IT understands them with a good percentage of direct costs (80 percent). The cost of specific software licenses (e.g. a Database Management System – DBMS) is still an indirect cost, being derived from the number of users of the services and not driven by the effective usage of the licenses. Getting to understand effective usage could mean introducing tools to monitor usage, producing ad hoc reporting and analysis. The costs associated with this enhancement could be significant so that the benefits for the majority of customers of more precise fees are outweighed by the new costs to be shared deriving from the introduction of the new technology and/or associated practices. Such a situation could be verified with a manual ad hoc analysis. In such a case, no further enhancements would be justified.

However, nothing stays still. The external and internal context change continuously, with increasing rapidity. In the previous example, a new service might be introduced for a specific customer. This is a very intensive DBMS dependent service with a relevant number of users that leads to increased costs, which are indirectly apportioned to old customers. The cost of introducing technology and practices to better measure the use of the DBMS remains unchanged but it may be split among a larger number of customers and is a lower proportion of the overall costs of DBMS management. To keep old customers satisfied, the option to change the apportioning criteria may emerge as an appropriate solution and therefore a relevant improvement. The business case for the implementation of the change has evolved and has become favorable because the cost of the new system could be amortized over a larger number of customers.

This example demonstrates that significant changes, occurring to business and IT organization contexts, should always be investigated for their effects and the possible improvement opportunities that they enable.

Because of the failure of many business process (or simply process) reengineering projects, new approaches have been suggested and introduced to deal with change. Among them, Kaizen is a leading approach. Kaizen (改善, Japanese for 'continuous improvement') is a Japanese philosophy that focuses on continuous improvement throughout all aspects of life. When applied to the workplace, Kaizen activities continually improve all functions of a business, from manufacturing to management and from the CEO to the assembly line workers. By improving standardized activities and processes, Kaizen aims to eliminate waste (see 'lean' manufacturing). Kaizen was first implemented in several Japanese businesses during the country's recovery after World War II, including Toyota, and has since spread to businesses throughout the world.

Kaizen is based on some assumptions that are quite contrasting to those underlying business process engineering:
• change is like a river; you cannot step into the same river twice; the area of the river may be the same but it is always changing
• change is a social construction
• change is a subjective experience
• change can be influenced but rarely managed

With the Kaizen approach:
• large-scale projects are replaced by smaller experiments
• no improvement is too small
• improvement starts from existing processes
• the 'doers' are involved in the improvement of their own activities
• process improvement becomes a natural part of the daily tasks and culture
• improvement is obtained by means of iterative process activities, e.g. Kaizen Events

Some organizations, adopting continuous improvement and the Kaizen approach, have abandoned the traditional business process reengineering approach. However, many organizations strive to achieve improvements by combining continual and continuous improvement approaches, implementing some steps by mean of projects while trying to adopt the Kaizen approach and establish clear roles and responsibilities for continuous improvement.

### 6.3.2 The ITIL approach for continuous (continual) improvement
The book Continual Service Improvement (CSI) of ITIL V3, describes a seven-step improvement process based on the Deming cycle and represented in Figure 6.4. This practice is introduced for IT service improvement; it is equally applicable to process improvement and, clearly, to IT financial management too.

It has to be remarked that the authors of ITIL have chosen the term 'continual' (which refers to a close and succession of things, rather than an absolute continuity) instead of 'continuous' (which denotes an interrupted flow) because 'an IT organization will not be continuously improving itself seamlessly, but rather it will be cyclical in nature'. However, in practical terms, the approach described in the book seems to be well suited to support a continuous approach more than a continual one. For example, a stable organization with roles and responsibilities clearly defined is encouraged to do continuous monitoring, analysis and action in line with the Deming cycle (Plan–Do–Check–Act).

Returning to the improvement cycle described in CSI, what should be remarked is the centrality of measures and targets as the basis for all improvements. The desired situation is defined and measures are identified to represent it. Progress is checked by means of these measures and actions are taken if results are not achieved.

Another basic concept of the improvement practice of CSI is the responsibilities for continuous improvement. In a service-oriented organization, responsibilities may lie at multiple levels. For example, global responsibility for overall improvement of IT services may be assigned to the continual service improvement manager, as suggested by ITIL V3. This role should work with others to manage improvements and, especially, service owners and practice owners. While the latter are responsible for specific domains of improvement, services and practices, the CSI manager should deal with cross-service and/or practice initiatives and coordinate overall improvement. Specific practice improvement responsibilities are normally assigned to practice owners, in our case typically to the IT financial manager or financial manager, depending on the scenario and as described in Chapter 5. It is common to find practice level responsibilities assigned, while it is still unusual to find overall roles as the one of CSI.

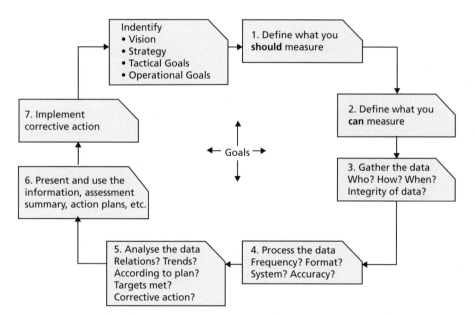

Figure 6.4 The seven-step improvement process (source OGC)

Linking goals to performance indicators and targets is a core activity for the owner of the improvement responsibility. The Balanced Scorecard, a technique developed by Kaplan and Norton in the mid-1990s, has demonstrated itself, over many years, to be an effective framework to support the definition of strategies and their implementation at any level. It works by establishing these relationships between goals and performance indicators. The Balanced Scorecards have typically been used to support the overall business strategy definition and implementation, although they can be successfully used in more restricted domains, such as IT or even specific practices (e.g. IT financial management). A Balanced Scorecard, applied to the IT financial management domain, would consider four perspectives:

- **Financial** – which should be the costs of IT financial management?
- **Client** – what do users (customers, proper users and managers) of IT financial management expect from it?
- **Internal processes** – what IT financial management should we excel at to satisfy stakeholders?
- **Learning and growth** – to achieve our vision, how do we sustain our ability to change and improve IT financial management?

For each of these perspectives, goals should be defined as well as performance indicators and their targets, which demonstrate their achievement. Figure 6.5 represents a sample Balanced Scorecard for IT financial management, assuming Scenario 2. Each column represents one of the Balanced Scorecard dimensions and, for each, goals and performance indicators are described. A Balanced Scorecard, with defined targets, is an optimal result of the preliminary step described in Figure 6.4: identify vision, strategy, tactical and operational goals. It is an optimal input for the following seven steps.

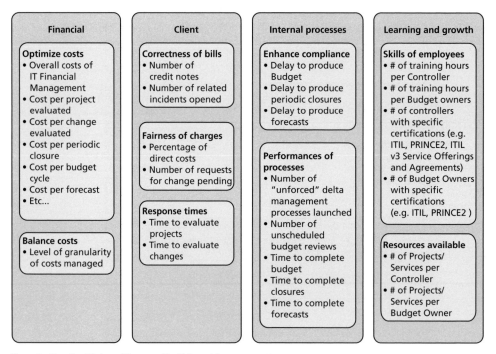

Figure 6.5 Sample of Balanced Scorecard for IT financial management.

As well as responsibilities for IT financial management practices (see Chapter 5) those for its continual improvement should be clearly assigned. Again, this may depend on the adopted scenario but in any case a referent should be clearly identified and appointed. He/she generally coincides with the practice owner, responsible for designing the practices and therefore their continual improvement too. In Scenario 1, this was probably the CFO (Figure 5.1); in Scenario 2, the IT financial manager (Figure 5.2) and, finally, in Scenario 3 the CFO again (Figure 5.3).

Among the responsibilities of the practice owner inherent to continual improvement, we find the following:
• defining the Key Performance Indicators (KPIs) to evaluate the effectiveness and efficiency of the practice
• reviewing KPIs and taking the required action following the analysis
• improving the effectiveness and efficiency of the practice
• reviewing any proposed enhancements to the practice
• providing input to the ongoing service improvement plan
• addressing any issues with the running of the practice

In service oriented and mature organizations, improvement is probably performed at all levels. A Service Improvement Plan (SIP), (that is, a formal plan to implement improvements to a practice or IT services) may be in place and practice owner(s) should assist in its preparation, management and maintenance. The overall management of improvements (all services, all practices) is usually assigned to the service level manager or to a specific dedicated role (for example, in ITIL V3 this is the continual service improvement manager), depending on the maturity and size of the organization. A complete picture is given in Figure 6.6, where the relationships among improvement responsibilities are shown.

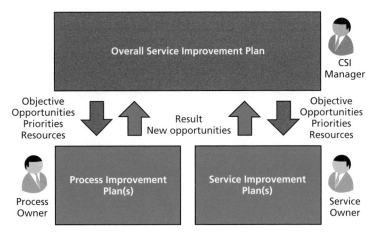

Figure 6.6 Relationships among improvement responsibilities and plans

An overall Service Improvement Plan, about all practices and services, coordinates and controls all improvement efforts, assigning resources when needed based on objectives and priorities. This ensures that dependencies are correctly managed, for example an improvement in the quality of budgets depending on enhancement of the capacity plan, and priorities / resources optimized based on overall business objectives. Each service or practice owner will then be given objectives, opportunities, priorities and resources and will manage their own plan, which will include them and add all other achievable, compatible and detected enhancement opportunities. Results, as well as opportunities (those requiring funds or across services and/or practices), will be passed back to the owner of the overall plan for evaluation and the definition of new inputs.

## 6.4   Organizational change management

Regardless of the type of improvement desired, continual versus continuous or both, organizational change management is a key point to be addressed. With this term, we do not refer to IT service management change management but to individual or organizational management of change. This has been proved to be a critical success factor for the implementation of any improvement project or initiative including, of course, those concerning IT financial management and previously described. In this and the following sections we will not concentrate on management of change for individuals although, in some cases, this can be an issue to be managed. For readers requiring more information on how to address this topic, the main models to be considered include: *Unfreeze-Change-Refreeze* (Kurt Lewin), the Kübler-Ross model (from Elizabeth Kubler-Ross's book, *On Death and Dying*), *Formula for Change* (Richard Beckhard and David Gleicher) and *ADKAR* (developed by Prosci).

Organizational change management includes processes and tools for managing the people side of the change at an organizational level. Organizational change management includes techniques for creating a change management strategy (readiness assessments), engaging senior managers as change leaders (sponsorship), building awareness of the need for change (communications), developing skills and knowledge to support the change (education and training), helping employees move through the transition (coaching by managers and supervisors), and methods to sustain the change (measurement systems, rewards and reinforcement). Organizational change management application in contexts where change is to be implemented improves the chances of achieving the desired results. Many of the components of organizational management, such as management of awareness, sponsorship, and communication, are embedded in some of the approaches previously described, especially Kaizen.

IT financial management is not just an IT discipline; it has strong relationships with business financial management. This reinforces the importance of organizational change management, as changes to IT financial management are often depending and/or influencing the business and vice versa.

### 6.4.1   Awareness and acceptance

Awareness is a key component of organizational change management; it is one of the most important components and steps of the implementing/improvement cycle that has been described in section 6.1. Defining where we are and where we want to be are key components of awareness. Culture is fundamental to facilitating the change: knowledge about the IT service management discipline and, in particular, IT financial management makes it much easier. This is why, initially, training and learning, in all possible forms, are key elements of awareness.

Awareness is mandatory for decision makers but it is useful at any other level of the organization that is involved in the change; and because continual improvement is never ending, managing awareness is also a continual activity. The organization's management should be continuously aware of progress made and of new targets to be achieved.

The key contents of awareness are generated by executing implementation projects and continual improvement activities. Managing awareness also depends very much on good communication, an aspect that we will examine more closely later.

Acceptance is another fundamental aspect of any IT service management initiative, including those that relate to IT financial management. Acceptance means different things depending on the level involved and perspective:
- For **customers** – approval of:
  - providers' interface roles and internally required ones
  - charging system
  - prices
  - bills
  - reporting
  - escalation activities
- For **users**:
  - providers' interface roles and internally required roles
  - charging mechanisms for requested services
  - reporting about requested services
  - level of support
- For the **IT department**:
  - roles, activities and procedures to be executed
  - tools to be used
  - KPIs, reporting
  - volumes of activities to be performed by the whole staff and individuals, for core tasks (e.g. budgeting, accounting) and complementary tasks (projects, risk management, etc.)
- For **management**:
  - key design decisions (see 6.5)
  - performances of activities
  - customers' and users' satisfaction
  - concerns that higher levels of maturity of IT financial management will lead to impersonal behaviors driven by a higher relevance of financial aspects

Achieving agreement and commitment of all stakeholders for all aspects is definitely not an easy task. After all, resistance is the primary reason why changes fail. Managing resistance should be a priority of top management and is a primary responsibility of the IT financial manager role. Different levels of resistance are possible, depending on the concerns of different stakeholders involved in the change:
- lack of understanding
- negative emotional response with no objective reasons
- lack of trust
- negative response based on objective reasons (ranging from small to relevant issues).

Table 6.5 shows actions to respond to each level of resistance. Actions that are appropriate for mitigating higher levels of resistance are generally useful also for the levels below. Nevertheless, a careful evaluation of the overall situation in terms of resistance (who is resisting and why) is always recommended when a project or changes are introduced; countermeasures should be planned in line with the evaluation, avoiding the use of inappropriate actions (too 'soft' or too 'hard' for the level of resistance to be managed).

| Level of resistance | Actions |
|---|---|
| **Lack of understanding** | • Explain the advantages and benefits of the new target situation for the organization; this should be done by adapting to different learning and communication styles |
| **Negative emotional response with no objective reasons** | • Explain personal advantages and benefits when existing or neutral effect<br>• Involve resisting people closely in the project or change if possible; people who feel they have helped plan the change will be more likely to help make the change, because they understand how and why it will occur |
| **Lack of trust** | • Use techniques for building trust (establish common ground, show that concerns are understood, use communication techniques)<br>• Implement quick-wins and communicate results<br>• Provide tailored training<br>• Show that concerns are addressed<br>• Achieve and publicly show top management commitment; employees will not support a change they feel is not fully supported by top management |
| **Negative response based on objective reasons** | • Create tangible benefits for key roles in transformation (e.g. with rewards for achieved, measurable objectives) and/or for the whole team and/or organization (e.g. bonus for success)<br>• Manage and identify appropriate ad hoc solutions for those specific situations where negative effects cannot be avoided (e.g. find a new role that is appropriate for resources losing their current role or no longer happy with it) |

Table 6.5 Level of resistance and progressive countermeasures

## 6.4.2 Communication

In the previous section, communication has been cited as a very important key element for the success of any initiative aimed at introducing and/or improving IT financial management. We have seen that communication will help to improve awareness and to overcome resistance. Communication may be optimized by means of a communication plan with the aim of building and maintaining awareness, understanding, enthusiasm and support among key influential stakeholders for the introduction or improvement of IT financial management practices.

When developing a communication plan, it is important to realize that effective communication is not just based on a one-way flow of information, and it covers more than just meetings. A communications plan must incorporate the ability to deal with responses and feedback from the target audiences.

A role should be identified to manage the communication plan, which means:
• designing and delivering communications to the different IT financial management roles, stakeholders such as other IT service management roles and identified target audiences
• identifying forums for customers' and users' feedback

- receiving and delivering responses and feedback to the project manager and/or team members

This role may be played by a specific temporary or permanently dedicated function or team (usually dealing with change management issues) in the context of a project or by the IT financial management practice owner when change occurs in a continual improvement context.

Key activities for building a communication plan include:
- identifying stakeholders and target audiences
- identifying the interests and degree of interdependence amongst stakeholders
- developing communications strategies and tactics
- identifying communication methods and techniques
- developing the communications plan (a matrix of who, what, why, when, where and how)
- identifying the project milestones and related communications requirements.

When developing a communication plan, it is important to understand how corporate communication works and the rules governing it. For example, in some organizations there are strict guidelines on who can communicate with the business. In many cases, this could be possible only for the demand and/or service level management and/or business relationship management practices and roles.

The final content of a communication plan is a list of communication actions, defining for each:
- the messenger of the communication
- the target audience
- content of the message
- method of communication (e.g. mail, meeting)
- date and frequency

Typical contents of messages are:
- program announcement
- start-up announcement
- achievement of goals
- status of activities
- announcements of completion of activities or of a project
- celebrating success

## 6.5 Design topics

When implementing IT financial management, many decisions will be taken during the design phase. Some are common to the other IT service management practices (for example designing roles and responsibilities), but many are specifically for IT financial management. We will examine these decisions in the next sections.

## 6.5.1  Charging perspectives

One of the most important decisions to be taken is whether to charge for the cost for supplying IT services. Charging is needed to recover costs but there can be different perspectives:

- **Accounting center** – Simply costing inputs with perhaps some element of budgeting. The benefit of this approach is that sound IT accounting focuses awareness on costs and enables investment decisions to be better founded, without the overheads of billing and bookkeeping. However, it is less likely to shape users' behavior and does not give the IT organization the full ability to choose how to financially manage itself, for example in funding IT investments.
- **Recovery center** – Costing outputs (services) and simply apportioning those costs. Organizations running as recovery centers are designed to account fully for all IT spend and recover it from the customers. These accounts include both cash and non-cash costs that, in effect, identify the full economic cost of running the business. The benefits of running as a recovery center (before charging is considered) include improved cost control over service provision, recognition of true costs by customers and consistency in approach by different organizations.
- **Profit center** – The full range of separate accounting. A profit center is a method of managing the IT organization in which it has sufficient autonomy to operate as a separate business entity (as an independent unit or with business objectives set by the organization to which the service provider belongs). The key characteristics are that:
  - deliverables or products are clearly identified and sold into a marketplace
  - each product or service carries a price tag

The above described perspectives are clearly related to the scenarios defined in section 2.3; Table 6.6 shows these relationships.

| Perspective / Scenario | Scenario 1 IT financial management for internal IT departments | Scenario 2 IT financial management for internal IT service providers | Scenario 3 IT financial management for market IT service providers |
|---|---|---|---|
| **Accounting center** | Generally adopted | Unsuited[5] | Unsuited |
| **Recovery center** | Usable, especially by organizations intending to move to Scenario 2 | Generally adopted | Unsuited |
| **Profit center** | Unusual | Usable, especially by organizations intending to move to Scenario 3 | Suited[6] |

Table 6.6 Relationship between charging perspectives and scenarios

The decision about the charging perspective will drive many other decisions, such as those about activities but also roles and responsibilities. For example, the existence of pricing and charging activities is related to the decision about the charging perspective.

Notional charging is about making a journal entry in the corporate financial system for the use of IT services. When organizations are switching from one charging perspective to a new one, it can be wise to evaluate the impacts before applying it. With notional charging, the effects of applying

---

[5]   In this scenario, it is not enough to understand the costs of inputs; it is important to fully understand the cost of services which, as a minimum, are transferred to internal customers.
[6]   In this scenario, organizations will need to make a profit, by selling IT services, in order to survive.

the charging perspective are measured (and in some cases communicated to the customers) but no actual charges are applied. The 'two book' method can be applied to manage this situation. Costs are recorded into the corporate financial system (for example with IT as a cost center) while in a second book revenues are determined and recorded with no effect on financial statements. Other important decisions related to charging are about the recipients and what to charge. The options are to charge for the whole IT costs, specific IT costs by customer or specific IT costs by service. This decision affects the charging system and also the whole accounting system as deciding to charge by customer or by service requires a method to determine costs for each customer or service. In Scenario 2, it is recommended to charge at least by customer. Charging by IT service is appropriate too, and recommended for Scenario 3. This because in a competitive environment customers will want to know the price of services in order to take decisions and service providers will determine their costs in order to make their offers.

*The decision is the charging perspective for IT, accounting, recovery or profit center, and all related details (notional charging, what to charge and the level of detail of charging).*

### 6.5.2 Organization
Organizational decisions are always among the most critical. They affect the roles, responsibilities and activities of many people. Decisions about the organization will also greatly depend on the scenario adopted for IT financial management. We will discuss each scenario separately.

**IT financial management for internal IT departments**
In this scenario a dedicated department is typically responsible for the financial management activities of the whole organization, including those of IT. Another frequent possibility is that the human resources department is responsible for IT. In the latter case, the following discussion is still applicable, by simply replacing the financial management department with the human resources department. This hypothetical organization is described in Figure 6.7.

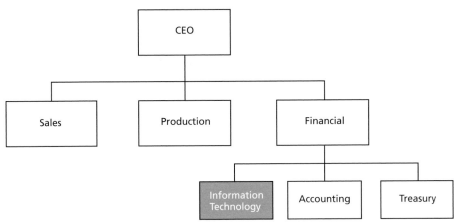

Figure 6.7 Hypothesis of organizational model for Scenario 1

In this context, some alternatives to assign the responsibilities of the typical IT financial management roles (discussed in Chapter 5) are reported in Table 6.7.

| Roles | FM department | IT manager | IT staff | IT line |
|---|---|---|---|---|
| IT financial manager | Suited | Possible for large IT organizations | | |
| IT financial controller | Suited | Only for small IT Organizations | Possible | |
| IT budget owner | | For overall IT budget | | For partial IT budgets |
| IT budget approver | Higher level of authorization | IT level authorization | | |

Table 6.7 Assignment of roles for Scenario 1

In larger IT organizations it may become convenient to specialize some positions to facilitate or perform some tasks of IT financial management activities such as, for example, assembling IT financial plans, budgets or forecasts, assisting in calculating the ROI of initiatives. These positions may be delegated to perform typical IT financial controller's activities too. Altogether, these responsibilities and staff may be grouped with other administrative tasks (e.g. order and contract management or goods and services receipts). This may lead to the creation of a back-office function in the IT department dedicated, among others, to support IT staff dealing with financial management practices and issues.

## IT financial management for internal IT service providers

In this scenario, IT is probably a department supplying services to business units (ITIL V3 describes it as a shared service unit) or other departments. The possible organizational situation is shown in Figure 6.8, where finance and administration correspond to the financial management department discussed previously.

The main decision to be taken by IT is whether to be independent, although integrated, or to rely on the financial management department's staff and systems. In the second case, the responsibilities will probably be assigned in line with the previous scenario, see Table 6.7. In the first case, Table 6.8 briefly summarizes alternatives to assign responsibilities. The final choice depends on the level of specificity/independence and some hybrid solutions are possible. This is probably the most difficult situation, as the need for independence of IT has to balance the needs for integrated processes and information at the organization's corporate level.

## IT financial management for market IT service providers

In this scenario, supplying IT services is the core business activity. This can be the mission of an independent business unit or a stand-alone legal entity. The financial department is working for the business and there is no differentiation between financial management and IT financial management. The organizational model may look like the one shown in Figure 6.9.

An internal IT department may still exist, supplying the internal IT services necessary to support the core business (which is the supply of IT services) but we are not referring to it when speaking of IT financial management in this scenario. Where it exists, this IT internal unit will probably be managed in line with Scenario 1 or 2 previously described.

Finally, Table 6.9 shows how responsibilities may be assigned for this scenario.

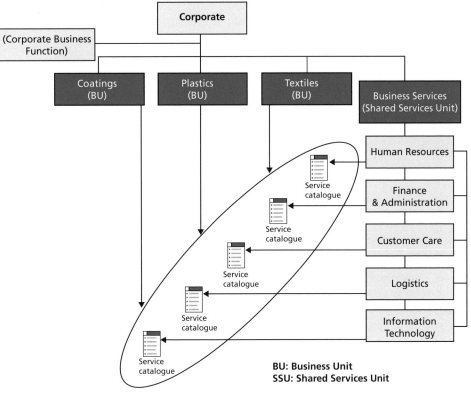

Figure 6.8 Hypothesis of organizational model for Scenario 2 (Source OGC)

| Roles | Other functions | IT manager | IT staff | IT line |
|---|---|---|---|---|
| IT financial manager | | Possible for small IT organization | Suited | |
| IT financial controller | | Possible for small IT organizations | Suited | |
| IT budget owner | | For overall IT budget | | For partial IT budgets |
| IT budget approver | Higher level of authorization | IT level authorization | | |

Table 6.8 Assignment of roles for Scenario 2

| Roles | Head of financial department | Financial department staff | Functions[7] |
|---|---|---|---|
| IT financial manager | Suited | | |
| IT financial controller | | Suited | |
| IT budget owner | | | Suited |
| IT budget approver | | | According to proxies |

Table 6.9 Assignment of roles for Scenario 3

7   Including the financial department.

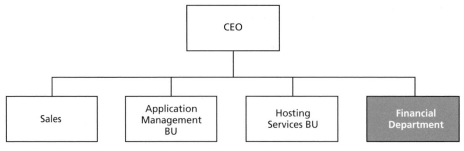

Figure 6.9 Hypothesis of organizational model for Scenario 3.

*The decision is the organizational structure and assignment of the typical roles of IT financial management.*

### 6.5.3  IT services

We have previously examined some important decisions to be taken about the charging perspective (6.5.1). If the final decision is to manage IT services for charging/accounting purposes, the IT department and customers should be clear about which services are involved. For this reason, it is strongly recommended that Service Catalog management and service level management practices have been put in place.

In ITIL V3, a distinction is made between business and technical IT services (see Figure 6.10). Business services are those services that are experienced (and eventually paid for) by the customers while technical services are those needed to support and run the business services. For example, a business service might be the mail service. This service is experienced by the customers and is probably paid on the basis of the number of mail boxes (prices could be differentiated upon the different types and size of mail boxes). In this context, there can be several technical services supporting the business service:

- **housing service**, to provide facilities for the servers needed
- **server management service**, in charge of the operating system and related components, which should be always up and ready to run the mail application
- **mail application management service**, aimed at running and managing the mail application properly (incident, change, problem management, etc.)
- **connectivity service**, in charge of assuring safe connection to the central mail server from mail clients or web browsers.

All these services mentioned above are technical, as the customer is not interested in their existence, although they are mandatory to supply the mail service: the final business service.

When accounting/charging by service is required, there are no decisions to be taken about business services, in the sense that the business Service Catalog will exist and that it should be possible to account for costs and, probably, charge for all IT services defined in it. Instead, a decision may arise about technical services. The IT organization could want to know the costs of these services too. Finally, the absorption of the costs of these services by the business services contributes to determine the full cost of the latter. Figure 6.11 shows how the cost of the mail box service can be determined based on the costs of the supporting technical services. Assuming

**The Service Catalogue**

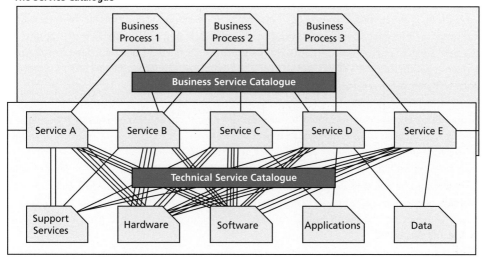

Figure 6.10 The business Service Catalog and the technical Service Catalog (source OGC)

a server is able to manage a certain number of mail boxes, with the described model the full cost per mail box can be determined.

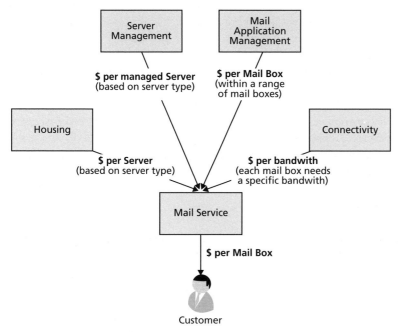

Figure 6.11 Cost of business services calculated on the basis of costs of technical services

The cost of the business service could be determined without referring to specific technical services, by apportioning the costs of IT to the business service. For example, the total cost of hardware maintenance should be known (for all servers). If one of 100 servers is used to provide the mail service, one percent of hardware maintenance costs could be apportioned to the mail service. Considering the other types of costs, the same reasoning can be applied to apportion costs to the business services.

Although costs can be apportioned to business services, there are several reasons for using and calculating the costs of intermediate technical services:
- the costs of technical services can be benchmarked with the market
- it can support a decision to outsource the service, and it gives the flexibility and level of detail that would be required to outsource it
- analysis to determine where opportunities for cost savings are becoming easier
- performance can be better linked to costs (each technical service will probably have some specific OLAs).

The whole IT activity can be decomposed in a set of services (business and technical), so the whole IT costs can be managed through this set of services. This approach will be more fully examined later in section 6.5.10.

*Starting from the architecture of IT services (which is an input for the design of IT financial management, deriving from IT services portfolio management and service catalog management activities) the decision is about for which services to perform financial management activities (e.g. budgeting, accounting).*

## 6.5.4  Activities
Activities for IT financial management have been described and discussed in Chapter 4. A theoretical model may be used as a reference but adaptations or more significant changes will probably be necessary in real environments. The existence and/or shape of activities depend on the scenario considered and on some other design decisions, such as those related to charging (see 6.5.1.) or pricing (see 6.5.11). For example, the decision to charge, or not, will determine the existence of the charging activity (see 4.4.1). Overall aspects to define are:
- execution of a specific activities
- frequency of execution (for example periodic closures, forecasting, etc.)
- execution of activities
- responsibilities.

Other aspects may be defined by means of procedures that detail:
- how to perform activities
- supporting tools
- structure and contents of input and output
- actors (who does the work).

*The decision is the execution and the detailed design of activities (and procedures) for IT financial management.*

## 6.5.5 General Accounting System versus Management Accounting System

The accounting systems is one of the core elements of financial management and therefore of IT financial management too. We can identify two major accounting systems. The first is the General Accounting System, also known as Financial Accounting System, which can be composed of several other sub-systems, such as the customers or Suppliers' Accounting Systems; the second is the Management Accounting System (MAS). By 'system', as we will see, we do not mean only specific software tools, although each is typically supported by at least one of them.

### General Accounting System

This is the set of accounting records that are used to log the facts with administrative relevance, when they occur. The relevant facts are those:

- referring to the relationship between the organization, as a legal entity, and other parties (clients, suppliers, employees, banks, etc.)
- having monetary value recognized by administrative documents (invoices, bank credit transfers, salaries, etc.).

The main objective of the General Accounting System is to support the preparation of the company accounts (annual or periodic) where the capital and the operating result of the organization are determined. The system is designed for decision makers who are not directly involved in the daily management of the organization. These users of the information are often external to the organization.

The General Accounting System has several recipients: contributors of capital, creditors, banks, employees, auditors, government and tax offices, and the organization's managers interfacing with all previously cited recipients. The financial data prepared for this purpose are governed by national regulations, such as the Generally Accepted Accounting Principles (GAAP) in the US, which provide consistency in the accounting data used for reporting purposes from one organization to another. This means that the accounting data used to compute the cost of goods, inventory values, and other financial accounting information used for external reporting must be prepared in accordance with these regulations, which vary from country to country. Topics such as products, services, and projects are generally not core information managed by the General Accounting System.

### Management Accounting System

This is the set of records, integrating those provided by the General Accounting System, needed to supply the requested information about the facts of economic relevance for the organization. The aim of the Management Accounting System is to record, apportioning, grouping, analyzing and demonstrating costs and revenues according to the needs of organization's management or authorized requesters. This is the system that is more affected by the scenarios described for IT financial management. It may be the case that the Management Accounting System designed to support the general business needs is not able to support those of IT financial management (especially when we consider Scenario 2). In such a case a specific Management Accounting System for IT could be designed and implemented.

Topics such as products, services, and projects are managed. So, for example, the Management Accounting System is able to provide information such as the costs, revenues and, therefore, profits of a specific service, including an IT service.

Typical output of the system, in the form of reports and analysis, are:
- balance sheets and reporting for fiscal and legal aims and auditors
- valuations of inventory of products and goods in progress
- comparison of line of business, products, services results
- comparisons of budgets and balance and analysis of delta
- calculation of performance and financial indexes and related analysis
- determination of periodic economic results.

The Management Accounting System can support a cost model, see 6.2.6, which will determine how well it can analyze data. In contrast to the General Accounting System, information managed by a Management Accounting System does not need to comply with national regulations, such as GAAP. Management is free to set its own definitions and rules although it should be possible to determine and explain different results obtained by using different accounting systems.

### Relationships between accounting systems
There are different possible relationships between the two accounting systems. We will synthesize them in three types:
- **Independent** – In the independent type, the two systems have autonomous life (for example, they run on separate platforms, such as an accounting software for the General Accounting System and a set of spreadsheet files for the Management Accounting System). The reconciliation of data is performed by the General Accounting System by means of reports and of cross-checking.
- **Based on accounting and separated** – In this type, data from the Management Accounting System are processed with a specific chart of accounts with the same software system used by the General Accounting System. Reconciliation of data is performed by means of the accounting system and specific linkage accounts.
- **Based on accounting and integrated** – In this type, data from the Management Accounting Systems are processed with a unique chart of accounts and the same software system used by the General Accounting System.

### Decisions about the accounting system
At least one General Accounting System exists in every organization and this system, with the set of its related activities, accounting rules and software, is managed by the financial department. All the facts with administrative relevance about IT are managed through this system. IT has minimal or no autonomy at all to define the principles and/or rules for it. Note that the output from the General Accounting System is of limited interest for IT; information managed at this level has little managerial relevance for IT. However, in Scenario 3, IT financial management for market IT service providers, the General Accounting System gives more relevant information to IT (the business) as it is focused on its needs.

Management, including IT, is more interested in the Management Accounting System to provide support for decision-making. Such a system is often present at the corporate level and managed by the financial department. IT is one of the functions of the organization and follows the principles, rules and activities defined by the financial department. The issue that might arise is that this system is built to control the relevant economic facts and perspectives of the business and that it might not feed all the information and details needed by the IT department. In such a case, the IT department has two options: asking the financial department to improve and adapt the Management Accounting System to fit its needs or building an internal and independent Management Accounting System. We will briefly outline the factors associated with a choice of option below.

Factors suggesting the use of the existing Management Accounting System of the financial department:
- economies of scale (tools, activities, staff) and investments
- easier integration of information (fewer systems to interface)
- quality of data (fewer sources to cross-check)
- minor ambiguity and confusion (fewer sources for reporting).

Factors suggesting the build of an MAS dedicated to IT needs:
- creation of specific competencies
- need for dedicated specific activities and tools
- availability of more valuable information for IT management.

These factors cannot be examined out of the context of the organization and of the IT scenario. Table 6.10 shows the influence that these variables have in the final choice of the Management Accounting System for IT.

| Financial department (FD) accounting systems relationships (GAS and MAS) | **IT financial management for internal IT departments** IT has limited specific needs compared to what FD can offer with its systems | **IT financial management for internal IT service providers** IT has significant specific needs compared to what FD can offer with its systems | **IT financial management for market IT service providers** financial systems and IT financial systems are the same |
|---|---|---|---|
| Independent | IT will opt for the FD's MAS; nevertheless (e.g. MAS based on Excel), it could be extended to cover IT specific needs by FD or IT | IT and/or FD will probably build a specific dedicated independent MAS for IT; FD will require to input data in both MAS and to cross- check data | MAS and GAS of FD are dedicated and fit with IT needs |
| Based on accounting and separated | IT will opt for the FD's systems | Either FD adapts GAS/MAS to accommodate IT needs (this is normally a significant effort due to specificities) or IT and/or FD builds a specific dedicated independent MAS; FD will require to input data in both MAS and to cross-check data | MAS and GAS of FD are dedicated and fit with IT needs |
| Based on accounting and integrated | IT will opt for the FD's systems | Either FD adapts GAS/MAS to accommodate IT needs (this is normally a significant effort due to specificities) or IT and/or FD builds a specific dedicated independent MAS; FD will require to input data in both MAS and to cross-check data | MAS and GAS of FD are dedicated and fit with IT needs |

Table 6.10 Options for the IT Management Accounting System

*The decision is: which Management Accounting System fits the IT department's needs best, giving optimal value on investments?*

## 6.5.6  Cash versus accruals based accounting systems

The simplest accounting system is the cash basis accounting system. Revenues and expenses are recognized as follows:
- revenue is recognized when cash is received
- expense is recognized when cash is paid.

In an accruals-based accounting system, revenues are recognized when earned and expenses are recognized when incurred (for example when a service is provided or a product is delivered). Under local regulations, such as GAAP, there may be specific provisions for recognizing revenues and expenses; for example:
- revenue is recognized when both of the following conditions are met
  - revenue is earned (when products are delivered or services are provided)
  - revenue is realized (means the money flow has occurred)
- expense is recognized in the period in which related revenue is recognized (this is the matching principle).

Accrual accounting is more accurate in terms of net income because it matches income with the expenses incurred to produce it. It is also more realistic for measuring business performance. A business can be in serious difficulties and still generate a positive cash basis income for several years by building accounts payable (accruing but not paying expenses), selling assets, and not replacing capital assets as they wear out. A business may be free to choose which method works best for it under certain constraints. For example, in the US companies with a turnover over 5 million dollars, or that keep an inventory of items to sell, are required by the IRS to use the accrual accounting method. These provisions depending on tax and government authority of each country and may change over time. Adopting one method or the other typically has an impact on taxation.

It is not the objective of this book to provide a method to choose the most appropriate accounting system, but Figure 6.11 summarizes the most likely benefits and disadvantages of both systems. Large organizations adopt sophisticated software and are able to manage both cash and accrual based accounting systems (and therefore statements) with unique accounting entries.

When adopting an accrual based accounting system, adjusting entries are performed. These are accounting journal entries that convert an organization's accounting records to the accrual basis of accounting. To demonstrate the need for adjusting entries, take the example of an amount that has already been recorded in the organization's accounting records, but the amount is for more than the current accounting period. Let us assume that on December 1, 2008 the company paid a supplier 24,000 euros for the provision of software maintenance fees. Maintenance fees cover the period from December 1, 2008 through November 30, 2008. The 24.000 euros transaction was recorded in the accounting records on December 1, but the amount represents twelve months of coverage and expense. By December 31, one month of the maintenance fee has expired. Hence the income statement for December should report just one month of software maintenance cost of 2.000 euros (24.000 divided by 12 months) in the account for software maintenance fees.

| | Cash accounting | Accrual accounting |
|---|---|---|
| **Benefits** | • Easy, simple to prepare, understand and interpret<br>• Costs less<br>• Much tighter control on spending<br>• Does not have adjustments (provision for doubtful debts) therefore not subjective | • Provides measures of economic goods and services consumed, transformed and earned<br>• Improved accountability for fixed assets<br>• Full cost of gov't activity is taken into account in pricing decisions<br>• Yields an income figure<br>• Yields a measure of capital<br>• Cannot be easily manipulated<br>• Permits recording of stock of goods maintained<br>• Provides adequate distinction between capital and revenue expenditure<br>• Gives a full financial picture<br>• Raise the level of transparency and accountability of government<br>• Fulfills the stewardship function of public sector organisations |
| **Disadvantages** | • Does not distinguish between capital and income<br>• Because no assets or liabilities are recorded, no measure of worth, no measure of capital<br>• Since income is the increase in capital there is no measure of income<br>• Excess of receipts over payments not income because receipts might include capital receipts.<br>• Excess of payments over receipts not loss because payments may include acquisitions of assets (capital)<br>• No opportunity to compare income with capital to yield a return on capital as a measure of business performance<br>• No opportunity to use income figure in any way as a comparative measure of performance | • Subjectivity – may be used to distort the true picture<br>• Demand high admin and accounting costs<br>• Financial control problem – an invoice need only be received |

Figure 6.11 Benefits and disadvantages of cash-based and accrual-based accounting systems

The balance sheet dated December 31 should report the cost of eleven months of the software maintenance fees that has not yet been used up in the asset account for software prepaid software maintenance fees. Since it is unlikely that the 24.000 euros transaction on December 1 was recorded this way, an adjusting entry will be needed at December 31, 2007 to make the income statement and balance sheet report this accurately.

There are two scenarios where adjusting journal entries are needed before the financial statements are issued:
1. Nothing has been entered in the accounting records for certain expenses or revenues, but those expenses and/or revenues did occur and must be included in the current period's income statement and balance sheet.

2. Something has already been entered in the accounting records, but the amount needs to be divided up between two or more accounting periods.

Adjusting entries almost always involves a balance sheet account (Interest Payable, Prepaid Software Maintenance Fees, Accounts Receivable, etc.) and a profit and loss statement account (Interest Expense, Software Maintenance Fees Expense, Service Revenues, etc.).

There are two major types of adjusting entries:
1. Accruals, for revenues and expenses that are recognized before the related financial transaction occurs.
2. Deferrals, for revenues and expenses that are recognized after the related financial transaction occurs.

Figure 6.12 shows examples of adjustment entries classified according to these two major types.

| Account | Financial transaction | Anticipated<br>Financial transaction (e.g. cash flow) occurs in a period before the one recorded in P&L, balance sheet | Postponed<br>Financial transaction (e.g. cash flow) occurs in a period after the one recorded in P&L, balance sheet |
|---|---|---|---|
| Revenue | | Deferred revenue; deferred credit; deferred liability; deferred income; prepaid income; unearned revenue; unearned income | Accrued earnings; accrued income; accrued revenue; accrued asset |
| Cost | | Deferred asset; deferred expenditure; deferred charge | Accrued cost; accrued charge; accrued expenses; accrued liabilities |

Figure 6.12 Example of adjustment entries

Typical IT accrued items for which adjusting entries may be made include:
• salaries
• past-due expenses
• unbilled revenue (the customer has started using the services provided and/or delivered products but has not paid yet).

Some deferred IT items for which adjusting entries may be made include:
• prepaid maintenance fees
• prepaid rent
• prepaid insurances
• depreciation
• unearned revenue (for example the customer is charged an amount before the service is activated).

The decision to be taken is whether the accounting system should be cash or accrual based. The decision is generally made by the financial department (which only in Scenario 3 coincides with IT financial management). A cash-based accounting system for the whole organization is probably only a viable solution for small organizations, depending on the regulations in force locally. In larger organizations the decision could be triggered when developing a specific Management Accounting System for IT needs only (such a situation may arise in Scenario 1 or 2).

*The decision is: which accounting system to implement when the IT department is developing its own, cash based or accrual based?*

### 6.5.7  Single-entry versus double-entry accounting systems

Single-entry bookkeeping makes a single entry in accounts for each transaction. This is sufficient to produce a profit and loss statement. Such an accounting system is valuable to smaller businesses, as it requires little or no bookkeeping or accounting knowledge.

The double-entry system derives its name from each transaction being recorded in at least two accounts. In particular, each transaction results in at least one account being debited and at least one account being credited, with the total debits of the transaction equal to the total credits. Some examples are helpful to understand. A sale is made that creates a record of income for the business. The double entry is the fact that the organization that bought the goods now owes the value of that sales invoice to the business. The double-entry system records the sales income and also the debt due from the customer or the debtor. On the other side, if a purchase is made that creates a record of expense for the business, the double entry will also create a record of credit due to the supplier, or creditor. With accounting software the two records are entered with a single activity.

The greatest value of double entry bookkeeping to a business is its ability to show in numerical terms the profitability of the business to generate improved financial performance and management while also producing a statement of assets and liabilities. Producing a balance sheet is generally a compulsory requirement for most organizations, depending on local regulations, and always for large organizations. This is one of the reasons why this system has become the standard one for General Accounting Systems.

Nevertheless, building a double-entry system may be an expensive task and requires specific accounting software, while a single-entry system can be managed simply with a spreadsheet. In Scenario 1 and sometimes in Scenario 2, when the decision has been taken to develop a specific Management Accounting System for IT needs and producing a balance sheet is not a requirement, the single-entry system may be a realistic option to evaluate.

*The decision is: which bookkeeping system to implement when IT is developing its own, single-entry or double-entry?*

### 6.5.8  Cost model

Cost stands for the sacrifice of resources. The price we pay measures the sacrifice we must make to acquire them. Whether we pay cash or use another asset, whether we pay now or later, the cost of the item acquired is represented by what we forego as a result and will be assigned to a specific accounting period. These resources are spent to acquire goods and services and specifically, in the IT service management context, they can be considered investments in service assets that increase business performance, as described in Figure 6.14.

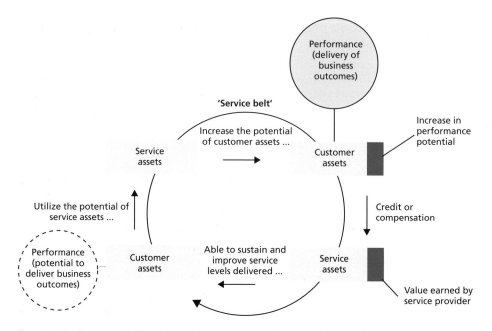

Figure 6.13 How investments in IT service assets increase customers' business performance (source ITIL V3 Service Strategy, OGC)

To calculate the costs of IT service provision, it is necessary to design a framework in which all known costs can be recorded and allocated to provide the different desired views of costs. This is called a cost model. Examples of required views of costs are by cost center, by organizational function, by customer, by service, by location, or by project. It is possible to support more than one view at a time but the trade-off is normally the complexity of data entry and/or calculations, as we will see later.

Each element of cost, for example staff's activity, hardware purchase, location contracts, etc. are classified according to various aspects of the cost model, required to provide information. The chosen cost model is supported by the Management Accounting System.

## Classification according to typology

It is useful to categorize costs to ensure that they are correctly identified and managed. This categorization should be consistent and easily understandable. For the aim of producing an IT cost model, a possible minimal categorization of costs is the following:
- hardware costs
- software costs
- people costs
- accommodation costs
- external services costs
- transfer costs.

The categories are often referred to as cost types (e.g. in ITIL).

Hardware and software costs are related to the purchase of goods and services. People costs are related to activities performed by internal resources. These costs can be simply managed in terms of number of assigned resources but, in Scenario 2 and especially in Scenario 3, they will probably be measured by means of time management processes and software. In this case, activities will probably be more detailed at project, service or even at process level (for example, incident management). Acquiring information at a more detailed level helps to reduce the volume of indirect costs but, again, it can become a very expensive task (for example, incident management costs may be directly related to the specific services).

External service costs need further explanation. It is now common to buy services from external parties (external services) that are a mixture of cost types, for example an outsourced service for providing application development that includes use of servers and middleware software. It may be difficult to break down this cost into each of the first four categories, as it is likely to contain elements that are indivisible or that the supplier will not wish to detail. It is easier and more usual to categorize this as an external service cost.

Finally, transfer costs are those representing goods and services that are sold from one part of an organization to the other. Transfer costs may be for:
- hardware (an IT organization buying PCs on behalf of a business customer)
- software (licenses centrally purchased in order to take advantage of economies of scale and transferred to each business unit based on usage)
- people (the HR overhead levied by the corporate HR department)
- accommodation (a charge made by the Facilities Management department).

Cost types are frequently exposed in reporting and they could be further articulated. For example, hardware costs could be divided into server costs, router costs, storage costs, etc. A sophisticated approach could be managing a hierarchy of cost types. Nevertheless, care should be taken so that the complexity and relative cost of managing classification of information does not become overwhelming. Further decomposition should be considered if information needs are evident and verified. ITIL suggests a hierarchy of three levels: cost types, cost elements and cost units. Cost types are the highest level of category to which costs are assigned in budgeting and accounting (typically, those previously listed). Cost elements are the middle level of category to which costs are assigned in budgeting and accounting (for cost type 'people', payroll, staff benefits, expenses, training, overtime etc. are examples of cost elements). Cost units are the lowest level of category to which costs are assigned. Cost units are usually things that can be easily counted (e.g. staff numbers, software licenses) or things easily measured (e.g. CPU usage, electricity consumed). Cost units are included within cost elements. For example a cost element of 'expenses' could include cost units of hotels, transport, meals etc.

## Direct versus indirect costs

Any cost that can be unambiguously related to a cost object is a direct cost of it. Conversely, those costs that cannot be unambiguously related to a cost object are indirect costs. If, for example, our analysis concerns cost centers, we would consider as direct all those costs that can be directly related to a specific cost center. Indirect costs would be those costs that are not clearly attributable to a specific cost center. If the desired result is to consider all costs apportioned to cost centers or services, it is necessary to find a method to apportion all costs to them. We will discuss how this can be done in further details in section 6.5.10, dealing with apportioning.

Direct or indirect costs do not depend on the type of cost but on the ability to relate it to the cost object. For example, if an IT service uses a dedicated infrastructure for a customer, the costs of it will be direct when related to the service. Conversely, if a service provider makes use of a common infrastructure, such as a mainframe or a storage area network, to supply different services it will be more difficult to establish direct costs for a specific customer and, probably, they will be managed as indirect cost and later apportioned to customers.

When evaluating the costs of a service or customer (cost object), the situation is much clearer when the majority or totality of costs are direct. However, when the majority of costs are indirect the assigned quota depends on the rules used to apportion them to the cost object. These rules may vary from time to time or depending on usage. For example, consider an IT service and its incident management process: the costs of people working on incidents can be either allocated directly, by means of timesheets and unit costs of resources, or indirectly apportioned, by means of the percentage of incidents occurring in the specific service when compared to the total number of incidents managed by incident management staff. Direct allocation of costs is always preferable, when possible, as it gives more accurate and reliable information (for example, the number of incidents may not reflect their relevance and related working time).

One difficulty is that costs may be directly related to one cost object and indirectly related to another. This is a common situation. Managing different types of cost objects may quickly increase the complexity or reduce the quota of costs that can be managed as direct (so finally the reliability of costs); this is a critical decision to be taken. In the previous example, if people solving incidents belong to a specific cost center, the allocation of their cost to it is direct while apportioning to IT service, as we have seen, may be indirect.

## Capital costs versus operational costs

Capital expenditures, or Capex, are expenditures incurred when a business acquires or improves long terms assets that create future benefits (benefits in more than one year). Capex is therefore investment in the business as assets are expected to contribute to it. Because of their use, assets become obsolete over time and therefore are depreciated so that their value eventually disappears.

For tax purposes, capital expenditures are costs that cannot be deducted in the year in which they are paid or incurred, and must be capitalized. In this context, the general (but not exhaustive) rule to identify these costs is that if the asset acquired or improved has a useful life longer than the taxable year, the cost must be capitalized. The capital expenditure costs are then amortized or depreciated (see also 6.5.9) over a predetermined period of time. The period identified by tax authorities may be different from the actual useful life of assets. For example, for PCs the useful life is often considered to be three years but in many countries depreciation, for taxation aims, is calculated over five years.

An operating expense (operating expenditure, operational expense, operational expenditure) or Opex is an ongoing cost for running a product, business, or system. If we consider an IT service,

Capex would be the cost of designing and implementing it while Opex would be the cost of running it.

The important effect of capitalizing is that the full cost of purchasing or improving the asset does not affect the profit and loss statement, thus affecting the profitability of the period when it is performed, but is recorded in the balance sheet. Only a depreciation quota of the asset is recorded and affects the profit and loss statement for each period. In general, capitalizing expenses is beneficial, as organizations acquiring new assets with a long-term lifespan can spread out the cost over a specified period of time. Organizations take expenses that they incur today and deduct them over the long term without an immediate negative impact on revenues.

Identification of Capex and depreciation methods are generally defined by country laws and tax regulations. This is to avoid the possibility of managing the operating results of an organization inappropriately. If an organization were to capitalize regular operating expenses, it would artificially boost its operating profit and loss statements and appear to be a more profitable company. Because an organization cannot hide its expenses forever, such a practice would, of course, fail in the long run.

Each country may have different approaches. Sometimes an organization might have to use different depreciation systems in order to satisfy different accounting models (for example one satisfying national regulations and one satisfying foreign regulations applicable to the holding company to which the organization belongs). Depreciation is a very complex subject and is normally one of the most relevant elements used to influence the operating results of a company. To understand this issue, just consider a simple cost unit, for example a server. It is normally considered a capital cost and therefore subject to depreciation. Nevertheless, this may depend upon the amount needed to buy the server: in some countries it may be established that, under a certain amount, the same type of cost (for example our server) should be managed as an operational cost. Furthermore, the same cost unit may be purchased with different financial options, such as lease or rent. Again, regulations will normally state that this cost should be managed as operational, and therefore without depreciation.

Even more complicated is the management of projects. A server can be bought separately or, for example, as an element of a very large project. Let us suppose that we want to provide a new CRM system. In this case the cost element will not be managed as a capital expenditure on its own but will be managed as the capital expenditure part of the whole project. Depreciation will start when the CRM system goes live for all the costs included in the project. Until then, all the costs related to the CRM system will be managed as assets, therefore affecting the company's balance sheet, but will not influence the operating result (profit and loss statement). Only after the go-live of the project, depreciation will start for the whole costs of the project and the corresponding value will be evident in the profit and loss statement, finally affecting operating results.

In Scenario 1 and 2 financial policies, including all depreciation aspects, are defined by the financial department or by the holding for the whole organization. We could say that these are out of scope for IT financial management. In Scenario 3, where IT financial management corresponds to the organization's overall financial management, they are clearly in scope.

Nevertheless, this subject requires deep understanding of accounting mechanisms and rules and it is influenced by local regulations; therefore it will not be described further in this book.

For the reasons discussed above, classification of costs as capital or operational may not always be easy and may vary depending on the existence of a project, the amount of the investment, the chosen method for funding and local regulations. As a result, even if relevant to determine the profit and loss statement, the distinction between Capex and Opex may not be especially important for the IT department. We explain this statement with an example. The IT department has budgeted for all the costs relating to the previously mentioned CRM system. Independently of whether a server is depreciated immediately or later, after buying it for the project, what is relevant for the IT department is that the cost of the server is aligned with its budget and occurs in the target accrual period. This is the core aspect that the IT department focuses on in Scenario 1 and 2. In Scenario 3 the other aspects (depreciation, leverage of financial options) play a relevant role too. In Scenario 1, and often in Scenario 2, the IT department focuses on the definition and control of costs and the financial department provides the rules to be followed to manage them as Opex or Capex or the financial option to be used (e.g. buy, lease, rent).

This highlights the differences between the scenarios. Financial policies will always influence the behavior of IT management even in Scenarios 1 and 2. For example, we might assume the following situation: an old information system has very expensive maintenance costs that could be reduced by buying a new server with a lower maintenance fee. Maintenance costs are operational costs while buying the new server is usually a capital expenditure. This option, buying the server outright, does not match the financial policies because of its high negative impact on cash flow. The best solution is in this situation is to acquire the server by means of a rental service, thus transferring the cost from capital to operational expenditure. All parties' needs are satisfied: the IT department has reduced ongoing costs and the financial department has achieved its aim of reducing Capex. Unfortunately, financial policies do not always have neutral impacts. In some cases the need for capitalizing costs may lead to inferior performance. For example, in order to capitalize, an organization may decide that no 'stand-alone' consulting services can be acquired (as these would be operational costs) but only products that can be capitalized, such as implemented systems. This may lead the IT department to reduce or do without external consulting services for the analysis and design of the solution before software purchase (as these consulting services may be difficult to justify for the aim of capitalizing). If there is a lack of internal knowledge, the purchasing decision (driven by financial constraints) could lead to ineffective decisions that have highly negative consequences for the project and for business performance because of the inappropriate choice and/or implementation of the target solution.

The following list gives typical examples of the cost elements, often classified into capital expenditure and operational expenditure:

**Capital expenditure**
- computer and network equipment
- software packages

## Operational expenditure
- staff costs
- maintenance of computer hardware and software
- consultancy services, rental fees for equipment
- software license fees
- accommodation costs
- administration expenditures
- electricity, water, gas, rates
- disaster recovery
- consumables

To simplify things for IT staff responsible for the data entry of cost elements while performing IT financial management activities (such as budgeting, accounting), it is usual to refine the classification of cost types and to link them directly to the use of the correct depreciation rules transparently. So, for example, 'hardware' costs could be articulated in 'purchased hardware' and 'leased or rented hardware'. Classifying a cost element in one category or the other would automatically and transparently define the use of a specific depreciation rule (including the 'no depreciation' rule). In the same way, other information could be defined in order to track depreciation in a transparent way, such as the project to which a cost element is related. In such cases, IT staff may not know if capitalizing is managed on a 'per cost element' basis or on a 'per project' basis, for a specific project. This could be determined and managed by a few specialized resources in the financial or IT department.

## Fixed costs versus variable costs
This is another typical way of classifying costs. Costs that do not change even when resource usage varies are referred to as fixed costs. The maintenance license costs of a software package are an example of fixed cost. Variable costs are those that vary with some factor, such as usage or time. An example of a variable cost could be storage, which increases with the number of managed records such as invoices or orders.

One characteristic of variable costs is that they are less predictable than fixed costs, as they are influenced by decisions made by the organization (e.g. the IT budget owner, project managers, cost center managers, etc.) or by service customers. From a funding point of view, this also means that cash flows of variable costs are more difficult to plan and can prevent proper operations if inadequately managed. It is very important to link variable costs to patterns of business activity. Fixed costs, on the other hand, are much easier to manage and plan. They tend to be less negotiable during the planning and budgeting cycles, because they often represent commitments that have already been made.

Sometimes it is necessary to view a cost as having a fixed element and a variable element. For example, storage will require a central unit and controllers that may be considered fixed costs. Disk drives that can be plugged into the storage unit are to be considered as variable costs. The cost of storage can be considered as made of a fixed part plus a variable part dependent on the space required. This remains true until the maximum limit of capacity of the storage unit is reached (for example the unit might accept a number of drives up to 2 terabytes of space). After that limit, the storage unit would be replaced and both fixed and variable costs of storage may vary.

The classification of fixed costs versus variable costs is mainly used for investment appraisal and purchase decisions. For example, a decision about which type of storage unit to buy might be based on the estimated use of disk space. Knowing variable costs is a valuable information when taking decisions about pricing and offers as revenues should cover at least variable costs

### Approach to validation of the cost model

It is now easy to understand that cost models can be very complex. It is important to validate cost models practically by means of simulating and checking results with real data before the full implementation of the Management Accounting System that supports the models. This can be done manually with the help of spreadsheets, but the data necessary to identify costs is not always readily available in most IT organizations. For example, it may be necessary to know, for each customer, the proportionate use of resources that are not currently accounted for, e.g. staff, accommodation, hardware, and software. Ideally, monitoring of resource usage should be automatic, using one or more software tools but some data is likely to be collected from paper records and reports or from stand-alone systems.

To validate the cost model, it is important to calculate and check the identified costs more than once. The model should be checked by performing a full balance check, including apportioning of costs if needed. This check should be made for all the cost objects, such as customers or services, to verify that the totals are equal and partial data look reasonable. In practice, this may be a time consuming activity, because of the lack of data and proper tools. The effort can be limited to a reduced scope, such as a small set of IT services (see also 6.3.5).

> *The decision is about the characteristics of the cost model: which cost types to consider, which are the direct/indirect costs, which are capital/operational costs, and how costs have to be managed.*

### 6.5.9  Depreciation

Depreciation is the measure of the wearing out, consumption or other reduction in the useful economic life of a fixed asset, whether from use, time or obsolescence due to technological or other environmental changes (e.g. regulations). Depreciation applies only to costs classified as capital expenditure. Depreciation should be calculated in order to charge a fair proportion of cost or valuation of the asset to each IT accounting period (typically the year) expected to benefit from its use.

The assessment of depreciation, and its allocation to IT accounting periods, involves the consideration of three factors:
- the actual cost (or valuation) of the asset
- the length of the asset's expected useful economic life to the business of the organization, having due regard to the likelihood of obsolescence
- the estimated residual value of the asset at the end of its useful economic life in the business of the organization.

The useful economic life of an asset may be:
- pre-determined, as in the case of a lease
- dependent on its physical deterioration through use or passage of time
- reduced by economic or technological obsolescence.

When determining the profit and loss sheet in line with national fiscal regulations, the economic life of assets is generally pre-determined.

The depreciation methods used should be those that are most appropriate when considering the types of assets and their usage in the business. The finance department should provide guidance on this, in line with the country laws and regulations that must be applied. This is true for Scenarios 1 and 2, while in Scenario 3 this aspect is also part of IT financial management.

The most common methods of assessing depreciation are:
- **Straight-line method** – Where an equal amount is written off the value of the asset each year. Usually a fixed percentage of purchase cost, this results in the item having zero net book value after a pre-set number of years (although it may continue to be used).
- **Reducing balance method** – Where a set percentage of the capital cost is written off the net book value each year. Often this is 40 percent in the first year, 30 percent in the second year and 30 percent in the last year.
- **By usage** – Where depreciation is written down according to the extent of usage during a period. It is usual to estimate the total useful 'life' of a device and to calculate the proportion of this 'life' that has been 'used' during the year. For example, a laser printer may be estimated to have a useful 'life' of 5,000,000 pages. If the average usage is 1,000,000 pages in a year, it can be depreciated by 20 percent in that year.

A typical problem of depreciation occurs when an asset becomes obsolete or is no longer used before it has been fully depreciated. This may happen, for example, because the economic life is defined by law, and because laws do not differentiate enough based on the type of assets (for example the economic life of a PC may be shorter than economic life of a server). The economic life of a PC may be defined as five years but its technical obsolescence may arise much earlier. In such a case, the decision to replace it could lead to specific bookkeeping entries determining a capital loss (a cost in the profit and loss statement corresponding to the net book value of the replaced asset). The contrary may also happen – that is, a fully depreciated asset (net book value equal to zero) may continue to be operationally used. As previously noted, the asset should not be removed from the Configuration Management System until actually discarded.

Calculating depreciation is a complex activity, which a General Accounting System and Management Accounting System should be able to perform. The methods and rules to be used to determine the profit and loss statement for fiscal duties can be different from those chosen by the organization to determine its balance sheet and profit and loss statement to evaluate its business performances. The General Accounting System would normally support different calculation methods for different aims. The Management Accounting System is not always required to be able to manage depreciation; when specifically developed for IT purposes and needs it could manage simplified rules for depreciation – or no rules at all, although this is probably not recommended. In Scenarios 1 and 2, the IT Management Accounting System may be different from the Management Accounting System of the financial department and may use very simple depreciation rules, such as the straight-line method.

*The decision is the depreciation model to be used for each type of cost.*

## 6.5.10 Cost apportioning model

Viewing IT financial data exclusively according to the cost types (see 6.5.8) classification or by the views provided by accounting reporting is generally not sufficient for the aim of forecasting, controlling and taking decisions about IT matters.

As a minimum, organizations in Scenarios 2 and 3 will need to view IT financial data according to different perspectives, such as customers, projects, and services. This perspective should align with those required by the financial department, typically about organizational functions, cost centers, products, line of business, etc.. The activity of assigning a share of the costs (which is applicable also to revenues) is called apportioning. In this activity, a cost object is any endpoint to which a cost is assigned, for example, a service, a department or a customer. A cost pool is a collection of costs that we want to assign to the cost object. The cost items belonging to a specific cost type as discussed in 6.5.8, such as hardware or software, are examples of cost pools. Finally the cost apportioning rule is the method or activity used to assign the cost in the cost pool to the cost object. A typical cost apportioning rule of IT is, for example, to apportion the cost of mainframe to customers based on CPU utilization.

Clearly, raw financial facts (data) cannot be classified according to all the possible and desired perspectives. let us take the example of an invoice. When recorded, the whole document or its single rows may be classified according to various perspectives, such as cost centers. Classifying the same document according to another perspective, for example a service, may be complex and time consuming. For example, if the document refers to the purchase of servers and its rows report three servers, the cost center might be the IT department purchasing them but the servers could be dedicated to supply different IT services. A convenient situation is when each server is dedicated to a specific service; in this case it could be simple, although time consuming, to enter three records, one for each server, related to the corresponding service and common cost center in the accounting system. By doing so, we have performed a direct imputation of costs to cost centers and to IT services. With many multiple perspectives, the number of registrations to be performed could quickly become overwhelming and it becomes necessary to choose only some of them. All other perspectives should be calculated by means of apportioning, although apportioning is a much less precise method if compared with direct assignment.

Choosing the perspectives to be managed directly is not a simple decision, as the perspectives that are useful for IT management could be in competition with those required by the financial department. This situation is typical of organizations in Scenario 2, where it may be difficult to convince the financial department to replace cost centers with services. In this case, the ideal situation occurs when the financial department can organize the IT services structure using the cost centers structure (as a part of it). If this does not happen, the IT department would have two options: agreeing to manage IT services by means of indirect costs and apportioning or building a specific Management Accounting System (see 6.5.5), where IT services are a core managed perspective with direct imputation of costs. In Scenario 1, the need for a dedicated Management Accounting System will be weak; apportioning costs to IT services or customers will probably be sufficient. In Scenario 3, the organization's accounting systems will be built around the needs of IT service management; IT services will be a core element of it with the possibility of charging costs directly to them. When the perspectives to be used for direct charges of costs (and revenues) have been defined, all other views of financial data would be determined by use of apportioning techniques, which we will analyze below.

Although apportioning may be applicable for revenues, it is used much more for costs and in this context it is known as cost apportioning. This is also because revenues are more simply assigned to the chosen perspectives, because of their nature – for example, a customer or a service where the billing activity directly generates records directly related to them.

The cost objects relevant for IT are traditionally cost centers, departments and customers. For service oriented companies, which adopt IT service management practices such as ITIL, and for those selling IT services in the market, the importance of knowing the cost by service is fundamental.

| Cost objects | IT financial management for internal IT departments | IT financial management for internal IT service providers | IT financial management for market IT service providers |
|---|---|---|---|
| Cost centers | Financial department requires this perspective (also used to manage cost of projects); normally costs are collected as direct. | Financial department requires this perspective (also used to manage cost of projects); normally costs are collected as direct. | This view is probably still required and costs may be collected as direct. |
| Departments | Financial department requires this perspective; normally costs of department are built as aggregation of cost centers and therefore they are collected as direct. | Financial department requires this perspective; normally costs of department are built as aggregation of cost centers and therefore they are collected as direct. | This view is probably still required and is generally built as aggregation of cost centers; an appropriate alternative is to determine the costs of departments by aggregation of services they own. |
| Customers | IT department may wish to know costs by customer; apportioning is frequent. | IT department needs this data, which can be built by means of apportioning of the costs of business services to customers. | Organization needs this data, which can be built by means of apportioning the costs of business services to customers. |
| Services | Unusual. | Mature service oriented organizations will feel the need for this perspective at least through apportioning, determining, as a minimum, the cost of business services. | Organization needs this data for pricing and decision-making; collecting costs directly is preferable because more precise. If not possible, apportioning would be used as a minimum. |

Table 6.11 Use of most relevant cost objects in scenarios

Cost apportioning has evolved from the aims of product costing and many different systems have been developed that are appropriate for a specific type of production. For example, in the custom boat sector, the costing system computes costs for the individual units (or small group of them), called jobs. In the paint factories the units of productions are identical, so the costing systems costs only large batches. Cost accountants use job costing and process costing to describe these two extremes. Many organizations use a hybrid of job and process costing, called operation costing, where an operation is a standardized method of making a product that is performed repeatedly in production. The cost is composed of a process costing for the common characteristics of products and of job costing for the specificities. This is typical of the automotive industry, for example. Activity-based costing is a two-stage-product costing method that assigns costs first to activities and then to the products, based on each product's use of activities, where an activity is a discrete task that an organization undertakes to make or deliver a product or service.

Organizations that manage services are the target of this book, although in the IT market some organizations are still focused on delivering products (hardware or software). These latter organizations will find the typical product costing models of the industrial world adequate for their purposes. Organizations involved in delivering IT services would find these models too simple and would be likely to build specific models starting from these basic industrial models.

The adopted costing model will depend on several factors. Table 6.11 shows some possible options that we will analyze further below.

## IT financial management for internal IT departments

The focus on costs is driven by the financial department, which defines cost objects and the required analysis according to the organization's core business needs. Cost centers are used to evaluate the performance of managers; the use of accounting for performance evaluation is often called responsibility accounting. This system classifies organizations' units (such as departments, functions, regions, stores) into centers based on the decision authority delegated to the center's manager. There are five types of centers: cost centers, discretionary cost centers, revenue centers, profit centers and investment centers.

Managers of cost centers are responsible for an activity for which a well defined relationship exists between inputs and outputs. Plant managers are a typical example of owners of cost centers. When managers are held responsible for costs but the input-output relationship is not well specified, a discretionary cost center is established. This is the typical case for IT departments in this scenario. Managers of revenue centers are responsible for selling products (this is typical of Scenario 3), while managers of profit centers are held accountable for profits and therefore manage both revenues and costs. Managers of investment centers have responsibility for profit and investment in assets. Investment centers are generally assigned to IT departments as well.

Figure 6.15 shows how costs are typically managed. Hardware and software maintenance contracts are typically assigned to the manager responsible for them as well as the cost of people they manage. Purchase of hardware and software, as well as of services, and use of resources (people) to implement a specific project are directly assigned to an investment center.

Cost centers are often grouped in hierarchical structures which enables, for example, a view of costs by department.

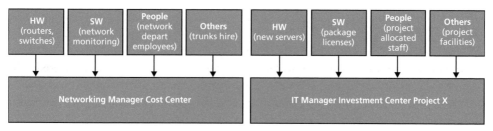

Figure 6.14 Allocation of costs to cost centers

A view of costs by customers may be required, to be able to transfer costs. This is often required by the business and organized by the financial department, although sometimes the initiator can be the IT department. Cost centers may be used for this purpose, for example creating specific cost centers for each customer.

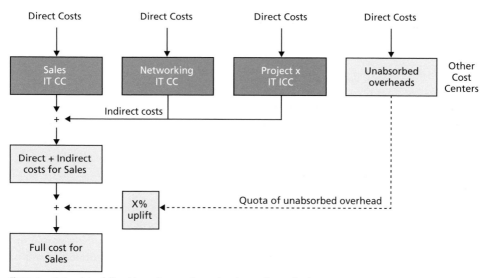

Figure 6.15 Determining full cost by customer using cost centers and apportioning

Figure 6.15 describes how determination of full cost by customer is possible using cost centers and apportioning of costs. In this example, the IT cost center Sales has been defined as the recipient for all the direct costs of the customer (the sales department of the organization, in this example). There could be more than one cost center dedicated to the customer (for example one for infrastructures and one for applications). Costs from other cost centers, such as networking, can be apportioned using specific drivers. Choosing the most appropriate driver is an important decision as there are nearly always several options. An appropriate driver should be one that is:

• easily measurable
• easy to understand
• fair
• non confidential

• enabling the implementation of an appropriate and cost effective measurement system for the driver

In our example, networking costs could be apportioned based on the number of users of the sales department or on bandwidth consumption (if this is measured). Some projects may be dedicated, for example the implementation of a new CRM system for sales agents, but often costs of projects are shared among many customers, for example the implementation of a new ERP (Enterprise resource planning) system. This is the case reported in Figure 6.15 and, again, the driver to apportion the costs of the project could be the number of users of the sales department or it could be an absolute percentage deriving from considerations about the relative importance of functionalities of the ERP system used by the sales department.

If drivers to apportion all costs of IT department to sales cannot be found for all the cost centers, there will be some unabsorbed overheads. These additional costs should be apportioned if we want to determine the full cost by customer. A commonly used method is to multiply the total of the direct and indirect costs for the cost center by a calculated percentage, which is based on the ratio of the total unabsorbed costs to the total absorbed costs. The uplift amount can be calculated with the following equation, which is very simple:

$$X\% \text{ uplift} = \frac{\text{Unabsorbed Costs}}{\text{All costs} - \text{Unabsorbed Costs}} \times 100$$

A high percentage of indirect costs and uplift means greater uncertainty about the full cost of the cost object – the IT sales department in our example. There should be an IT financial management policy that sets upper limits to control the risks related to this uncertainty.

## IT financial management for internal IT service providers

The focus on costs is still driven by the financial department but the IT department starts to have specific needs too. Cost center management as described for the previous scenario will probably be still in place, as well as management by customer if the business requires it. However, in this scenario, management of IT services is likely to be an emerging need too. Attention will be initially focused on business services (see 6.5.3). In practice, the approach may be similar to the one illustrated to determine the full cost by customer and described in Figure 6.17.

The number of services can be considerably larger than the number of customers and this may add complexity (this is especially true for organizations in Scenario 2, dealing with a captive market). The view by customer can be derived from the view by service by grouping services (this is easy when services are dedicated to specific customers). This is probably the most common case, although it can be possible that some business services are supplied to more than one customer (this mainly depends on the definition of a specific service and the related Service Catalog structure). In such cases, the costs of the shared services should be apportioned to customers with specific drivers.

At this point, the cost center approach and apportioning may not be sufficient any more. The IT department might not have enough information (for example the cost of managing a specific category of servers is not clear and useful for management), or it might want to determine the

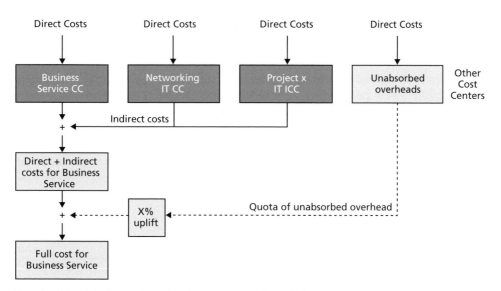

Figure 6.17 Determining full cost by service using cost centers and apportioning

costs of the technical services as well as the business services center. Although the relationship with the financial department has been successfully managed up to this point, probably retrieving information from the Managerial Accounting System, it will no longer be possible to merge the IT department's requirements with those of the financial department. A service oriented organization would need to organize responsibilities and budget around the concept of service, which would emerge as the main cost object to focus on. The Managerial Accounting System of the financial department might not be able to include the new cost object or to manage more than one cost object at a time, which could lead to higher costs to manage information (for example order entry or invoice recording).

In the next scenario, we will present an advanced approach for managing IT costs by service. Such a solution could be taken into consideration in this scenario too, but with more difficulties, as the IT department would probably need to implement a specific Managerial Accounting System.

## IT financial management for market IT service providers

Although it is possible to find IT service providers controlling their costs by means of one of the methods suggested for the previous scenarios, this situation provides the opportunity to make a step ahead toward becoming a service-oriented organization. A service can be seen as a center of responsibility, costs and, generally, profit. Financial management is focused on IT as the core business of the organization and is therefore able to adopt the most appropriate solutions to provide the required information to management. In this scenario, the service should achieve the relevance of a product in the industrial domain. Figure 6.18 describes how the full cost of services (both business and technical) can be calculated. Instead of cost centers, service centers are the core cost objects managed. Service centers are normally related to IT services but they are also appropriate for managing projects. Costs are directly allocated to service centers, whenever possible. For example, the cost of locations or electricity can be directly assigned to a housing service, the cost of purchasing a server to server management service, the cost of management office applications to PC applications management service, etc. Service architecture is developed at such a level to ensure that every cost has a service to which it can be directly assigned. Staff activities can also be related to services. For example activities performed by the HR department can be considered as a specific service, HR Service, which includes activities such as resource recruitment, payment of wages, etc.

The full cost of business services can be determined by means of apportioning. For example, the service cost of fleet management can be entirely apportioned to workstation service but housing is apportioned to server management on the basis of a driver, such as the space occupied by the server or the number and type of servers. Any unabsorbed costs for the business services can be managed, once again, with the uplift method previously described.

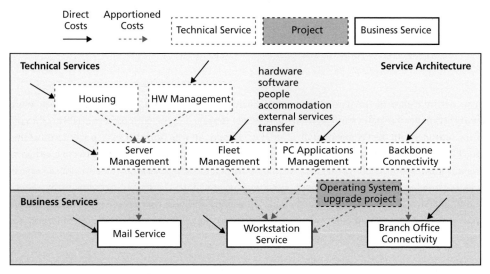

Figure 6.18 Managing all costs through services

## Apportioning metrics and associated costs

Regardless of the scenario, cost apportioning metrics have to be defined. Recipients (cost center, customer or service) have to be aware, understand and accept the metric. The metric depends on the specific recipients considered. Typical metrics are:
- absolute percentage – a fixed percentage of costs is apportioned to the recipient
- number of users – typical for application services but very frequent also for systems
- CPU usage
- number of components – PCs, servers, routers, etc.
- storage usage
- bandwidth utilization
- activity – number of service requests, incidents, changes, releases, etc.
- hours of work.

Most of the metrics are based on volumes and a specific activity should be in place to regularly determine actual values (at least before closures and charging are performed). Reviews of all used metrics should be regularly performed to check their effectiveness and their efficiency compared with possible new emerging or suggested metrics.

The total cost apportioned to a recipient is generally determined by the actual value of the driver multiplied by its associated cost. There are different methods to calculate this cost. Generally a period is taken into consideration and the cost associated with the driver for the period is determined by dividing the total cost of the period by the quantity of the driver. For example, if the cost of the service server management in a month has been 60,000 euros to manage 300 servers, the cost per server will be 200 euros.

When systems change, underlying costs also change. For example, after defining the unit cost of the driver, a new server might be bought and added. Because of economies of scale, the new values might change very little when recalculating the unit cost associated with the driver for the following period (in this case less than 300 euros per server). Depending on the purpose and rules of the Management Accounting System, there are several ways to report the cost: average and standard are the most frequent.

With average cost, the unit cost is calculated for each period and the result used. The main disadvantage of this method for the recipient is that the cost is not only related to the specific use of the resources but also to the overall usage. Let us take the situation that in a specific period the recipient uses fewer servers. If this happens for other recipients too, the total cost is divided by a smaller number of servers. In such a case, the recipient could pay more for less servers because the unit cost would be higher. The advantage of this method is that the total cost is always considered if cost recovery is a target. To apply this method successfully, it is recommended that demand management is set up and properly working, thus optimally regulating the request of capacity and avoiding excessive fluctuations.

With the standard cost method, the unit cost is defined by estimating the costs of the resources necessary to meet an estimated capacity. The calculated unit cost is used for a certain number of periods regardless of the changes occurring to the components of the service. From time to time, if the objective is exact cost recovery, it will be necessary to manage adjustments. This can be done by specific positive or negative allocations of costs, which should be monitored by means of KPIs (for example the percentage of adjusted costs compared with total costs charged). When adjustments are made, the unit cost may be kept unchanged or newly defined. This method is appropriate when prices need to be defined in the Service Catalog.

*The decision is the choice of cost objects and the design of the cost apportioning model to be used for them.*

## 6.5.11 Pricing

After the core decision about the charging perspective has been taken (see 6.5.1) the pricing question may arise. In Scenario 1, IT financial management for internal IT departments, IT is usually considered as an accounting center and there is generally no charging to business units or to customers. In Scenario 2, IT financial management for internal IT service providers, IT will probably be considered as a recovery center and the transfer price mechanism is likely to be used to determine the amount to charge for each customer. In Scenario 3, IT financial management for market IT service providers, the IT service organization will sell its services for a specific price, defined for each service. In this scenario, a market price approach reflecting the value of services is appropriate.

The transfer price is the value or amount recorded in an organization's accounting records when one business unit, in our case the IT department, sells (transfers) goods or services to another business unit. In Scenario 2, if we assume that the final objective is cost recovery, the transfer price is easy to define: the outlay cost. It can be more difficult to decide on how to split the costs among customers when this is required. A driver needs to be defined; typical options are:
the number of users of IT services in the customer organization
the number of employees in the customer organization
the turnover of the customer organization.

For further information on this subject, see section 6.5.10 where a detailed description has been provided. Effectively, the transfer price is all about apportioning costs.

In Scenario 3, the market and the performance (often profitability) targets will be the main drivers to define tariffs for services. The price-quality strategy, together with the theory of demand curve and price sensitivity of customers (Kotler), market pricing, is generally used in this scenario. Some common service offer models are:
- **Tiered subscription** – For shared services (among many customers), where a set of different discrete levels of warranty and/or utility is offered (for example bronze, silver and gold levels) for specific prices.
- **Metered usage** – Where a price per unit for a shared service (among many customers) is determined, usually depending on the customer's demand.
- **Ad-hoc configurations** – Where the customer's dedicated infrastructures and applications are managed.
- **Value based** – Where the customer is paying for the perceived value of services.

Table 6.12 shows which pricing method is applicable for each service offer model. There are a number of cost-plus pricing models. The basic form is:

*Price = cost + x percent*

The mark-up (x percent) is set by the organization as a standard target return, comparable with returns on other business investments. The use of the cost plus method should be carefully applied as it may drive the organization away from market behavior. In particular, if the organization is not performing optimally, the desired mark-up may be not compatible with the prices offered by competitors.

ITIL version 3 has focused attention on the two main drivers creating value to the customers' of IT services: utility (or fit for purpose) and warranty (or fit for use). Analyzing (see Figure 6.19) the way by which value is created for customers and enabling IT services to provide it, justifies higher prices for these services, independently from market behavior. Value based price, what the customer is willing to pay for the recognized value of services, is another option for pricing that is applicable in Scenarios 2 and 3.

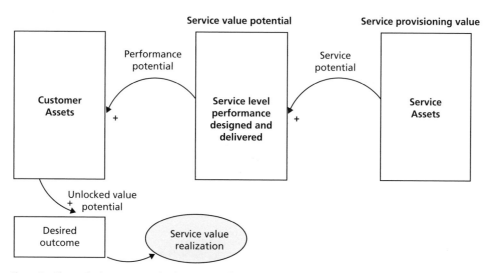

Figure 6.19 The mechanism to create value for customers (source ITIL V3, OGC)

Organizations in Scenario 2 may also opt for the mechanisms described for Scenario 3. These mechanisms often manage ad hoc configurations, so the cost plus method is frequently appropriate for them. In this case, the mark-up percentage may be defined to encourage the use of strategic applications or technologies. For example, if a mainframe platform has high maintenance costs and needs to be replaced, the mark-up percentage can be determined to influence the customer's behavior.

| Type of offering | Possible pricing models |
|---|---|
| Tiered subscription | Market pricing (recommended), cost plus |
| Metered usage | Market pricing (recommended), cost plus |
| Ad hoc configurations | Cost plus (Scenario 2), value based (Scenario 3) |

Table 6.12 Models of service offer and pricing options for organizations adopting Scenario 3

*The decision is the pricing mechanism when charging is required (transfer price versus market price) and the definition of tariffs or rules to define the amounts to charge.*

## 6.5.12 Cycles

Many of the activities described previously in Chapter 4 have specific frequencies (cycles). Their periodicity should be defined; this can be derived, to a great extent, from the financial cycles of the business (this is true, in particular, for Scenarios 1 and 2).

| Activity | Typical frequency |
|---|---|
| Planning | Each business cycle, for example every three years. In some cases, planning cycles can be rolling with annual reviews. |
| Budgeting | Budgeting is typically an annual activity. Reviews of budget can be performed during the year (for example each semester or quarter). |
| Accounting | The accounting cycles are typically monthly. Frequency can also depend on the probability and value of deviation from target performance (budget) and on how activities are funded. For Scenario 2 with low criticality and autonomous Management Accounting System, accounting cycles can be trimesters or quarters. For Scenario 3, accounting cycles will be monthly at minimum, but shorter frequencies are not unusual. |
| Forecasting | Forecasting also depends on criticality (probability and absolute value of potential deviations from budgets) and funding mechanisms. The forecasting cycle depends on the availability of actual data so maximum frequency is the same as accounting cycles. Because forecasting is a time-consuming activity for the management and key roles of IT service management, its frequency can be less often than accounting, especially for Scenario 2. For example, it is not unusual to have monthly accounting cycles and forecasting each quarter. |
| Investment evaluation | This activity is generally performed together with budgeting cycles and also every time a new investment arises. |
| Reporting | The frequency of reporting varies with each report. Some derive from the above-mentioned activities. So, for example, the budget profit and loss statement is produced at each budgeting activity. Some reports may be independent from those activities and have specific frequencies (sometimes they may be produced on request). |

Table 6.13 Typical frequencies for IT financial management activities

*The decision is the frequency of each IT service management activity.*

## 6.5.13 Reporting

One of the key decisions concerns the reports financial management should be providing. Several aspects should be considered: perspectives and time (periods to which analysis and reporting will refer), sources of data (the type of documents to which analysis and reporting will refer), models to be used (accounting, cost, cost apportioning), maximum level of detail of data (this will influence the level of detail of analysis and reporting), contents and lay-out of reports. We will analyse all these aspects in further detail.

In this book we have concentrated our attention on reporting directed to internal management, aimed at supporting decision making, planning and controlling of the business. Organizations in Scenario 3 and independent legal entities in Scenario 2 also have to deal with reporting for external stakeholders in addition to internal management, such as investors, banks, government bodies, etc. This is a required perspective that has not been considered in this book and is typically supported by financial management.

### Time perspectives and periods

Financial data may refer to the past or to the future. When we consider the past, we normally refer to balance (or actual) values. The past can be divided in periods, such as months, quarters, semesters or years. The decision to be taken is which periods we want to analyze and manage.

For many reports, such as the organization's profit and loss or balance sheet statements, this decision may be taken by the financial department; the decision will also depend on the scenario considered.

Managing periods may appear strange, at first sight, for someone not acquainted with financial management. With a good software tool available, it may appear very simple to extract data within a desired time range and to run reports on them. In financial management, however, this may be not so simple for several reasons. First, data relative to the selected period may be incomplete because the underlying supporting activities have not yet been completed. There is another important reason, which is typical of financial management, which is that some required operations (such as calculation of depreciation and accruals) cannot be managed (or are not conveniently managed) on a record by record and/or daily basis, but are achieved or optimized if managed at a specific point in time. These instances occur after the end of the period we want to report and, when all activities are performed, this period (and its data) can be considered closed and ready to be used for reporting and analysis. Therefore, the time periods to be considered for financial analysis are an important decision to be taken. An example of typical periodicity for a profit and loss statement report is a month or a year. Nevertheless, a defined rule for periodicity should not become an excuse to deny useful requests of information.

For the future we might consider different perspectives or dimensions, each corresponding to a specific set of figures. Typical dimensions are planning, budgeting and forecasting. The planning dimension is used to support long-range business previews, exploring the financial impact related to the business plans. It normally contains data at a high level, lacking details, and is related to a long time frame (three or five years, for example). Internally, this long time frame can be divided in sub-periods, such as for example the year or semester. The second dimension, budgeting, used to set the objectives of the organization for the financial year defined in the company charter. It usually has more detail than normal planning, but not always, corresponding to the one of balance data. Again, it can be divided into smaller periods, such as months, quarters, etc. Finally, forecasting, the third dimension, is used to is used to estimate the expected financial results for a target period and may be performed several times with specified frequency or based on needs. The forecasted time frame may correspond to the overall planning time frame, the financial year, a specific month, etc. Forecasts often have the same level of detail as budget.

Decisions about which time perspectives and periods to manage are very important as accounting systems will have to acquire and manage data in line with these decisions. Changing decisions is not recommended as it can be very difficult to rebuild the financial history for the new required perspectives and/or periods, if data has not been managed and stored at a sufficient level of detail.

Deciding on short financial periods (e.g. a month or less) enables better control and therefore the reduction of risks. This has to be balanced with the costs of assuring that these periods are managed (consider the difference of budgeting by year and by month, where each period needs specific input and closures). The final decision depends on the absolute relevance of the budget and on environmental risks. Scenario 3, IT financial management for market IT service providers, requires tighter control as revenues, depending on the market, are more risky than in other scenarios and determine the organization's ability to survive. The decision about time dimensions and periods also drives the frequency of execution of the IT financial management activities.

For the purpose of this book, we will consider the following perspectives, each characterized by its specific (competence) periods: planned, budgeted, actual, and forecasted. The General Accounting System is typically concerned with the actual perspective while the Management Accounting Systems is concerned with all of them.

## Types of documents

Financial records may refer to different types of documents. Typically they are, for the passive side: order requests, orders, invoices, and payments. For the active side: confirmed offers, orders, invoices, and payments. Often, the same report may refer to different data, for example revenues based on orders or invoices. Table 6.14 lists the typical dimensions deriving from the documents that we might consider when operating analysis and reporting.

| Reporting dimensions | Passive documents | Active documents |
|---|---|---|
| Committed | Requests for Purchase | Confirmed offers |
| Ordered | Orders | Orders |
| Invoiced | Invoices | Invoices |
| Paid | Payments | Payments |

Table 6.14 Financial dimensions based on type of documents

Not all dimensions are managed equally by accounting systems. General Accounting Systems are used to deal with Ordered, Invoiced and Paid. Management Accounting Systems are used to deal with all of them, although this depends on the type of Management Accounting System. For example, if the Management Accounting System is not strongly related to the General Accounting System (see 6.5.3) it will be uncommon to find the Paid (and in many cases Invoiced) dimensions managed.

## Accounting models

The economically relevant facts are recorded in the accounting systems, for example invoices or payments. Accounting systems process these data to determine information and reports in line with accounting models (an accounting system may support more than one of these at the same time). Each accounting model is a set of principles (for example a defined chart of accounts) and rules that are be applied to the facts (for example for which facts an account shall be used). So for example when considering a balance sheet statement, starting from the same raw facts, the results can be significantly different if we consider and apply the accounting model required to fulfil GAAP requirements or if we apply IFRS (International Financial Reporting Standards). Any organization, for example, will use a specific accounting model to determine the operating results and, in particular, the profit and loss and the balance sheet statements.

Among accounting models, particular attention should be paid to those adopted by the General Accounting System (at least one compliant with national fiscal regulations) and those adopted by the Management Accounting System (at least one chosen by the organization's management to determine and analyze operating results). Reconciliation of data reported by different systems adopting different accounting models, when necessary, might be a complex and time consuming task.

The accounting models often include which type of documents should be considered. The analysis of the structure and the definition of the contents of an accounting model is a complex topic, which is out of scope for the purposes of this book. It is important to remember that reporting, when performing calculation on data, should be coherent with the applicable accounting model. Performing calculations is more typical of MAS (for example when based on spreadsheets) than of General Accounting System, where reporting often simply reads and formats pre-calculated data.

## Types of report

We will now examine the most used financial reports: the balance sheet statement, the profit and loss statement and the cashflow statement.

Together, these statements give a picture of the organization's operations and financial position. Some of these can be applied to the whole organization, a department or function (such as IT), a cost center, a customer, a product or service, etc.

### Balance sheet

This represents a 'snapshot' of the financial position of an evaluated company. The balance sheet is generally produced at the end of each financial year but it can be at other times to meet the needs of stakeholders, investors, authorities (such as exchange). It is normally generated for the whole organization and reflects daily changes (such as changes in inventories, fixed assets or bank loans). The balance sheet is composed of two parts: assets and liabilities (see also Figure 6.20). Assets are 'items' that the organization owns and they are listed in order of 'liquidity' (the length of time it takes to convert them to cash). Liabilities represent the claims that various groups have against the company value, listed in the order in which they must be paid. The amounts shown in the balance sheet are called book values as they represent the amounts recorded by bookkeepers when assets are purchased or liabilities are incurred. The market value of a company can be very different from its book value. This is normally due to the effect of 'intangible' assets, which are assets that book keeping cannot record such as reputation or brand value. The balance sheet can refer to the actual or budget position; it is less usual to prepare a balance sheet forecast. The balance sheet is normally prepared for a whole company but, in certain cases, it can be prepared for business units or departments too (this may happen, for example, when a line of business and its departments are sold). Finally, the balance sheet statement is normally produced by the General Accounting System.

IT is usually a significant component of both assets and liabilities as IT investments and maintenance costs can be relevant. Of course, this depends on the business industry and on the value that management gives to IT. In every case, IT is part of the value and liabilities of the organization and this has to be managed in each of the scenarios that we have initially examined. In Scenarios 1 and 2, the financial department involves the IT department in the same way as any other of its functions/departments to produce the organization's balance sheet. In Scenario 2, it could happen that a specific balance sheet for the IT service organization is required. In Scenario 3, the balance sheet of the IT service organization corresponds to the company's balance sheet and is therefore mandatory.

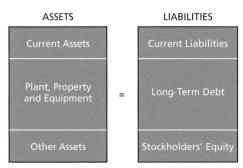

Figure 6.20 Assets and liabilities of a balance sheet.

## Profit and loss statement

The profit and loss statement (P&L) measures performance and can refer to the whole organization, a department or function (such as IT), a cost center, a customer, a product or service, etc..

Unlike the balance sheet, which is a 'snapshot' at a certain instant, the profit and loss statement reflects results for a specific period. The profit and loss statement may be organized in many different ways and with different levels of detail, depending on the cost and accounting models used (and their related principles), the purpose (for example evaluation of the organization's performance versus evaluation of an IT service) and also the style and culture of managers who require it.

A typical profit and loss statement is organized with the following sections:
a. sales (or revenues)
b. operating costs excluding depreciations and amortization
c. EBITDA (Earnings Before Interest, Taxes, Depreciation and Amortization) = a – b
d. depreciation
e. amortization[8]
f. EBIT (Earnings Before Interest and Taxes, or operating income) = c – d – e
g. interests
h. EBT (Earnings Before Taxes) = f – g
i. taxes
j. net income before preferred dividends = h – i
k. preferred dividends
l. net income = j – k
m. common dividends
n. addition to retained earnings

This is a comprehensive high-level profit and loss statement structure that can be adapted to specific purposes. For example, the sections before EBITDA can be developed to provide evidence of gross margin (an example is reported in Table 6.15) or contribution margin (an example is reported in Table 6.16).

---

[8]  In accounting, amortization refers to the expense of the acquisition cost minus the residual value of intangible assets (often intellectual property such as patents and trademarks or copyrights) in a systematic manner over their estimated useful economic lives so as to reflect their consumption, expiry, obsolescence or other decline in value as a result of use or the passage of time. Under International Financial Reporting Standards, guidance on accounting for the amortization of intangible assets is contained in International Accounting Standard 38, intangible assets. Under the United States' Generally Accepted Accounting Principles (GAAP), the primary guidance is contained in the statement of financial accounting standards No. 142, goodwill and other intangible assets.

| Revenue | 90.000,00 euros |
|---|---|
|     Variable IT service delivery costs | 46.000,00 euros |
|     Fixed IT service delivery costs | 12.000,00 euros |
| **Gross margin** | **32.000,00 euros** |
|     Variable marketing and administrative costs | 8.000,00 euros |
|     Fixed marketing and administrative costs | 14.000,00 euros |
| **Operating profit (EBITDA)** | **10.000,00 euros** |

Table 6.15 Profit and loss statement evidencing gross margin

| Revenue | 90.000,00 euros |
|---|---|
|     Variable IT service delivery costs | 46.000,00 euros |
|     Variable marketing and administrative costs | 8.000,00 euros |
| **Contribution margin** | **36.000,00 euros** |
|     Fixed IT service delivery costs | 12.000,00 euros |
|     Fixed marketing and administrative costs | 14.000,00 euros |
| **Operating profit (EBITDA)** | **10.000,00 euros** |

Table 6.16 Profit and loss statement evidencing contribution margin

There is no reason to restrict managers to the above details and approach and, typically, profit and loss statements will cover many aspects: those required by the accounting principles and those required by management for decision-making. Figure 6.21 shows an example of a profit and loss statement developed for the purpose of monitoring a specific IT service, a mail service, appropriate to the management style of the organization.

*Cash flow statement*

The amount of cash available to an organization is influenced by several factors, as net income can be used in a variety of ways, such as to pay dividends, to increase inventories, to finance account receivables, to invest in fixed assets, to reduce debt, etc. The statement of cash flow summarizes any changes in an organization's cash position. The statement separates activities into three categories:

1. operating activities (net income, depreciation, etc.)
2. investing activities (investments in or sales of fixed assets)
3. financing activities (selling investments or issuing debt, stock operations, etc.)

The cash flow statement is derived from the profit & loss statement and the balance sheet. Net earnings from the profit & loss statement is the figure from which the information on the cash flow statement is deduced. As for the balance sheet, the net cash flow in the cash flow statement from one year to the next should equal the increase or decrease of cash between the two consecutive balance sheets that apply to the period that the cash flow statement covers (for example, if you are calculating a cash flow for the year 2009, the balance sheets from the years 2008 and 2009 should be used).

This statement is generally of interest for IT service organizations in Scenario 3.

## Structure, contents and layout of reporting

Decisions about the previous aspects will define which data, with which rules and in what time frames will be available to support financial management. The dream of any IT manager, which

| Profit & loss statement for Mail Service Period January 2008 | Value (euros) |
|---|---:|
| **Revenues** | **100.000,00** |
| Customer A | 50.000,00 |
| Customer B | 35.000,00 |
| Customer C | 20.000,00 |
| **Costs** | **92.000,00** |
| **Hardware:** | **12.000,00** |
| Rental | 10.000,00 |
| Maintenance | 2.000,00 |
| **Software:** | **10.000,00** |
| Purchase | 0,00 |
| Maintenance | 10.000,00 |
| **Activities:** | **60.000,00** |
| Internal resources | 60.000,00 |
| External services | 0,00 |
| **Telecommunications:** | **5.000,00** |
| WAN connection | 5.000,00 |
| **Other costs:** | **5.000,00** |
| Travels | 1.500,00 |
| Others (disaster recovery) | 3.500,00 |
| **Operating profit (EBITDA)** | **8.000,00** |
| **Depreciation:** | **8.000,00** |
| Hardware | 4.000,00 |
| Software | 4.000,00 |
| **Operating profit (EBIT)** | **0,00** |

Figure 6.21 Example of simple profit and loss statement for an IT service

business intelligence tries to transform into reality, is to allow users to be free to create their own analysis/reporting based on consistent data and calculation rules. In each case, a structured predefined set of reports should always exist, to support the activities, decisions and deliverables of IT financial management as well. One of the core products of financial management is its set of reports and analysis.

Defining the set of reports to be produced is one of the key decisions of financial management planning. Typical elements to be defined, for each report, are:
- name of the report
- type (e.g. profit and loss)
- owner (in charge of its definition and improvement)
- short description
- purpose
- perspectives included (e.g. balance, budget)
- time periods to which the report may refer (e.g. month, year)
- time frequency for which the report can be requested
- authorized requester
- filtering criteria available (for example, list of projects or projects by client, range of periods included)
- distribution list (to whom the report is available or distributed)
- models to be used (accounting, cost, cost apportioning)
- source systems (e.g. General Accounting System, Management Accounting System or others)

- detailed description of content
  - description of sections
  - layout style (possibly with reference to unified, agreed templates)
  - for each section
    ◇ if table (content of rows, content of columns)
    ◇ if graphic (type of graphic, content of series)

Financial reports typically show actual figures against budget, for the recent period (e.g. last month) and also year to date, with comparisons against the previous year. Forecasts for the full year totals are also compared to the budget and previous years. Summary reports are provided to each budget owner and to those responsible for cost objects (e.g. cost centers, services, customers). Detailed reports showing all transactions for the period are also provided so that any unexpected variances can be investigated and mis-postings more easily identified.

*The decision is about the reports to be produced and their characteristics (frequency, contents, etc..).*

## 6.5.14 IT accounting and charging continuity aspects

It is possible that, in the event of a major disaster, the IT service continuity plan is to stop delivering IT accounting and charging service entirely. If this is not the case, then IT accounting and charging must be tested as part of the disaster recovery testing.

The IT service continuity plan should reflect the organization's use of IT accounting and charging. Simply holding paper copies of spreadsheets and bills does not provide sufficient contingency in the event of, say, a spreadsheet corruption. The dependency of the organization on IT accounting and charging varies with the type of organization (increasing from Scenario 1 to 3).

IT financial management should determine which reports and plans are indispensable to the organization and ensure that they can be produced in the event of a major incident affecting the IT accounting or charging systems. The contingency arrangement for IT accounting and charging must be regularly reviewed.

The impact of a disaster is minimized by keeping off-site back-up of all required data and by maintaining standby or spare equipment to run the IT accounting and charging systems, but the data sources on which they rely may not be available in the event of a disaster. Another important aspect to take care of is the availability of resources with the proper profiles and qualifications in IT financial management.

*The decision is which approach is most suitable to ensure IT financial management continuity in case of disaster.*

An optimal approach to be evaluated is considering IT financial management as a service, therefore including it in the IT service continuity scope of interest.

## 6.5.15 Investment appraisal techniques

Investment appraisal has long been recognized as an essential prerequisite to sound financial management, both in the public and private sectors. The importance of investment appraisal has grown in recent years as an aid to decision-making in its broadest sense, as a means of identifying efficiency savings and controlling investment expenditure to maximum effectiveness.

There is often a trade-off between capital investment and running cost expenditure: i.e. between maximising effectiveness in the long-term and the risk of failing to achieve short-term goals. Capital investment decisions are essentially longer-term decisions, and thus it is more difficult to hold management responsible and accountable for such decisions. However, because the performance of a manager is often measured on the efficient and effective use of allocated resources within a budget period (of one year), there are only limited ways of holding managers responsible for investment decisions: this is why sound investment appraisal procedures are essential to an organization.

From the viewpoint of the business manager, IT investment and the supply of IT services are the same as any other planned expenditure or allocation of resource in that it is measured in terms of its contribution to the effective, efficient and economic achievement of business goals. It must enable the business to determine whether, for example, the returns would be better from a new IT system or from increased advertising.

Investment appraisal activities have been described in Chapter 4. Besides the activities, decisions should be taken about which technique is most suitable to be used for investment appraisal. In the following sections, we will examine some of the most frequently used techniques:
- Return On Investment (ROI)
- Total Cost of Ownership (TCO)
- Net Present Value (NPV)
- payback
- Internal Rate of Return (IRR)
- cost-benefit analysis
- anchor values

Now, we will try to give a quick guide on how to choose the most appropriate method among those described.

## Return On Investment (ROI)

ROI is based on the assumptions that costs and benefits of IT can be expressed and measured in terms of cash. ROI may be applied to a whole organization, department (for example IT) or a specific project/investment. When it is applied to a whole organization, the time horizon is typically a year and we speak of Return On Invested Capital (ROIC), which is computed as follows:

$$\text{ROIC (\%)} = \frac{\text{Net Operating Profit After Taxes (NOPAT)}}{\text{Operating Capital}}$$

When applied to a project/investment, the time horizon may be several years and it is computed as follows:

$$\text{ROI (\%)} = \frac{\text{Profit}}{\text{investment}}$$

Profit is calculated as revenues (real income or the prevention of costs[9] or loss of revenues) less investments (capital, one-off, and operational, ongoing). For convenience, the ROI of a project/investment should be greater than those of competing projects/investments, if resources are limited, or the cost rate of investing the same amount of money for the same period, if resources are unlimited.

## Total Cost of Ownership (TCO)

The Total Cost of Ownership has been initially developed by Gartner Group in 1987. TCO is applied to a specific category of items which, in IT domain, may be either hardware, software or combination of both (e.g. technologies). For example, TCO may be calculated for desktop PCs, laptops, PDAs, smartphones, printers, virtualization software, ERPs, etc.

TCO is the full cost of buying and managing the specific item over its whole lifecycle. This includes all type of costs. For example, for a PC this should include: purchase cost, HW maintenance cost, software purchase and its related maintenance cost, administration activities, user and IT training, disposal costs, incident and change management costs.

TCO is calculated for the different available alternatives. Continuing with the example of laptop PCs, alternatives could be letting user free to manage it against locking the device and managing it centrally. TCO for this two approaches or intermediate levels between the extremes may be calculated and be the basis for decision making.

## Net Present Value (NPV)

This method also assumes that benefits and costs can be expressed in terms of cash. Net Present Value (NPV) relies on Discounted Cash Flows (DCF) technique. NPV is computed as follows:

$$NPV = CF_0 + \frac{CF_1}{(1+r)^1} + \frac{CF_2}{(1+r)^2} + \ldots + \frac{CF_n}{(1+r)^n}$$

In this formula CF is the net cash flow (positive or negative outflows) at period n and r is the cost of capital. Finally n is the project/investment's life. Figure 6.22 illustrates the calculation of NPV for a four-year project with 10 percent as the cost of capital.

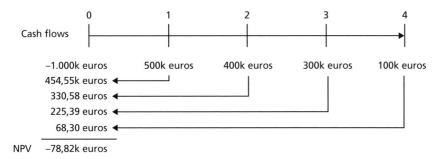

Figure 6.22 Example of NPV calculation

---

[9]  Cost avoidance is deemed a benefit and is often categorized as either Hard Dollar or Soft Dollar avoidance. Hard Dollar avoidance enables the organization to avoid a cost that would otherwise be certain (e.g. investing in a system for regulatory compliance enables it to avoid penalties or restrictions of trade). Soft Dollar avoidance has less certainty about affecting the bottom line and the organization has options to work around incurring the cost (e.g. implementing a new air conditioning system will be likely to decrease illness by 5 percent and therefore increase productivity accordingly).

The chosen capital cost (or discount rate) is critical and is generally determined by the cost of capital for the organization, the level of inflation and the level of risk (higher if more risky). The investment, to be beneficial, should have an NPV greater than zero. In some cases, projects/investments are performed to achieve results with little or no ability to determine positive related cash flows. When this situation occurs, comparison made using the NPV method will select a project/investment with higher value (less negative). Although NPV depends on discount rate and, therefore, may vary depending on it, it is the most reliable and least questioned measure of investment return.

## Payback period

This is the amount of time that a project/investment takes to recover the original investment. In its simplest form, it is computed as follows:

$$\text{Payback} = \text{Year before full recovery} + \frac{\text{Unrecovered cost at end of recovery year}}{\text{Cash flow during recovery year}}$$

Figure 6.23 illustrates the calculation of payback for the project previously considered for NPV calculation.

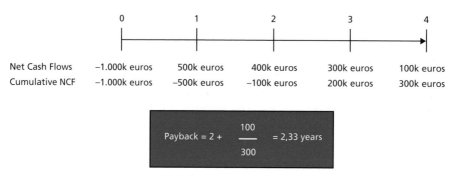

| | 0 | 1 | 2 | 3 | 4 |
|---|---|---|---|---|---|
| Net Cash Flows | −1.000k euros | 500k euros | 400k euros | 300k euros | 100k euros |
| Cumulative NCF | −1.000k euros | −500k euros | −100k euros | 200k euros | 300k euros |

$$\text{Payback} = 2 + \frac{100}{300} = 2{,}33 \text{ years}$$

Figure 6.23 Example of payback period calculation

A variant of payback period is discounted payback period, which is similar except that the expected cash flows are discounted by the cost of capital. Figure 6.24 illustrates the computation of a discounted payback period compared to the previous (not discounted).

The major problem of payback, even in its discounted version, is that it ignores what happens after the payback point. Projects/investments with high initial net cash flows could be predicted as a good investment decision but this might not be true in a longer timeframe.

## Internal Rate of Return (IRR)

This is the discount rate that will discount a cash flow to give a Net Present Value of zero. IRR is the rate that forces the NPV to equal 0:

$$CF_0 + \frac{CF_1}{(1 + IRR)^1} + \frac{CF_2}{(1 + IRR)^2} + \cdots + \frac{CF_n}{(1 + IRR)^n} = 0$$

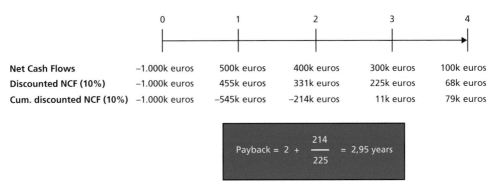

Figure 6.24 Example of discounted payback calculation

IRR cannot be calculated by means of a formula, so a trial and error approach is applied. IRR is difficult and time consuming to determine without a financial calculator. As an example project with its NPV and payback period, IRR is equal to 14.5 percent. If the cost of capital is 10 percent, the project seems to be a worthwhile investment and should be accepted, unless resources are not available. Because NPV and IRR are based on the same formula, the two methods will always lead to the same decisions. This occurs because if NPV is positive, IRR must exceed r (cost of capital).

## Cost-benefit analysis

In cost-benefit analysis the approach is to use money as a metric. Transforming benefits and cost into money is an appealing but difficult task. This approach is always time consuming and requires expertise. The benefits of a project/investment that can be translated into money generally are:

- productivity (for example increments of the output of employees, generating a total greater output)
- throughput (reduction of staff by incrementing productivity while keeping output volumes)
- reduced inventory
- faster turnaround of operations (which can lead to better utilization of resources, reducing overtime, etc.)
- quality of service (which can lead, for example, to higher prices or lower costs to manage defects)
- intangibles (benefits that can be only measured by asking people to give them a value).

Once benefits have been expressed into money, one of the previous methods can be applied to calculate ROI, NPV, payback or IRR. Cost-benefit analysis can be considered a synergistic approach.

## Anchor values

Anchor values is another approach that can be used for IT investment evaluation. A set of metrics is defined and used to measure the impact of IT expenditure. Productivity or similar measures are used, for example:

- transactions per employee
- turnover per employee

- incidence of IT costs on turnover
- market share
- sales per employee.

Anchor values have the big advantage that they can be used to measure intangible benefits and can be linked to the final performance of the business. Another advantage is that they can often be used to compare the organization's performance with that of other organizations.

## Choosing the most appropriate investment appraisal method

First, it is important to consider what has to be evaluated. When the objective is to measure the performances of an organization, a department or function, ROIC and anchor values can be used. ROIC is most suitable when a transfer price or, preferably, a market price is applicable. This is typical of Scenario 3 and sometimes of Scenario 2. When the target is to evaluate the performance of an investment, academics prefer NPV (Brigham & Ehrhardt, 2005), while many executives prefer IRR (probably because they find it more relevant to evaluate investments in terms of percentage rates of returns than money). Table 6.17 summarizes possible choices.

| Method | Target of evaluation: IT service organization | Target of evaluation: IT investments |
|---|---|---|
| Scenario 1: IT financial management for internal IT departments | Not frequent, anchor values is preferable although the relationship between the organization's performance and IT may be questioned | NPV, discounted NPV, IRR |
| Scenario 2: IT financial management for internal IT service providers | If the IT department is charging for its services: ROIC If not, anchor values | NPV, discounted NPV, IRR |
| Scenario 3: IT financial management for market IT service providers | ROIC | NPV, discounted NPV, IRR |

Table 6.17 Preferred appraisal method based on scenario and target evaluated

The drivers for investments are also important. If the investment is mandatory (for example because of obsolescence, as for Year 2000 and euro projects), evaluation is less relevant, although recommended. If the drivers are cost savings, cost avoidance or revenue generation, ROI, NPV, IRR or payback will be the preferred methods. If the driver is the improvement of decision support, customer satisfaction measurement is often the most effective approach. When the drivers are service enhancement or strategy, besides customer satisfaction, anchor values is the most suitable evaluation method.

Regardless of the method used, the quality of the evaluation depends on a thorough and complete assessment of benefits and costs. Some specific steps should be performed to achieve reliable results (Bannister, 2004):
- the reason for the investment should be spelled out
- all costs, initial and ongoing, direct and hidden, should be identified
- all benefits should be identified

- the timing for each cost and benefit should be projected
- where the reason is mandatory, justifying the investment may not be required
- where applicable, additional revenue, cost avoidance and cost savings should be identified
- where there are intangible benefits, these should be quantified (by users, for example)
- when all the above steps have been performed the evaluation method can be chosen and applied

Regardless of the method, it is also important to note that for many reasons the reliability of the assumptions made in the analysis is almost always called into question. (Financial resources are often limited and competing projects will make strong cases for investment.) It is advisable to make conservative estimates that are aligned with the organization's tolerance for risk.

### 6.5.16 Regulatory compliance

IT financial management is the IT service management practice that is most affected by regulatory issues. Regulations can apply to different targets: the whole organization, the IT department and employees.

We have already mentioned that GAAP, IRFS, corporate or management's established principles may apply to General Accounting Systems and Management Accounting Systems. This is true for all types of IT service organization, regardless of the scenario they adopt (see 2.3).

When considering the IT service organization, some regulations may also derive from the best practices or standards adopted – for example, ISO 9000 or ISO/IEC 20000. In particular the latter ISO standard has recommendations, both 'shall' (mandatory) and 'should' (desirable), applicable to budgeting and accounting for IT.

At a professional level, ethical issues may arise. Design of cost systems is about the assignment of costs to activities, services, projects and departments; this may affect prices, reimbursement, payments, etc. With some limitations, the accountant's choices may affect company performance as well as their own evaluation. In an attempt to positively influence the accounting profession, many of its professional organizations such as the Institute of Management Accountants (IMA), Institute of Internal Auditors (IIA) and the American Institute of Certified Public Accountants (AICPA) have developed codes of ethics to which their members are expected to adhere.

## 6.6 Challenges, possible problems, critical success factors and risks

Risk is defined as uncertainty of outcome, whether positive opportunity or negative threat. Managing risk is generally considered important, although many organizations do not perform risk management with a visible, repeatable and systematic approach. In the context of risk management, problems can be defined here as the underlying causes generating uncertainty of outcome – in other words, risks.

A consistent and generic framework for risk management is described in Figure 6.25. This is the approach suggested by M_o_R, Management of Risk methodology from OGC.

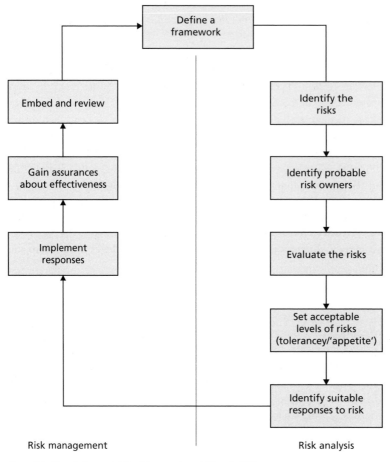

Figure 6.25 Generic framework for risk management (M_o_R, OGC)

Depending on the size of the organization, its maturity in IT financial management practices, the target scenario and many other factors there can be several problems while implementing or improving IT financial management. Risk management, defined as the task of ensuring that organizations make cost effective use of risk handling activities, is recommended for projects and programs to minimize the possibility of failing to achieve desired outcomes and targets.

In the following part of this section, we will analyze the most common problems generating risks while implementing or improving IT financial management. Properly managing these problems is the challenge and therefore the critical success factor of any implementation.

One of the typical and most critical problems is faced by organizations in Scenario 2. The temptation to re-use existing tools, activities and skills may be very strong and lead to considering the service dimension simply as a new reporting topic. Financially managing IT services cannot be simply done by means of apportioning Indirect Costs. It requires a new approach, where an appropriate proportion of cost is directly assigned to IT services; this can be incompatible with the pre-existing arrangement and its supporting systems. Organizations should recognize this potential problem as soon as possible and should analyze carefully the risks related to keeping the existing approach.

Another problem derives from the length of the project, which will take a long period of time (from six to twelve months) to be completed. During this period it will be necessary to keep senior management commitment and attention high; this is normally the task of the project board. Attention and commitment should also be raised at lower levels of the organization by all those affected and involved in the new activities. Staff should understand the importance of recording timesheets on schedule or of being precise with data entry and should be collaborative. At operational level, the effort of running financial management functions could increase, but this would be balanced by savings deriving from valuable and reliable reporting or from better decision-making. These benefits are experienced mainly by management and therefore the introduction of the new IT financial management functions can be unpopular. To limit possible problems and impacts and to maximize the level of support it is important to start the awareness campaign from the beginning of the project (see 6.3.2), to continuously monitor staff opinion and to intensify communication when needed. "Quick fixes" are effective, such as premiums for employees or, at least, allocating key roles in the project.

Skill of resources is perhaps the most important topic. It is not easy to find the right mix of skills, which should include both financial management matters and IT knowledge. It is usual to find experienced accountants with little knowledge of IT or IT resources with no knowledge of financial topics. Finding suitable resources is usually the biggest challenge for project and process related roles, and the main reason for failure or unsatisfactory results. The project team should not only be competent but also properly empowered by top management. Assembling the wrong people or missing empowerment will have a negative influence on the quality of results and generate relevant problems such as:
- IT accounting and charging that is over-complex or ineffective
- IT accounting and charging activities that are so elaborate that the cost of the system exceeds the value of the information produced.

Impact in terms of effort is another problem that is often underestimated. Managing information about a detailed cost model of IT may require additional effort compared to the situation in place before its introduction. Effort related to the project is normally considered and evaluated but impact on the roles responsible for running the day-to-day activities and, most of all, on those peripherally affected (such as roles managing passive cycle activities) is often under estimated. An example that has been mentioned before is the impact on passive order entry. The definition of the cost model may complicate the structure of the orders and create additional lines to be managed. This impact of this should be carefully evaluated and discussed with the purchasing department.

Another issue may reside in tooling. Because of initial lack of knowledge or budget pressure, it is often believed that the existing tool(s) supporting financial management will fit and support IT financial management as well. This is possible, of course, but it does not always happen depending on the rigidity of the existing software. Advanced and newer solutions will enable different arrangement of information and needs (such as apportioning) but, typically, older accounting software or closely integrated solutions, such as ERP systems, will probably have difficulties. This issue should be investigated as soon as possible. Another typical problem about tooling comes when discussing the benefits of IT financial management, such as those promised by investments analysis for better decision-making. Many of these benefits become possible as far as tools properly support the underlying processes. Charging is another typical area of issues when it is based on prices and the resources used. In this case tools should be available, typically in the domain of monitoring, flexible enough and interfaced with the charging module to provide all the required information. Often this does not happen and further investments become necessary. Chapter 8 will explore the tooling topic in more detail.

Finally, an overall underestimation of IT financial management complexity and related difficulties is a frequent error. It is often considered one of the easiest service management practices to implement. After all, organizations have been doing budgets and accounting, including IT aspects, for many years and they often consider what they have to be sufficient. This is likely to be true for Scenario 1, but when moving to Scenario 2 or 3, IT financial management should be considered as a totally new practice and careful attention should be given to it. Failure to understand the increasing difficulty and specific requirements of new scenarios is likely to lead to allocation of insufficient budget and underestimates of the effort necessary to achieve them and, as a consequence, into project failure.

Besides the general problems related to the project, previously described, there are other possible problems:
- Some relevant practices, such as planning, Service Catalog or capacity management, may be not mature enough and supplying the needed information. For example, for organizations attempting to implement Scenario 2, if the Service Catalog is not well designed or widespread, defining the correct apportioning model and reporting may become very difficult and the results will probably be unsatisfactory.
- Senior business managers may not recognize the benefits of IT accounting and charging and may resent the administrative overheads and the workload of related activities.
- The IT organization may not be able to respond to changes in users' demands once costs become an influence.
- The monitoring tools that provide resource usage information may be inaccurate, irrelevant or cost too much to develop and maintain.

# 7 Managing finances

## 7.1 Operational management

Day-to-day operations of IT financial management are clearly focused on the execution of the reference activities described in Chapter 4. In addition, there are 'routine' activities that are not easily referenced or described by means of processes. In this chapter we will give an overview of all the activities performed by IT financial management from an operational perspective.

### 7.1.1 Daily/weekly activities

There is a number of activities, related to IT financial management, that need to be performed or are used to be triggered daily. We will examine each of them.

**Supporting correct recording of data**

We have already remarked that passive cycle activities are responsible for recording economically relevant facts, for example orders, reception of goods and services, passive invoices. We have not considered these activities as part of IT financial management; however, key roles of IT financial management are often involved in these tasks, mainly with a supporting and consulting remit. Staff performing these activities may need help to enter records properly that are related to IT aspects, such as the example of cost centers or the choice of depreciation rule. The controllers are usually IT financial management staff responsible for supporting those who should perform the activities.

Entering records is often a tedious activity and players of passive cycle activities tend to be late and/or 'quick' in performing this task. It is recommended to keep the progress and quality of these activities under control. This may be done by means of weekly reports, which give hints to IT financial management staff to enter records promptly and correct mistakes.

**Supporting demand, change and delta management activity execution**

IT service management best practices recommend that any change should be evaluated for its financial impact. This may affect IT financial management staff. Staff involved in evaluation of the costs associated with changes may require the support of IT financial management staff (e.g. IT financial controllers) to complete their evaluation. If changes lead to additional costs, it is also necessary to check if there are resources (budget) available for them. Again, IT financial management staff may support this task, if required. If the budget is not sufficient, the delta management activity (see 4.2.4) should be invoked. IT financial management staff will have a leading role in its execution.

Similar activities derive from the demand management function. Here too some customers' requests may need to be evaluated and later lead to delta management execution.

## Performing evaluation of investments

This is another typical daily task of IT financial management staff, in particular involving (IT) financial controllers. Support for the activity or much more extensive involvement also depends on the level of expertise of resources in charge of the proposals of investment.

## Ad hoc analysis and reporting

It has been remarked that one of the drivers for the adoption of IT financial management is better information to support management's decision making processes. This will mean that management will look at IT financial management as a valuable source of information about financial topics when normal reporting is not sufficient. Requests coming from management or authorized personnel will sometimes lead to analysis and ad hoc reporting.

## Opening Requests for Change

As part of continual improvement, another activity may be opening Requests For Change to modify IT financial management practices and/or systems. Typical examples are those needed to update the structure of cost centers, master data of services and projects and, less frequently, cost or cost apportioning models.

## Meetings

Meetings are a frequent activity at all levels of IT financial management staff. The IT financial manager is likely to be involved in Change Advisory Board (CAB) meetings, while controllers will probably be invited to periodic review meetings of projects and/or services. Weekly staff meetings are also typical to update on news and to communicate and agree on priorities for IT financial management.

### 7.1.2   Monthly activities

There are other activities, related to IT financial management, that need to be performed or are used to be triggered on a monthly basis.

## Periodic closures

Monthly is a typical and appropriate frequency for periodic closures, which have been previously discussed as an activity. The typical activities performed are to:
• collect data, perform preliminary checks and rectify if necessary
• run cost apportioning system (if present), calculation of depreciation and accruals
• produce reports
• check that costs are in line with predictions and explain any variances
• activate delta management activities if necessary
• produce and circulate all agreed reports (e.g. balance sheet, profit and loss statement)

## Charge customers

The charging activity depends on agreements with customers, especially for Scenario 3; however a monthly frequency is typical for this activity. Activities to be performed have been discussed in section 4.4.1. The following is a summary of the main tasks to be completed:
• gather information to enable charging (consumptions of the charging drivers)
• charge customers (prepare documentation and/or invoices)
• check and distribute charging documentation

- prepare reports
- analyze data and explain deviations against targets
- distribute reports and analysis

### 7.1.3   Quarterly/semi-annual activities

#### Periodic forecasting

Frequency of forecasting activities depends on each organization, in particular on their culture, policies, and size and on the budget relevance. Typical frequencies for forecasting are quarterly or every trimester but, in some cases, the activity could be even monthly (this is appropriate for organizations in Scenario 3). Preparing forecasts requires having reliable balance data and, therefore, these activities generally follow those of a periodic closure (see 7.1.2). Activities to be performed are:

- check balance data
- analyze and predict trends
- prepare forecasts
- distribute reports.

#### Budget review

Budget review is performed at least once a year. Reviewing the budget requires reliable balance data and, therefore, this activity follows a periodic closure (see 7.1.2). Activities to be executed are:

- acquire updated objectives and constraints
- prepare initial information and reports (budget, balance, available forecasts)
- perform budget review
- calculate depreciations, accruals, run apportioning and reporting
- approve reviewed budget
- distribute reports

The elapsed time of these activities depends on the size of the organization and the relevance of the budget. It generally takes several weeks to review and gain agreement (and sign-off) for a budget.

### 7.1.4   Annually

#### Budgeting

The budgeting activity is a typical annual activity. It is performed some months before the start of the upcoming financial year. Activities to be performed are:

- acquire objectives and constraints
- prepare initial information and reports (planning data for the year to budget, previous year budget, current balance, available estimations to complete current year)
- prepare budget estimations for next year
- calculate depreciations, accruals, run apportioning and reporting
- approve budget
- distribute reports

Iterations and reviews are possible. The budget involves the whole organization and aggregations of more detailed level of budgets will be performed. For these reasons, it generally takes several weeks to review and gain agreement (and sign-off) for a budget.

### Annual closure

Annual closure is very similar to periodic closures (see 7.1.2). Very often execution of the last periodic closure and of annual closure are integrated in a single activity. The activities are similar to those reported for monthly closures:
- collect data, perform preliminary checks and rectify if necessary
- run cost apportioning system, calculation of depreciation and accruals
- produce reporting
- check that costs are in line with predictions and explain any variances
- activate delta management activities if necessary
- produce and circulate all agreed reporting (e.g. balance sheet, profit and loss statement)

Annual closure reporting is typically more complete and detailed than reporting of periodic closures.

### Planning

Organizations' strategic or industrial plans are generally prepared every three to five years. Activities to be executed may be similar to those of the budgeting activity with the differences that the forecast period includes several budget periods and that the level of detail of data is lower. This means that appropriate effort is needed. To keep alignment with the evolving marketplace/customer requirements plans should be frequently updated, at least annually or when major events or profit warnings require it.

## 7.2   Controls

The purpose of controls is to demonstrate that:
- formal practices and procedures are followed
- activity maturity has reached the planned level
- IT financial management is delivering the expected benefits (it is efficient, effective and cost-justified)

The post-implementation review and subsequent periodic reviews of IT financial management practices and systems should check these they are working effectively. Responsible management should also periodically review the system and identify and correct deficiencies. The implementation and execution of a continual improvement approach should be part of the controls and reviews.

Formal controls may be performed by internal staff or by external auditors. However, management should not rely solely on formal checks but should verify that practices and systems run properly and policies are respected. Independent controls such as audits (see also 7.5.2) should confirm this from time to time.

Frequency of formal internal controls depends on many aspects: maturity of IT financial management, existing issues, criticality of IT for the business, frequency of internal audits, etc. Formal external audits should be performed at least annually. Internal reviews should be performed quarterly or, at least, every semester. Where possible, reviews should be synchronized with those of service level management and capacity management so that it is possible to understand quickly where the problems lie when issues are found affecting the important interfaces between IT financial management and these practices.

## 7.2.1  Detailed controls for budgeting

Controls should confirm that:
- budgets are provided for all activities/aspects and are developed according to models (accounting, cost, cost apportioning models)
- senior managers (across the organization and within IT services) and staff are satisfied with the reports produced
- budgets are reviewed as scheduled
- differences between actual and budgeted costs and/or revenues are promptly identified and managed according to policies and practices

## 7.2.2  Detailed controls for accounting

Controls should check that:
costs are accurately accounted each month and at the end of the year.
- all costs (hardware, software, people, accommodation and transfer), including unexpected costs, are accounted for according to the cost model
- apportioning, depreciations and accruals are correctly performed
- senior managers (across the organization and within IT services) and staff are satisfied with the reports produced
- the accounting system is understood, customers and staff are satisfied with how it operates.
- interfaces to configuration management, capacity management and service level management are effective and provide the necessary workload information
- the CMDB (Configuration Management Database) provides needed information for decision making related to financial management (e.g. all configurations items of a specific service are correctly identified and their status updated)
- change management and problem management procedures are strictly followed

When a check of deviations is not performed by means of forecasts but by means of the budget (that is, the budget is articulated into periods at a sufficient level of detail to enable identification of deviations, e.g. a budget for the whole year and for each month) the following checks are also recommended:
- deviations between actual spend and budget are clearly and easily identified
- where there are deviations, actions are taken according to defined practices and procedures

## 7.2.3  Detailed controls for forecasting

Controls should check that:
- costs and revenues are accurately forecasted when scheduled
- apportioning, depreciations and accruals are correctly performed

- senior managers (across the organization and within IT services) and staff are satisfied with the reports produced
- interfaces with capacity management and service level management are working and provide the necessary information
- deviations between balance plus forecast data and budgets are clearly and easily identified
- where there are deviations, actions are taken according to defined practices and procedures

### 7.2.4 Detailed controls for pricing

Controls should check that:
- the effect on charges is considered fair by customers
- price lists are available and prices are correctly defined (aligned to market conditions in Scenario 3), communicated and any changes to the charges or price lists are implemented within target timescales
- if included in the Service Catalog, prices are up to date

### 7.2.5 Detailed controls for charging

Controls should check that:
- bills are simple, clear, accurate and issued on time
- income is collected on time
- customers are neither under-charged nor overcharged for their IT services
- the price list is correctly defined (and aligned to market conditions in Scenario 3)
- discrepancies in charges are identified quickly and resolved with customers
- senior managers (across the organization and within IT services) and staff are satisfied with the reports produced
- cost recovery plans are on target (cost recovery provides a barometer of how well prices have been set in relation to predicted costs of IT usage)
- interfaces to capacity management and service level management are effective

### 7.2.6 Controls for audit

An audit will usually examine and test most of the previously mentioned controls. As a minimum, it should:
- check that regular reviews are carried out regularly and non-conformances followed up
- randomly select bills to test for clarity, accuracy and timeliness
- examine cost recovery projections and revenue to assess the accuracy of the system
- ensure that audit trails are provided
- ensure that revenues are collected and properly accounted for
- check that all documentation is accurate, up-to-date and complete

Examples of audit evidences that are collected and checked are the following:
- relevant policies
- practices and procedures
- responsibility and authority matrices
- cost types and definition
- cost model
- cost apportioning model
- reports

- financial decisions based on financial reports
- actions from review meetings that demonstrate effective management
- financial analysis of changes
- approval for changes based on impact assessment of costs of services
- communication of price lists

## 7.3    Metrics for IT financial management

### 7.3.1    Why are metrics needed?

There are many reasons to measure. ITIL V3 Continual Service Improvement identifies four reasons. Although they were mainly intended for IT services improvement globally, they are equally applicable to specific practice improvement too and, therefore, to IT financial management. These reasons are:
- **to validate** – monitoring and measuring to validate previous decisions
- **to direct** – monitoring and measuring to set direction for activities in order to meet set targets. It is the most prevalent reason for monitoring and measuring
- **to justify** – monitoring and measuring to justify, with factual evidence or proof, that a course of action is required
- **to intervene** – monitoring and measuring to identify a point of intervention including subsequent changes and corrective actions

Brooks, Van Bon and Verheijen have identified another set of valuable reasons:
- metrics provide the instrumentation necessary to control an organization
- metrics make it easier to concentrate on important matters
- well presented metrics make it easy to spot danger in time to correct it
- metrics can improve morale in an organization
- metrics can stimulate healthy competition between process owners
- metrics help to align IT with business goals.

As an example to show how metrics can provide the instrumentation to control IT financial management, in section 6.3.2 we have seen the use of KPIs in a Balanced Scorecard to give meaningful comprehension of the situation and of how well the objectives are being achieved.

### 7.3.2    Who should be responsible and who should use metrics

Since metrics are designed to allow an organization to control, it is important that somebody is responsible for each metric. This means controlling the status and trend of a metric and taking action when necessary.

We can distinguish between metrics related to the financial performance of the services provided (their costs, revenues) and metrics related to the performance of the IT financial management function and processes. IT service management managers should be owners of the metrics related to service performances. Service owners (accountable for a specific service, as introduced in ITIL V3 Continual Service Improvement) are usually the most appropriate owners for metrics specific to services (at least in Scenario 1 and 2, while in Scenario 3 the situation can be much more articulated, e.g. for the presence of a sales force). The metrics for overall IT costs and revenues are typically owned by the IT manager while IT financial management performance related metrics should be owned by the roles identified in chapter 5, in particular the IT financial manager and IT financial controllers. However, especially for Scenario 1, in some cases owners can also be identified in the financial department (e.g. controllers).

Metrics have no value if they are not actually used. The owner is not the only individual interested in them and there should be proper communication according to the different needs of recipients: IT management, process and service managers and staff.

IT management (management in Scenario 3) strives to align IT with business needs and takes decisions. Metrics should support these tasks: they should be clear (understanding should be immediate), comprehensive (the level of detail should be appropriate to the recipient's needs; management is generally interested in high level KPIs although providing drill-down navigation of figures is recommended), relevant (only KPIs which are of interest to the recipients should be provided), timely (warnings and alerts should be communicated as soon as they occur; anticipated trends analysis should provide early warnings) and reliable (information should be accurate). Managers in IT service management will usually receive a mix of metrics – that is, metrics about the financial performance of services together with metrics about SLAs. A Balanced Scorecard helps to provide management control.

Service and process managers should, as a minimum, receive the metrics they own. They will want to receive an explanation of what has already occurred and to take corrective action if required; they should be strongly committed in order to anticipate trends and make proactive decisions. The IT financial manager is one of these managers and he/she is likely to be the owner of many of the specific metrics identified in section 7.3. Again, metrics should be clear, comprehensive, relevant, timely and reliable. A specific Balanced Scorecard for the IT financial management function, such as the one illustrated in 6.3.2, is a good example of the use of metrics.

All other members of the IT department need to understand what the process metrics, KPIs and SLAs are, especially those applying to their own area of activity. Staff should be aware of their meaning and of their trend and should actively contribute to improvements. In some cases, this can be achieved by linking metrics to rewards against the achievement of target results.

### 7.3.3   Which metrics?

In this section, we will explore in detail some typical metrics for IT financial management activities, which can be used in the internal perspective of a Balanced Scorecard. Although metrics have been tuned and designed for the activities described in Chapter 4, many can be used in any context. Metrics will be illustrated on a per activity basis (see Chapter 4, in particular Figure 4.1, for the reference model).

For each metric, the following information will be detailed:
- **name** – name of KPI
- **description** – a description of the KPI
- **basis for computation** – this describes the scope of the KPI
- **frequency of usage** – this information gives the typical frequency of utilization (when the KPI is calculated and reported)

- **polarity** – this information gives the appropriate trend (positive vs. negative) when applicable
- **comments** – any further useful information about the KPI under examination

The information is organized in a table for each metric. The tables with blue backgrounds show metrics that measure efficiency; the tables with red backgrounds show metrics that measure effectiveness of the practices.

## 7.3.4 Metrics for IT financial management implementation

These metrics give evidence of the status of adoption of IT financial management practices.

| Name | Number of services/projects managed |
|---|---|
| Description | This is the absolute number of services/projects managed with IT financial management practices. |
| Basis for computation | Projects and services that have been active during the observation period. |
| Formula | Count of the number of services/projects managed according to IT financial management services. |
| Polarity | Positive |

| Name | Percentage of services/projects managed |
|---|---|
| Description | This is the percentage of services/projects managed with IT financial management practices. |
| Basis for computation | Projects and services that have been active during the observation period. |
| Formula | $\dfrac{\text{(\# Services/Projects managed according to ITFM processes)}}{\text{(\# Service/Projects)}} \times 100$ |
| Polarity | Positive |

## 7.3.5 Investment evaluation

| Name | Number of investment evaluations |
|---|---|
| Description | This is the number of evaluations performed. |
| Basis for computation | Annual budget or n months rolling. |
| Formula | # of investment evaluations performed |
| Polarity | Positive. |

| Name | Percentage of services/projects evaluated |
|---|---|
| Description | This KPI gives evidence of the percentage of new or significantly changed services/projects formally evaluated. |
| Basis for computation | Annual budget or n months rolling. |
| Formula | $\dfrac{\text{(\# of new or changed/projects evaluated through process}}{\text{(\# of new or changed services/projects)}} \times 100$ |
| Polarity | Positive. |

| Name | Activity costs percentage |
|---|---|
| Description | This measures the costs of the investment evaluation activity, compared to the value evaluation required. |
| Basis for computation | Annual budget or n months rolling. |
| Formula | $\dfrac{\text{Costs of all evalutions performed}}{\text{Costs of all services/projects evaluated}} \times 100$ |
| Polarity | Negative (diminishing). |

| Name | Average evaluation lead time |
|---|---|
| Description | This is the time needed to perform an evaluation (from request to official results available). |
| Basis for computation | All the evaluations performed in the annual budget or n months rolling. |
| Formula | $\dfrac{\Sigma \text{ (Time of availability of results – time of request)}}{\text{\# of evaluations performed}}$ |
| Polarity | Negative (diminishing). |

| Name | Percentage of post evaluations |
|---|---|
| Description | This measures the number of new/changed services/projects with a post implementation review (PIR). The post implementation review does not necessarily include an evaluation of returns of investments. |
| Basis for computation | All new or significantly changed services/projects closed in an annual budget or n months rolling. |
| Formula | $\dfrac{(\text{\# of new or significantly changed services/projects with PIR})}{(\text{\# of new or significantly changed services/projects})} \times 100$ |
| Polarity | Positive. |
| Comment | This KPI may be modified to use other investment evaluation techniques (e.g. Internal Rate of Return). |

| Name | Accuracy of evaluations |
|---|---|
| Description | This measures the accuracy of performed evaluations in terms of ratio between the returns beforehand and afterwards |
| Basis for computation | All evaluated services/projects closed relative to annual budget or n months rolling. |
| Formula | $\dfrac{\text{Sum of effective ROI}}{\text{Sum of planned ROI}} \times 100$ |
| Polarity | Positive. |
| Comment | This KPI may be modified to use other investment evaluation techniques (e.g. Internal Rate of Return). |

| Name | Percentage of success |
|---|---|
| Description | This measures the percentage of evaluated services/projects that are achieving the target, which could be the forecasted ROI or IRR. |
| Basis for computation | All evaluated services/projects closed relative to annual budget or n months rolling. |
| Formula | $\dfrac{\text{\# of evaluated services/projects achieving target}}{\text{\# of evaluated services/projects}} \times 100$ |
| Polarity | Positive. |
| Comment | This KPI may be modified to use other investment evaluation techniques (e.g. Internal Rate of Return). Care should be taken as positive performances of some services/projects may compensate negatively for others (a possible solution is to ignore positive results). |

## 7.3.6 Metrics for budgeting

### Annual budget

| Name | Percentage of budget managed |
|---|---|
| Description | This is the percentage of the overall IT organization budget managed according to IT financial management practices. |
| Basis for computation | All initiatives (projects and services) included in the annual budget. |
| Formula | $\dfrac{\text{Budget of Services/Projects managed according to ITFM processes}}{\text{(Budget of Services/Projects)}} \times 100$ |
| Polarity | Positive |

| Name | Percentage of budgets on time |
|---|---|
| Description | This is the percentage of budgets of services/projects that have been defined by the given initial deadline. This measures the project manager's or service owner's performances. |
| Basis for computation | All services/projects included in budget and managed according to IT financial management practices. |
| Formula | $\dfrac{\text{(\# of services/projects budgeted on time)}}{\text{(\# of services/projects)}} \times 100$ |
| Polarity | Positive. |

| Name | Number of reviews |
|---|---|
| Description | This is the number of unplanned budget reviews performed. |
| Basis for computation | Duration of budget year. |
| Formula | Number of unplanned reviews performed. |
| Polarity | Negative (diminishing). |

| Name | Initial variance |
|---|---|
| Description | This is the percentage deviation between the first suggested budget and the approved budget. It gives evidence of the quality of input data and guidelines. |
| Basis for computation | All costs included in budgets (initial and/or approved). |
| Formula | $\dfrac{\text{(Initial Suggested Budget – Approved Budget )}}{\text{(Approved Budget)}} \times 100$ |
| Polarity | Negative (diminishing). |
| Comment | This KPI should be applied separately to costs and revenues. When relevant events occur, deriving from the context (such as change of economics trends) or unforeseen circumstances (such as new rules in GAAP applications or capitalizing policies), this KPI may become no longer applicable, because the variance no longer indicates the quality of the activity. |

| Name | Approval cycles |
|---|---|
| Description | This is the number of cycles performed to approve the budget (internal to IT management). |
| Basis for computation | Time from official budget start to final approval. |
| Formula | Number of approval cycles executed. |
| Polarity | Negative (diminishing). |

| Name | Delay in budget presentation |
|---|---|
| Description | This is the delay (days) between the scheduled date of budget presentation for approval and actual presentation date. This measure is an important aspect of effectiveness of the activity. |
| Basis for computation | Annual budget activity. |
| Formula | Date of actual budget presentation – Scheduled date of budget presentation. |
| Polarity | Negative (diminishing). When relevant events occur, deriving from the context (such as change of economics trends) or unforeseen circumstances (such as new rules in GAAP applications or capitalizing policies), this KPI may become not applicable, because the variance is no longer indicating the quality of the activity. |

| Name | Percentage of costs apportioned automatically |
|---|---|
| Description | This measures the percentage of costs that are automatically apportioned to services/projects. |
| Basis for computation | Services/projects budgeted in an annual budget. |
| Formula | $\dfrac{\text{(budgeted costs automatically apportioned to services/projects)}}{\text{(budgeted costs apportioned to services/projects)}} \times 100$ |
| Polarity | Positive. |

| Name | Acitivity costs percentage |
|---|---|
| Description | This measures the costs of the budgeting activity, compared to those of the managed budget. This is an important aspect of efficiency. |
| Basis for computation | Annual budget. |
| Formula | $\dfrac{\text{Costs of annual budgeting process}}{\text{Costs included in approved budget}} \times 100$ |
| Polarity | Negative (diminishing). |

| Name | Final variance |
|---|---|
| Description | This is the percentage deviation between the initial annual budget and the final balance. It gives evidence of the predictive capacity and accuracy of the budgeting activity. This measure is an important aspect of effectiveness of the activity. |
| Basis for computation | All costs with competence in the annual budget. |
| Formula | $\dfrac{\text{(Budgeted costs – Balance of costs)}}{\text{(Budgeted costs)}} \times 100$ |
| Polarity | Negative (diminishing). |
| Comment | This KPI should be applied separately to costs and revenues. When some relevant events occur, deriving from the context (such as change of economics trends) or unforeseen circumstances (such as new rules in GAAP applications or capitalizing policies), this KPI may become not applicable, because the variance is no longer indicating the quality of the activity. |

| Name | Number of deltas generated |
|---|---|
| Description | This is the number of occurrences of delta management activity (see section 4.2.4 for details) generated during forecasting. |
| Basis for computation | Time from official forecast start to end of activity. |
| Formula | # of delta management activity instances generated (an instance is generated for each forecasted service/project out of tolerance). |
| Polarity | Negative (diminishing). |

| Name | Percentage of forecasts with deltas |
|---|---|
| Description | This is the percentage of forecasting activities affected by the need of managing at least one delta (project and/or service with forecasts deviated from budget and out of tolerance). |
| Basis for computation | Annual budget period or n months rolling. |
| Formula | $\dfrac{(\text{\# of forecasts affected by deltas to be managed})}{(\text{\# of forecasts})} \times 100$ |
| Polarity | Negative (diminishing). |

| Name | Percentage of costs managed by deltas |
|---|---|
| Description | This shows the amount of costs managed by exception compared to the initial budget. |
| Basis for computation | Annual budget period. |
| Formula | $\dfrac{\text{Sum of all costs approved by delta management process instances}}{\text{Costs included in approved budget}} \times 100$ |
| Polarity | Negative (diminishing). |

| Name | Budgeted unit cost of services |
|---|---|
| Description | This measures the cost of each service per unit of consumption when this is applicable. |
| Basis for computation | Each service where unit cost can be calculated. |
| Formula | $\dfrac{(\text{budgeted costs of service})}{(\text{budgeted delivered units of service})} \times 100$ |
| Polarity | Negative (diminishing). |

| Name | Variance of costs of projects/services |
|---|---|
| Description | This measures the difference between the actual and budgeted costs of services/projects. |
| Basis for computation | Services/projects budgeted and accounted at each closure period. |
| Formula | $\dfrac{(\text{actual costs of services/projects})}{(\text{budgeted costs of services/projects})} \times 100$ |
| Polarity | Negative (diminishing). |
| Comment | This KPI may be applied to each service/project separately. The budget should enable the budgeted costs at the closure period to be determined. If this is not available the actual costs of services/projects can be substituted by actual costs of services/projects plus their forecasted costs to completion. |

| Name | Percentage of direct costs |
|---|---|
| Description | This measures the costs that are directly allocated to services/projects. |
| Basis for computation | Services/projects budgeted in an annual budget. |
| Formula | $\dfrac{(\text{costs directly allocated to services/projects})}{(\text{budgeted costs of services/projects})} \times 100$ |
| Polarity | Positive. |

## Budget review

Metrics described for the annual budget may be applied to budget reviews too:

- approval cycles (review)
- delay in budget (review) presentation
- activity costs (review) percentage
- final variance (reviews performed at the same time in each budget cycle, for example first quarter, should be compared to verify trends)
- number of deltas generated (reviews performed at the same time in each budget cycle, for example first quarter, should be compared to verify trends) after review.

### 7.3.7 Metrics for planning

Metrics for planning are very similar to metrics for budgeting where the basis for computation changes (planning period instead of budget period, etc.). The following are typical KPIs that may be used:

- percentage of planned costs managed
- initial variance
- approval cycles
- delay in plans presentation
- percentage of costs apportioned automatically
- activity costs percentage
- final variance
- number of deltas generated
- percentage of planned costs managed by deltas
- planned unit cost of services
- variance of costs of projects/services
- percentage of direct costs

In addition, a specific KPI for planning may be the following.

| Name | Frequency of review of cost (and/or apportioning) model |
|---|---|
| Description | This is the elapsed time between a change of cost (and/or apportioning) model and the next review. |
| Basis for computation | Planning period. |
| Formula | $\frac{\text{Number of day between end and start of planning period}}{\text{Number of reviews of Cost (and/or Apportioning) Model}} \times 100$ |
| Polarity | Negative (diminishing). |

### 7.3.8 Metrics for periodic forecasting

| Name | Percentage of services/projects managed |
|---|---|
| Description | This is the percentage of services/projects for which the forecast activity is active among those managed with IT financial management practices. |
| Basis for computation | Projects and services that are managed with IT financial management practices. |
| Formula | $\frac{(\text{\# Services/Projects managed forecasted})}{(\text{\# Services/Projects})} \times 100$ |
| Polarity | Positive. |

| Name | Percentage of forecasts on time |
|---|---|
| Description | This is the percentage of services/projects forecasts prepared by the due date. This measures the project manager's or service owner's performances. |
| Basis for computation | Annual budget period or n months rolling. |
| Formula | $\dfrac{\text{(\# Services/Projects forecasts on time)}}{\text{(\# Services/Projects forecasts prepared)}} \times 100$ |
| Polarity | Negative (diminishing). |

| Name | Forecast reporting delay |
|---|---|
| Description | This is the delay (days) between the due date for forecast reporting and the actual date. |
| Basis for computation | Time from official forecast start to end of activity. |
| Formula | Date of actual forecast reporting presentation – Scheduled date of forecast reporting presentation. |
| Polarity | Negative (diminishing). |

| Name | Activity costs percentage |
|---|---|
| Description | This measures the costs of the forecasting activity, compared to those of the managed budget. This is an important aspect of activity efficiency. |
| Basis for computation | Annual budget. |
| Formula | $\dfrac{\text{Sum of all costs related to forecast process instances}}{\text{Costs included in approved budget}} \times 100$ |
| Polarity | Negative (diminishing). |

| Name | Percentage of costs apportioned automatically |
|---|---|
| Description | This measures the percentage of costs that are automatically apportioned to services/projects. |
| Basis for computation | Forecast. |
| Formula | $\dfrac{\text{(forecasted costs automatically apportioned to services/projects)}}{\text{(forecasted costs apportioned to services/projects)}} \times 100$ |
| Polarity | Positive. |

## 7.3.9  Metrics for delta management

| Name | Number of requests from passive cycle |
|---|---|
| Description | This measures the number of requests for delta management (corresponding to instances of the activity) generated by the passive cycle (when the required budget is not available). |
| Basis for computation | Annual budget period or n months rolling. |
| Formula | # of requests for delta management raised. |
| Polarity | Negative (diminishing). |

| Name | Percentage of requests approved |
|------|------|
| Description | This measures the percentage of requests for delta management (corresponding to instances of the activity) with a positive result (approval for delta requested) compared to the total number of requests. |
| Basis for computation | Annual budget period or n months rolling. |
| Formula | $\frac{\text{\# of requests with final approval}}{\text{Total \# of requests processed}} \times 100$ |
| Polarity | Positive. |

| Name | Delta management lead time |
|------|------|
| Description | This measures the average time required to manage deltas. |
| Basis for computation | Annual budget period or n months rolling. |
| Formula | $\frac{\Sigma \ (\text{Time of approval} - \text{time of request})}{\text{\# of instances of delta management process}}$ |
| Polarity | Negative (diminishing). |

| Name | Activity costs percentage |
|------|------|
| Description | This measures the costs of the delta management activity, compared to those of the managed budget. This is an important aspect of activity efficiency. |
| Basis for computation | Annual budget. |
| Formula | $\frac{\text{Sum of all costs related to delta management process instances}}{\text{Costs included in approved budget}} \times 100$ |
| Polarity | Negative (diminishing). |

## 7.3.10 Metrics for periodic closures

| Name | Percentage of timesheets on time |
|------|------|
| Description | This measures the percentage of timesheets (the records of time spent to perform activities declared by staff and external resources in providing services and executing projects) that are completed by the due date. This count can be based on people for each period. |
| Basis for computation | Annual budget or n months rolling or period. |
| Formula | $\frac{\text{\# of timesheet completed on time}}{\text{\# of timesheet completed}} \times 100$ |
| Polarity | Positive. |

| Name | Percentage of services/projects on time |
|------|------|
| Description | This measures the percentage of services and/or projects that have costs loaded and verified by the due date. This count may be performed for each period. |
| Basis for computation | Period. |
| Formula | $\frac{\text{\# of services/projects completed on time}}{\text{\# of services/projects managed}} \times 100$ |
| Polarity | Positive. |

| Name | Periodic closures reporting delay |
|---|---|
| Description | This is the delay (days) between the due date for accounting reporting and the actual date. |
| Basis for computation | Time from official periodic closure start to end of activity. |
| Formula | Date of actual accounting reporting presentation – Scheduled date of accounting reporting presentation (Periodic closure). |
| Polarity | Negative (diminishing). |

| Name | Activity costs percentage |
|---|---|
| Description | This measures the costs of the accounting (periodic closure) activity, compared to those of the managed budget. This is an important aspect of activity efficiency. |
| Basis for computation | Annual budget. |
| Formula | $\dfrac{\text{Sum of all costs related to periodic closures}}{\text{Costs included in approved budget}} \times 100$ |
| Polarity | Negative (diminishing). |

| Name | Percentage of costs apportioned automatically |
|---|---|
| Description | This measures the percentage of costs that are automatically apportioned to services/projects. |
| Basis for computation | Services/projects managed at each periodic closure. |
| Formula | $\dfrac{\text{(accounted costs automatically apportioned to services/projects)}}{\text{(accounted costs apportioned to services/projects)}} \times 100$ |
| Polarity | Positive. |

## 7.3.11 Metrics for annual closures

| Name | Annual closures reporting delay |
|---|---|
| Description | This is the delay (days) between the due date for accounting reporting and the actual date. |
| Basis for computation | Time from official periodic closure start to end of activity (annual closure). |
| Formula | Date of actual accounting reporting presentation – Scheduled date of accounting reporting presentation. |
| Polarity | Negative (diminishing). |

| Name | Activity costs percentage |
|---|---|
| Description | This measures the costs of the accounting (annual closure) activity, compared to those of the managed budget. This is an important aspect of activity efficiency. |
| Basis for computation | Annual budget. |
| Formula | $\dfrac{\text{Sum of all costs related to annual closure}}{\text{Costs included in approved budget}} \times 100$ |
| Polarity | Negative (diminishing). |

| Name | Percentage of costs apportioned automatically |
|---|---|
| Description | This measures the percentage of costs that are automatically apportioned to services/projects. |
| Basis for computation | Services/projects managed at each annual closure. |
| Formula | $\dfrac{\text{(accounted costs automatically apportioned to services/projects)}}{\text{(accounted costs appotioned to services/projects)}} \times 100$ |
| Polarity | Positive. |

## 7.3.12 Customer charging

| Name | Activity cost |
|---|---|
| Description | This measures the costs of the charging activity. This is an important aspect of activity efficiency. |
| Basis for computation | Annual budget or n months rolling. |
| Formula | Sum of costs of charging activity. |
| Polarity | Negative (diminishing). |

| Name | Number of disputes (claims) for charging reasons |
|---|---|
| Description | This gives evidence of any problems with the charging activity. |
| Basis for computation | Annual budget or n months rolling or for each execution of charging activity. |
| Formula | # of disputes (claims) raised by customers regarding charging. |
| Polarity | Negative (diminishing). |
| Comment | Depending on the meaning of dispute and claim for organizations, two KPIs could be managed. |

| Name | Disputed value percentage |
|---|---|
| Description | This measures the relevance of disputed charges by customers. |
| Basis for computation | Annual budget or n months rolling. |
| Formula | $\dfrac{\text{Value of claims raised}}{\text{Values of charges}} \times 100$ |
| Polarity | Negative (diminishing). |

## 7.3.13 Additional metrics and final considerations

### Additional metrics

An obvious measure that IT financial management practices are defined properly may be the perceptions of stakeholders (customers, users, management, etc.). This can be measured by means of satisfaction surveys. Surveys can cover important aspects such as:

- charges, where applied, are seen to be fair
- the IT organization is provided with the expected income/level of profits.

Additional KPIs are suitable for continual improvement activities, such as:

- timeliness of audits
- number and timeliness of review meetings
- the number (and severity) of changes required by the IT accounting system

- the number of changes made to the charging algorithm (where appropriate)
- other KPIs are suitable, depending on the actual scope of IT financial management practices

Examples of KPIs related to practices and activities not included in the reference model are:
- number of requests of ad hoc reports and analysis
- timeliness to prepare ad hoc reports and analysis
- number of inventory checks performed
- timeliness of inventory checks
- number of adjustments to be performed after inventory
- value of adjustments to be performed after inventory

Ad hoc reports and financial analysis become necessary when available outputs (those designed and implemented as part of the financial management set) are not supplying the required information. Standard reports cannot fulfill all needs and therefore a certain amount of requests is to be expected. However, requests for new reports are time consuming and often place extra work pressures on IT staff when they are urgent. If this situation becomes frequent it may be a symptom of several issues: the standard reporting has been poorly designed, reporting tools are not flexible and/or user-friendly enough and, finally, requests are not properly evaluated and filtered (for example because they are considered effortless or because no knowledge is available about their associated costs). Such a situation needs to be analyzed and a solution found. If the problem relates to poor design or problems with tools) and time is needed to identify a definitive solution, a temporary mitigation action can be to ask for payment for requests (either notional or real charging) while the reporting system is being improved. This is likely to be the only solution when the problem relates to difficulties of requesters in clearly stating their information needs or to the fact that no cost/benefit evaluation is performed when raising requests.

## Final considerations

In the previous sections we have described a significant number of metrics and KPIs for IT financial management practices. Some may not be suitable for all organizations, for example if some of the activities are not performed (e.g. charging). Many may not be applicable when certain events occur, deriving from the business context (such as change of economic trends) or unforeseen circumstances (such as new rules in GAAP applications or capitalizing policies). Implementing and maintaining each of the above measures is generally a relevant effort: each measure should be analyzed in the context of the target organization and its definition tuned accordingly. For example, for approval cycles (KPI), it will be necessary to clearly define the official start time and the official final approval time.

After analysis, it will be necessary to define how to calculate KPIs. Automation is generally the best option but this implies an initial effort to design, implement, customize or configure a solution and related investments. In order to compute KPIs, changes to accounting and, more generally, IT service management support tools may be needed. For example, the budgeting system could be updated with a new functionality to record the start and end dates of each budgeting cycle.

When the reporting and all other support systems are in place, they will need to be maintained. This happens because of the changes normally affecting all practices and systems. For example, it will be necessary to update the lists of recipients of reports. Or, a change in the number of managed statuses of projects and services could lead to the need for updating the calculation rules of KPIs (simply because they would use status transitions to determine dates). It is frequent to see errors in reporting because changes have not been analyzed and managed for impact.

In conclusion, it is mandatory to introduce KPIs to control and improve IT financial management, but there is a significant associated cost that is rapidly increasing with the number and complexity of adopted metrics. Organizations should have a clear understanding of the trade-off; they should implement only those metrics that are really needed and aligned with the scope, maturity and objectives of IT financial management.

# 8 Tooling

## 8.1 Requirements for IT financial management tools

Except for small IT service organizations, it is not practical to attempt IT accounting without suitable applications or software tools. Automated solutions range from the use of legacy systems, which often support financial practices, to customized applications; the choice of solution depends on the complexity and size of the organization.

In the next sections, we will list some major requirements for automated solutions. Requirements will be organized and presented in relation to supported practices. Some general and cross-platform requirements should be added but have not been analyzed here: for example requirements for supplier, technical architecture, localization, etc.

### 8.1.1 Requirements to support accounting

The main requirements for automation to support accounting activities are:
- management of the company calendar (e.g. fiscal years different from calendar year)
- management of ledgers
- support of the chosen cost model
- user friendly data entry (especially to enter common records)
- management of apportioning (support of cost apportioning model) and, when necessary, interface with the systems feeding balance data of apportioning drivers (e.g. the number of users)
- automatic calculation of capitalizing, amortization, depreciations, accruals
- interfaces with the financial department's general ledger and purchasing systems
- ability to freeze periods
- interface with budgeting in order to input data

The possible options to supply these functionalities are:
- using the system in use by the financial department
- building a new system that is specific to the IT department and interfacing it with the general ledger of the financial department.

### 8.1.2 Requirements to support budgeting and planning

In addition to the suggested requirements to support accounting activities, the main requirements for automation to support budgeting and planning activities are:
- interfaces to load data series to support budgeting and planning (e.g. the balance for the previous year)
- ability to budget revenues as well as costs
- user friendly data entry features to manage budget per accrual period (e.g. distribution of a total value per period based on seasonality derived from the previous year)
- support of simulations (e.g. what happens if unit costs change or automatically simulate a reduction of costs by x percent)
- ability to aggregate and freeze the budget

- management of several budgets (e.g. to support reviews or to compare options) for the same period
- comparisons between different budgets
- support of budgeting and planning activity workflows (e.g. preparing a service budget of direct costs within deadline) and notifications

In some organizations, the budgeting activity is still extensively supported by a spreadsheet. Not all ERP or accounting systems are fulfilling the requirements listed above, in particular user-friendliness and simulation. In some cases, the financial department has developed a budgeting solution based on specialized packages or custom applications. The IT department may adopt these solutions or opt for its own solution, which will need to be interfaced with the financial department's solution.

### 8.1.3   Requirements to support forecasting and delta management

The main requirements for automation to support forecasting and delta management activities are:

- interfaces with the general ledger, purchasing, pricing, charging and/or budgeting/planning system in order to load all the required data (budgets, actual)
- interface with the accounting module to feed balance data
- user-friendly support of forecast determination (for example automatic suggestions based on balance, budget and/or trends)
- workflow to manage authorizations of deviations from forecast (the approved amounts should be varied in the purchasing system automatically)
- ability to aggregate and freeze forecasts

Forecasting is often supported by the same automation solution that supports budgeting activities.

### 8.1.4   Requirements to support charging

The main requirements for automation to support charging activity are:

- management of contracts, at a minimum providing the information needed to issue bills (e.g. tariffs, frequency and method of payment)
- management of required charging rules (e.g. computation of charging based on fixed prices or based on quantities and tariffs)
- interface with systems feeding balance data of charging drivers (e.g. the number of users)
- manual and/or batch charges computation
- management and automatic warning based on thresholds (e.g. the maximum agreed utilization of resources has been passed)
- issuing of invoices and credit/debit notes
- finalization of provisory issues and credit/debit notes and interfaces with the general ledger to record them
- management of attached documentation to justify bills to customers
- interfaces with accounting, budgeting and forecasting systems to transfer data about charges issued

Tools needed to feed charging drivers are not usually found in the domain of IT financial management. More often, they belong to the domain that monitors service management support applications (such as tools for availability management, capacity management and incident management).

### 8.1.5 Requirements to support pricing

The main requirements for automation to support pricing activity are:
- management of a price list according to supported commercial rules (e.g. quantity discounts, specific price lists for customers)
- ability to print the price list for commercial use or to publish prices (e.g. into web portals).
- tracking of changes
- workflow to manage authorizations of new or changed prices
- interfaces with budgeting, forecasting and charging systems

### 8.1.6 Requirements for reporting

Reporting is a central element of any financial management system. The reporting system should be able to provide all the defined reports (see 6.5.13 for a list) and it should be flexible enough to accommodate future needs. Possible requirements for a reporting system are:
- ability to interface different sources of data (e.g. separated accounting and/or budgeting systems)
- ability to manage a dedicated data warehouse where required information is copied for reporting aims (e.g. to allow detailed analysis with no impact on performance)
- ability to design the required set of reports, to define their recipients, the frequency of report generation, related filtering options (range of dates to consider, IT services to include, etc.) and rights of access to data (e.g. the IT service owner will access a specific set of reports and, within them, only information about the assigned services).
- support of tabular layouts as well as of graphic layouts for data presentation
- possibility to freeze and distribute reports (e.g. by mail or web access) and the data contained in reports
- scheduling batch execution and provision of reporting
- ability to provide controlled navigation of reports (e.g. drill-down of information)
- ability to provide controlled design functionality of new reports to authorized users

## 8.2 Architecture and options for IT financial management tools

There are several possible scenarios for the IT financial management system architecture. The choice of architecture and the relationship established between the Management Accounting System and General Accounting System are correlated. We will consider planning, budgeting, forecasting, reporting modules, each supporting the corresponding activity, as components of the Management Accounting System and we will describe some typical architectures.

The simplest option and architecture is described in Figure 8.1, where an integrated financial management system deals with both IT and non-IT aspects. This could be part of a wider ERP system, which could also include some of the modules that have been shown as external in Figure

8.2 (e.g. purchasing). If this is the case, the relationship between the General Accounting System and Management Accounting System will probably be of the type 'based on accounting and integrated' or 'based on accounting and separated' (see section 6.5.5 for details). The reporting module is likely to be used to produce all reporting, independently from the source module of information. This architecture is more frequent in Scenario 1, when IT financial management is part of financial management and pricing and charging modules have not been implemented, and Scenario 3, where financial management is IT financial management.

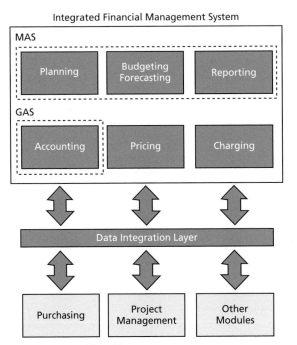

Figure 8.1 Integrated financial management system

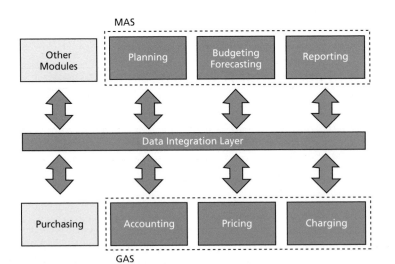

Figure 8.2 Modular IT financial management system

A more complex architecture is shown in Figure 8.2. In this case we have more independent systems: an accounting package supports the General Accounting System and pricing/charging modules. A customized application supports the Management Accounting System. The level of sophistication of this latter application may vary from a simple set of inter-related spreadsheets to a very complete set of carefully designed functionalities. Again, some additional modules may be provided by the accounting system (e.g. purchasing), which could evolve in an ERP system. The reporting module will usually be dedicated to the Management Accounting System but all other modules will at least have an autonomous predefined set of reports. This architecture is possible for all scenarios but it is most frequent in Scenario 2.

## 8.3    How to evaluate and select a tool

The use of tools to support financial management practices is almost mandatory if the organization is not very small. As we have seen in the previous section, it is possible that more than one tool is used to support all the activities. The general aspects to be considered when choosing tools are:

- compatibility of hardware and middleware requirements with architectural policies and standards
- data structure, data handling and integration
- integration capability with existing and future new systems
- compliance to international open standards
- flexibility in implementation, usage and data sharing
- usability – the ease of use permitted by the user interface
- conversion requirements for previously tracked data
- data backup, control and security
- support options provided by the tool vendor
- scalability for increasing of capacity (the number of users, volume of data and so on).

To these general aspects we should add the requirements previously discussed (see 8.1). A Statement of Requirements (SoR) is recommended, if there is to be a formal evaluation or to guide the implementation of a chosen solution that already exists.

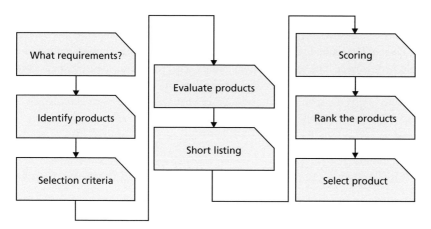

Figure 8.3 Tool evaluation according to ITIL V3 (source OGC)

If there is a formal evaluation, a suggested approach is described in Figure 8.3. A key step of the activity is to evaluate the product according to the selection criteria. A possible method is to categorize requirements using the MoSCoW approach:

- M – MUST have this
- S – SHOULD have this if at all possible
- C – COULD have this if it does not affect anything else
- W – WON'T have this time but WOULD like in the future

To make the final decision, the following rules could be used:

- 80 percent fit to all functional and technical requirements (MUST and SHOULD)
- a meeting of ALL mandatory requirements (MUST)
- little (if any) product customization required
- adherence of tool and supplier to service management best practice (e.g. ISO/IEC 20000 certification)
- administration and maintenance costs within budget
- availability of training and support services (e.g. in local language and for the territories where the solution will be deployed)

Other requirements should be taken into account, not just the technical requirements. They should include all the general aspects initially listed and many others related to the supplier, such as: revenues and profitability, completeness of offer, vertical knowledge and references in target industries, references, age and stability of the solution, staff, reputation, etc.

Another approach for evaluating products is to use a weighting and scoring system for requirements. Each requirement has a weight and a scoring system to measure how much it is achieved (e.g. fully natively achieved, achieved with portable customization, achieved with non-portable customization, not achievable; non-portable customizations means that in newer versions of the tool they should be newly implemented). Requirements can be grouped in sections that could be weighted too. The final result of this approach is an absolute score that can be used to rank alternative products. In every case, even if using this method, the mandatory requirements should be identified and matched. For example, if the cost model would not be supported this should lead to the rejection of an accounting system.

The advantage of this second model is that it gives an absolute, objective final score that can be used to make the choice. The main disadvantage is that if the scoring system is poorly tuned, the final choice would be incorrect. The scoring system should reflect real priorities; the final score should match with the general view about the evaluated solutions. If not, the reasons should be investigated and, if necessary, the scoring system should be changed to reflect actual priorities.

# 9 Terminology and definitions

## 9.1 Definitions list

| | |
|---|---|
| Accounting | A set of activities that are part of IT financial management aimed at determining actual costs and revenues relating to IT at specified instants of time and according to all applicable rules (e.g. defined cost model) and regulations. As a result a set of predefined reports is produced. Recording of economically relevant facts has been considered part of other practices, such as the passive cycle or financial management practices. |
| Accounting center | A type of IT organization that identifies the costs of providing services, and may do some budgeting. The focus is on measuring performance and conducting investment assessment. |
| Accounting model | A set of basic assumptions, concepts, principles and procedures that determine the methods of recognizing, recording, measuring and reporting an entity's financial transactions. The definition of the rules underlying the accounting model may be influenced by IRFS. |
| Accounting system | General Accounting System or Management Accounting System. An Any Accounting System supports a specific Accounting Model. |
| Accrual accounting | A system of accounting in which revenue is recognized when it is earned and expenses are recognized as they are incurred. |
| Accruals | Accounts on a profit and loss statement and/or balance sheet that represent liabilities and non-cash-based assets used in accrual-based accounting. These accounts include, among many others, accounts payable, accounts receivable, goodwill, future tax liability and future interest expense. The use of accrual accounts has greatly increased the amount of information on accounting statements. Before the use of accruals only cash transactions were recorded on these statements. Cash transactions do not give information about other important business activities, such as revenue based on credit and future liabilities. By using accruals, an organization can measure what it owes looking forward and what cash revenue it expects to receive. It also allows a company to show assets that do not have a cash value, such as goodwill. |
| Adjusting entries | Adjusting entries are journal entries usually made at the end of an accounting period to allocate income and expenditure to the period in which they actually occurred. |
| Allocated cost | Referring to a cost object, a direct cost of it. |
| Amortization | Accounting procedure that gradually reduces the cost value of a limited life asset or intangible asset through periodic charges to income. For fixed assets the term used is depreciation, and for consuming assets (natural resources) it is depletion, both terms meaning essentially the same thing as amortization. Most companies follow the conservative practice of writing off, through amortization, intangible assets such as goodwill. |
| Anchor values | An investment appraisal technique. |
| Apportioned cost | Referring to a cost object, an indirect cost of it. The cost is shared among different cost objects of the same type. |
| Apportioning model | See cost apportioning model. |
| Asset | According to ITIL V3, an asset is defined as 'any resource or capability. Assets of a service provider include anything that could contribute to the delivery of a service. Assets can be one of the following types: management, organization, process, knowledge, people, information, applications, infrastructure, and financial capital.' |

| Asset management | According to ITIL V3, asset management is defined as 'the practice responsible for tracking and reporting the value and ownership of financial assets throughout their lifecycle. Asset management is part of an overall service asset and configuration management process.' |
|---|---|
| Assessment | According to ITIL V3, assessment is defined as 'inspection and analysis to check whether a standard or set of guidelines is being followed, that records are accurate, or that efficiency and effectiveness targets are being met'. |
| Audit | According to ITIL V3, audit is defined as 'formal inspection and verification to check whether a standard or set of guidelines is being followed, that records are accurate, or that efficiency and effectiveness targets are being met. An audit may be carried out by internal or external groups.' |
| Balanced Scorecard | According to ITIL V2, this is defined as 'an aid to organizational performance management. It helps to focus, not only on the financial targets but also on the internal practices, customers and learning and growth issues'. |
| Balance sheet | A report representing a 'snapshot' of the financial position of an evaluated company. Balance sheets may also be produced for any cost object, such as departments, services, etc. |
| Budget | According to ITIL V3, budget is defined as 'a list of all the money an organization or business unit plans to receive, and plans to pay out, over a specified period of time'. |
| Budget year | An accounting period covering twelve consecutive months. |
| Budgeting | One of the IT financial management activities ensuring that the correct finance is defined for the provision of IT services. Budgeting can be broken down in annual budget and budget review activity. |
| Business | According to ITIL V3, a business is defined as 'an overall corporate entity or organization formed of a number of business units. In the context of ITSM, the term business includes public sector and not-for-profit organizations, as well as companies. An IT service provider provides IT services to a customer within a business. The IT service provider may be part of the same business as their customer (internal service provider), or part of another business (external service provider).' |
| Business (IT) service | An IT service that is known by customer(s). |
| Business Service Catalog | Part of the Service Catalog containing those IT services visible to the customers. |
| Business unit | According to ITIL V2, a business unit is defined as 'a segment of the business entity by which both revenues are received and expenditure are caused or controlled, such revenues and expenditure being used to evaluate segmental performance'. |
| Cash accounting | A system of accounting in which revenues and costs are recognized when they actually occur (according to the related financial transaction, e.g. cash payment). |
| Change | According to ITIL V3, change is defined as 'the addition, modification or removal of anything that could have an effect on IT services. The scope should include all IT services, configuration items, processes, documentation etc.' |
| Change Advisory Board | According to ITIL V3, this is defined as 'a group of people that advises the change manager in the assessment, prioritisation and scheduling of changes. This board is usually made up of representatives from all areas within the IT service provider, the business, and third parties such as suppliers'. |
| Charging | One of the IT financial management activities aimed at charging customers for the supplied IT service. |
| Chart of Accounts | System of accounting records developed by every organization to be compatible with its particular financial structure, and in agreement with the amount of detail required in its financial statements. It consists of a list of ledger account names and numbers showing classifications and sub-classifications, and serves as an index to locate a given account within the ledger. |

| | |
|---|---|
| Capability Maturity Model (CMM) | According to ITIL V3, this is defined as 'the Capability Maturity Model for software (also known as the CMM and SW-CMM) is a model used to identify best practices to help increase process maturity. CMM was developed at the Software Engineering Institute (SEI) of Carnegie Mellon University. In 2000, the SW-CMM was upgraded to CMMI® (Capability Maturity Model Integration). The SEI no longer maintains the SW-CMM model, its associated appraisal methods, or training materials.' |
| Capability Maturity Model Integration (CMMI) | According to ITIL V3, this is defined as 'Capability Maturity Model® Integration (CMMI), a process improvement approach developed by the Software Engineering Institute (SEI) of Carnegie Mellon University. CMMI provides organizations with the essential elements of effective practices. It can be used to guide practice improvement across a project, a division, or an entire organization. CMMI helps integrate traditionally separate organizational functions, set practice improvement goals and priorities, provide guidance for quality practices, and provide a point of reference for appraising current practices. See http://www.sei.cmu.edu/cmmi/ for more information.' |
| Capacity management | In ITIL V3, this is defined as 'the process responsible for ensuring that the capacity of IT services and the IT infrastructure is able to deliver agreed service level targets in a cost effective and timely manner'. |
| Capacity manager | Practice owner of capacity management practices. |
| Capacity Plan | According to ITIL V3, this is defined as follows: 'a Capacity Plan is used to manage the resources required to deliver IT services. The plan contains scenarios for different predictions of business demand, and costed options to deliver the agreed service level targets.' |
| Capex | Capital expenditures, or Capex, are expenditures incurred when an organization acquires or improves long-term assets that create future benefits (benefits in more than a year). |
| Capitalization | Not to be confused with Capitalizing, capitalization may refer to the sum of a corporation's long-term debt, stock and retained earnings (also called invested capital) or the market price of an entire company, calculated by multiplying the number of shares outstanding by the price per share (also called market capitalization). |
| Capitalizing | In ITIL V3, this is defined as 'identifying major cost as capital, even though no asset is purchased. This is done to spread the impact of the cost over multiple accounting periods. The most common example of this is software development, or purchase of a software license.' In a financial context, capitalizing is an accounting method used to delay the recognition of expenses by recording the expense as long-term assets. Capitalized expenditures (or Capex) are depreciated or amortized (see Depreciation and Amortization). |
| Cash flow statement | The statement of cash flow is a financial report summarizing any changes in a company's cash position. |
| Change | In ITIL V3, change is defined as 'the addition, modification or removal of anything that could have an effect on IT services. The scope should include all IT services, configuration items, processes, documentation etc.' |
| Change management | One of the IT service management processes. In ITIL V3, it is defined as 'the process responsible for controlling the lifecycle of all changes. The primary objective of change management is to enable beneficial changes to be made, with minimum disruption to IT services.' It is described in the Service Transition book. |
| Change manager | Process owner of the change management process. |
| Charging | One of the IT financial management activities aimed at charging customers for the use of IT services. |

| | |
|---|---|
| Chief Financial Officer | The Chief Financial Officer (CFO) of a company or public agency is the corporate officer primarily responsible for managing the financial risks of the business or agency. This officer is also responsible for financial planning and record keeping, as well as financial reporting to higher management (in recent years, however, the role has expanded to encompass communicating financial performance and forecasts to the analyst community). The title is equivalent to finance director, commonly seen in the United Kingdom. |
| Chief Information Officer | The Chief Information Officer (CIO) is a job title for the board level head of Information Technology within an organization. |
| Configuration item | In ITIL V3, this is defined as 'any component that needs to be managed in order to deliver an IT service'. |
| Configuration management | According to ITIL V3, this is defined as 'the process responsible for maintaining information about configuration items required to deliver an IT service, including their relationships'. |
| Configuration Management Data Base (CMDB) | According to ITIL V3, this is defined as 'a database used to store configuration records throughout their lifecycle'. |
| Control Objectives for Information and related Technology (CobiT) | According to ITIL V3, this is defined as 'Control Objectives for Information and related Technology (CobiT), which provides guidance and best practice for the management of IT Processes. CobiT is published by the IT Governance Institute. See http://www.isaca.org/ for more information.' |
| Cost apportioning model | Set of principles and rules used to apportion costs to cost objects. A cost apportioning model is often considered part of a cost model. |
| Cost benefit analysis | An investment appraisal technique. |
| Cost center | A segment of a business or other organization, in which costs can be segregated, with the head of that segment being held accountable for expenses. Cost centers are established in large organizations to identify responsibility and to control costs. |
| Cost element | According to ITIL V3, this is defined as 'the middle level of category to which costs are assigned in budgeting and accounting. The highest level category is cost type. For example a cost type of "people" could have cost elements of payroll, staff benefits, expenses, training, overtime etc. cost elements can be further broken down to give cost units. For example the cost element "expenses" could include cost units of hotels, transport, meals etc.' |
| Cost model | In order to calculate the costs of providing service it is necessary to design and build a framework in which all costs can be recorded and allocated or apportioned to specific customers or other activities. Such 'cost models' can be developed to show, for example, the cost of each service, the cost for each customer or the cost for each location. The usual start point is to develop a cost-by-customer cost model. |
| Cost object | Any end to which a cost is assigned. Typical examples of cost objects are IT services, departments, customers. |
| Cost pool | A collection of costs that are assigned to a cost object. Hardware or software are typical examples of cost pools. |
| Cost type | According to ITIL V3, this is defined as 'the highest level of category to which costs are assigned in budgeting and accounting. For example hardware, software, people, accommodation, external and transfer.' |
| Cost unit | According to ITIL V3, this is defined as 'the lowest level of category to which costs are assigned, cost units are usually things that can be easily counted (e.g. staff numbers, software licenses) or things easily measured (e.g. CPU usage, electricity consumed). Cost units are included within cost elements. For example a cost element of "expenses" could include cost units of hotels, transport, meals etc.' |

| | |
|---|---|
| Customer | According to ITIL V3, a customer is defined as 'someone who buys goods or services. The customer of an IT service provider is the person or group who defines and agrees the service level targets. The term "customers" is also sometimes informally used to mean users, for example "this is a customer focussed organization".' |
| Delta management | One of the IT financial management activities with the objective to manage deltas (deviations) between forecasted (balance at a date plus estimations to the end of budget period), or actual, versus budgeted costs and revenues. |
| Demand management | According to ITIL V3, this is defined as 'activities that understand and influence customer demand for services and the provision of capacity to meet these demands. At a strategic level demand management can involve analysis of patterns of business activity and user profiles. At a tactical level it can involve use of differential charging to encourage customers to use IT services at less busy times.' |
| Deming cycle | Synonym of Plan-Do-Check-Act. |
| Depreciation | Depreciation is the measure of the reduction in the useful economic life of a capital item or asset. It will take into account the current value of the asset, the expected remaining length of life and any residual value of the asset at the end of its useful life. Finance departments will give guidance on the method of depreciation to be employed. |
| Direct cost | A cost that is incurred for, and can be traced in full to a cost object. |
| Discounted payback (period) | A variant of payback technique. |
| Discretionary cost center | A classification of an organizational unit being responsible for costs whose relationships with revenues are existing but not well specified. |
| Economy of scale | According to ITIL V3, this is defined as 'the reduction in average cost that is possible from increasing the usage of an IT service or asset'. |
| Economy of scope | According to ITIL V3, this is defined as 'the reduction in cost that is assigned to an IT service by using an existing asset for an additional purpose – for example, delivering a new IT service from existing IT infrastructure'. |
| Financial Accounting System | See General Accounting System. |
| Financial controller | A financial controller is a person who supervises accounting and financial reporting within an organization. A financial controller is an accountant in a business who oversees accounting and the implementation and monitoring of internal controls. In the United States, the United Kingdom, and Canada, a financial controller is a senior position within most companies, often reporting to a Chief Financial Officer. |
| Financial management | This term may refer to a discipline and/or an organizational function and/ or responsibilities and practices depending on the context in which it is used. Regardless of the subject (discipline, organizational function or responsibilities and practices), financial management deals with the raising of capital to finance an organization's operations and its careful use. |
| Financial management for IT services | The set of practices responsible for managing an IT service provider's budgeting, accounting and charging requirements. |
| Financial year | See budget year. |
| Fiscal year | A period of twelve months that is reported for economic results by organizations in order to define the amount of taxes to be paid. |
| Full cost | According to ITIL V2, this is defined as 'the total cost of all the resources used in supplying a service – that is, the sum of the direct costs of producing the output, a proportional share of overhead costs and any selling and distribution expenses. Both cash costs and notional (non-cash) costs should be included, including the cost of capital.' |

| | |
|---|---|
| General Accepted Accounting Principles (GAAP) | The overall conventions, rules, and procedures that define accepted accounting practice at a particular time in the United States. |
| General Accounting System | The set of accounting records that are used to log, when they occur, the facts having administrative relevance. |
| Incident | According to ITIL V3, this is defined as 'an unplanned interruption to an IT service or a reduction in the quality of an IT service'. |
| Incident management | According to ITIL V3, this is defined as 'the process responsible for managing the lifecycle of all incidents. The primary objective of incident management is to return the IT service to users as quickly as possible.' |
| Indirect cost | A cost incurred in the course of making a product, providing a service or running a cost center or department, but which cannot be traced directly and in full to the product, service or department. Indirect costs are also referred to as overheads.' |
| Internal Rate of Return (IRR) | An investment appraisal technique. |
| International Accounting Standards | Many of the standards forming part of IFRS are known by the older name of International Accounting Standards (IAS). IAS was issued between 1973 and 2001 by the board of the International Accounting Standards Committee (IASC). In April 2001 the IASB adopted all IAS and continued their development, calling the new standards IFRS. |
| International Accounting Standards Board (IASB) | Standard setting body responsible for the development of International Financial Reporting Standards (IFRSs). |
| International Financial Reporting Standards | A set of international accounting standards stating how particular types of transactions and other events should be reported in financial statements. IFRSs are issued by the International Accounting Standards Board. IFRS are sometimes confused with International Accounting Standards (IAS), which are the older standards that IFRS replaced. (IASs were issued from 1973 to 2000.) The goal with IFRS is to make international comparisons as easy as possible. This is difficult because, to a large extent, each country has its own set of rules. For example, the United States GAAP is different from Canadian GAAP. Synchronizing accounting standards across the globe is an ongoing process in the international accounting community. |
| Investment center | A classification of an organizational unit being responsible for investments. |
| Investment evaluation (appraisal) | An activity with the objective to determine the appropriateness of investing money to implement an initiative. When applied to IT projects, investment evaluation can be included in the set of IT financial management activities. |
| ISO/IEC 19770-1:2006 | ISO specification for software asset management. |
| ISO/IEC 20000 | ISO Specification and Code of Practice for IT service management. ISO/IEC 20000 is aligned with ITIL best practices. |
| IT budget approver | A person responsible for approving a part or the total budget together with the related IT budget owner(s) (who can be the same person). |
| IT budget owner | A person responsible for the budget inherent to a specific IT area or all IT. The budget owner authorizes expenditures within its domain and available budget. |
| IT financial controller | A financial controller specializing in IT related topics. |
| IT financial management | This term may refer to a discipline and/or an organizational function and/ or responsibilities and practices depending on the context where it is used. Regardless of the subject (discipline, organizational function or responsibilities and practices), IT financial management deals with the evaluation, planning, funding, controlling and charging of IT investments and costs. For organizations in Scenario 3, IT financial management corresponds to financial management and acquires a much wider scope that includes the previous. |
| IT financial manager | Practice owner of IT financial management function. |

| | |
|---|---|
| IT financial planning | One of the IT financial management activities, element of planning. |
| IT Infrastructure Library (ITIL) | A set of best practice guidance for IT service management. ITIL is owned by the UK Office of Government Commerce (OGC) and consists of a series of publications giving guidance on the provision of quality IT services, and on the practices and facilities needed to support them. See www.itil.co.uk for more information. |
| IT service | In ITIL V3, this is defined as 'a service provided to one or more customers by an IT service provider. An IT service is based on the use of Information Technology and supports the customer's business processes. An IT service is made up from a combination of people, processes and technology and should be defined in a Service Level Agreement.' |
| IT service management | In ITIL V3, this is defined as: 'the implementation and management of quality IT services that meet the needs of the business. IT service management is performed by IT service providers through an appropriate mix of people, process and Information Technology.' |
| IT service provider | In ITIL V3, this is defined as 'a service provider that provides IT services to internal customers or external customers'. |
| Kaizen | Kaizen (改善, Japanese for 'continuous improvement') is a Japanese philosophy that focuses on continuous improvement throughout all aspects of life. When applied to the workplace, Kaizen activities continually improve all functions of a business, from manufacturing to management and from the CEO to the assembly line workers. |
| Kaizen Event | Any action whose output is intended to be an improvement to an existing process. Kaizen Events are commonly referred to as a tool that: 1) gathers operators, managers, and owners of a process in one place 2) maps the existing process (using a deployment flowchart, in most cases) 3) improves on the existing process 4) solicits buy-in from all parties related to the process. |
| Key Performance Indicator (KPI) | According to ITIL V3, this is defined as 'a metric that is used to help manage a practice, IT service or activity. Many metrics may be measured, but only the most important of these are defined as KPIs and used to actively manage and report on the practice, IT service or activity. KPIs should be selected to ensure that efficiency, effectiveness, and cost effectiveness are all managed'. |
| Management Accounting System | Set of records, integrating those provided by the General Accounting Systems, needed to supply the requested information about the facts of economical relevance for the company. |
| Market price | Definition of the price of goods and services based on the market offer and competition. |
| Maturity | In ITIL V3, this is defined as 'a measure of the reliability, efficiency and effectiveness of a practice, function, organization etc. The most mature practices and functions are formally aligned to business objectives and strategy, and are supported by a framework for continual improvement.' |
| Maturity level | In ITIL V3, this is defined as 'a named level in a maturity model such as the Carnegie Mellon Capability Maturity Model Integration'. |
| Metrics | A standard for measuring or evaluating something. |
| Net book value | The net book value of an asset is the capitalized cost minus the depreciation written-off to date. |
| Net present value | An investment appraisal technique, which calculates the difference between the present value of the future cash flows from an investment and the amount of investment. |
| Notional charging | In ITIL V3, this is defined as 'an approach to charging for IT services. Charges to customers are calculated and customers are informed of the charge, but no money is actually transferred. Notional charging is sometimes introduced to ensure that customers are aware of the costs they incur or as a stage during the introduction of real charging.' |

| | |
|---|---|
| Operating capital | Also known as working capital, it is equal to net liquid assets computed by deducting current liabilities from current assets. Sources of working capital are net income, long-term loans (non-current liabilities), sale of capital (non-current) assets, and injection of funds by the owners (stockholders). The amount of available working capital is a measure of an organization's ability to meet its short-term obligations. |
| Operational Level Agreement (OLA) | In ITIL V3, this is defined as 'an agreement between an IT service provider and another part of the same organization'. |
| Opex | An operating expense (operating expenditure, operational expense, operational expenditure) or Opex is an ongoing cost for running a product, business, or system. |
| Overheads | See Indirect cost. |
| Passive cycle | A set of related activities, starting from the identification of the need for buying something and terminating with the payment of the goods/services purchased, including all the intermediate steps, e.g. ordering, receipts management, invoice control, accounting and supplier management. |
| Payback (period) | An investment appraisal technique. |
| Periodic closure | One of the accounting activities with the objective to determine and report actual costs and revenues relating to IT at the end of each reporting period (e.g. month) into which a budget year has been divided. |
| Periodic forecast | One of the IT financial management activities with the objective to define the costs and revenues from a certain instant (e.g. when a forecast is required) to the end of a period (e.g. a budget period). |
| Pilot | In ITIL V3, this is defined as 'a limited deployment of an IT service, a release or a process to the live environment. A pilot is used to reduce risk and to gain user feedback and acceptance'. |
| Planning | A business activity with the objective to define initiatives and to predict and control the spending of money to achieve the business objectives in the medium/long term. |
| Plan-Do-Check-Act | According to ITIL V3, this is defined as 'a four stage cycle for process management, attributed to Edward Deming. Plan-Do-Check-Act is also called the Deming Cycle. PLAN: Design or revise processes that support the IT services. DO: Implement the plan and manage the processes. CHECK: Measure the processes and IT services, compare with Objectives and produce reports ACT: Plan and implement changes to improve the processes.' |
| Policy management | One of the IT financial management activities with the specific objective to define and maintain the related policies. |
| Pricing | One of the IT financial management activities with the objective to determine the selling price of IT services. |
| Profit and loss statement | A financial report used to provide evidence of company performance. It can be referred to any evaluated object, such as the whole company, a department or function (such as IT), a cost center, a customer, a product or service, etc. |
| Profit center | In the IT service management context, this is a type of IT organization that acts as a business in its own right, although its objectives are set by the organization as a whole. IT is run as a business with profit objectives. In accounting, this is a classification of an organizational unit that is responsible for profit and therefore for both costs and revenues. |
| Projects IN Controlled Environment 2 (PRINCE2) | The standard UK government methodology for project management. See http://www.ogc.gov.uk/prince2/ for more information. |
| RACI | According to ITIL V3, this is defined as 'a model used to help define roles and responsibilities. RACI stands for Responsible, Accountable, Consulted and Informed.' |

| | |
|---|---|
| Recovery center | Where an IT unit analyses its full expenditure and investments so that they may be recovered from customers, usually by formal charging but without profit. |
| Request For Change (RFC) | In ITIL V3, this is defined as 'a formal proposal for a change to be made. An RFC includes details of the proposed change, and may be recorded on paper or electronically.' |
| Return On Investment (ROI) | An investment appraisal technique. |
| Revenue center | A classification of an organizational unit that is responsible for revenues. |
| Scenario(s) | In this book we use the term 'scenario' to mean one of the possible contexts which influence the characteristics of IT financial management. In particular, three scenarios have been identified: 1. IT financial management for internal IT departments 2. IT financial management for internal IT service providers 3. IT financial management for market IT service providers |
| Service | See IT service. |
| Service Catalog | In ITIL V3, this is defined as 'a database or structured document with information about all live IT services, including those available for deployment'. |
| Service Improvement Plan | A formal plan to implement improvements to a process, practice, or IT service. |
| Service level | In ITIL V3, this is defined as 'measured and reported achievement against one or more service level targets. The term "service level" is sometimes used informally to mean "service level target".' |
| Service Level Agreement (SLA) | In ITIL V3, this is defined as 'an agreement between an IT service provider and a customer. The SLA describes the IT service, documents service level targets, and specifies the responsibilities of the IT service provider and the customer. A single SLA may cover multiple IT services or multiple customers.' |
| Service level management | In ITIL V3, this is defined as "The process responsible for negotiating Service Level Agreements, and ensuring that these are met". Service level management is responsible for ensuring that all IT service management activities, Operational Level Agreements, and Underpinning Contracts are appropriate for the agreed service level targets. Service level management monitors and reports on service levels, and holds regular customer reviews. |
| Service level manager | Process owner of service level management process. |
| Service level target | According to ITIL V3, this is defined as 'a commitment that is documented in a Service Level Agreement'. |
| Service portfolio | According to ITIL V3, this is defined as 'the complete set of services that are managed by a service provider'. |
| Service portfolio management | According to ITIL V3, this is defined as 'the process responsible for managing the service portfolio. Service portfolio management considers services in terms of the business value that they provide.' |
| Service provider | In ITIL V3, this is defined as 'an organization supplying services to one or more internal customers or external customers. "Service provider" is often used as an abbreviation for "IT service provider".' |
| Software Asset Management (SAM) | According to ITIL V2, this is defined as 'Software Asset Management (SAM), which is all of the infrastructure and processes necessary for the effective management, control and protection of the software assets within an organization, throughout all stages of their lifecycle'. |
| Standard cost | According to ITIL V2, this is defined as 'a pre-determined calculation of how much costs should be under specified working conditions. It is built up from an assessment of the value of cost elements and correlates technical specifications and the quantification of materials, labor and other costs to the prices and/or wages expected to apply during the period in which the standard cost is intended to be used. Its main purposes are to provide bases for control through variance accounting, for the valuation of work in progress and for fixing selling prices.' |

| | |
|---|---|
| Statement of Requirements (SoR) | According to ITIL V3, this is defined as 'a document containing all requirements for a product purchase, or a new or changed IT service'. |
| Supplier | According to ITIL V3, this is defined as 'a third party responsible for supplying goods or services that are required to deliver IT services'. |
| Technical service | An IT service that is not known by customer(s) and is supporting other IT services. |
| Technical Service Catalog | Part of the Service Catalog containing those IT services not directly visible to the customers but supporting other IT services. |
| Third party | According to ITIL V3, this is defined as 'a person, group, or business that is not part of the Service Level Agreement for an IT service, but is required to ensure successful delivery of that IT service. For example a software supplier, a hardware maintenance company, or a facilities department. Requirements for third parties are typically specified in underpinning contracts or Operational Level Agreements.' |
| Total Cost of Ownership (TCO) | In ITIL V3, this is defined as 'a methodology used to help make investment decisions. TCO assesses the full lifecycle cost of owning a configuration item, not just the initial cost or purchase price.' |
| Transfer price | The amount recorded in a company's accounting records when one business unit sells (transfers) a good or service to another one. |
| Underpinning contract | According to ITIL V3, this is defined as 'a contract between an IT service provider and a third party. The third party provides goods or services that support delivery of an IT service to a customer. The underpinning contract defines targets and responsibilities that are required to meet agreed service level targets in an SLA.' |
| User | According to ITIL V3, a user is defined as 'a person who uses the IT service on a day-to-day basis. Users are distinct from customers, as some customers do not use the IT service directly.' |
| Variance analysis | According to ITIL V2, this is defined as 'an analysis of the factors that have caused the difference between the pre-determined standards and the actual results'. |
| Annual closure | One of the accounting activities with the objective to determine and report actual costs and revenues relating to IT at the end of the budget year. |

# 9.2 Acronyms list

| | |
|---|---|
| BSC | Balanced Scorecard |
| BU | Business unit |
| CAB | Change Advisory Board |
| CFO | Chief Financial Officer |
| CI | Configuration item |
| CIO | Chief Information Officer |
| CMDB | Configuration Management Data Base |
| CMM | Capability Maturity Model |
| CMMI | Capability Maturity Model Integration |
| CobiT | Control Objectives for Information and related Technology |
| CSI | Continual Service Improvement |
| DCF | Discounted Cash Flow |
| FD | Financial department |
| GAAP | General Accepted Accounting Principles |
| GAS | General Accounting System |
| IAS | International Accounting Standards |
| IASB | International Accounting Standards Board |
| IFRS | International Financial Reporting Standards |
| IRR | Internal Rate of Return |
| IT | Information Technology |
| ITFC | IT financial controller |
| ITFM | IT financial management |
| ITIL | IT Infrastructure Library |
| KPI | Key Performance Indicator |
| MAS | Management Accounting System |
| NPV | Net Present Value |
| OLA | Operational Level Agreement |
| PDCA | Plan-Do-Check-Act |
| PMF | Process Maturity Framework |
| PRINCE2 | Projects IN Controlled Environments 2 |
| P&L | Profit and loss statement |
| RFC | Request For Change |
| ROI | Return On Investment |
| ROIC | Return On Invested Capital |
| SAM | Software Asset Management |
| SIP | Service Improvement Plan |
| SLA | Service Level Agreement |
| SoR | Statement of Requirements |
| TCO | Total Cost of Ownership |

# 10 Templates

## 10.1 Levels of maturity according to the Process Maturity Framework

This section illustrates the characteristics of the maturity levels according to the process maturity framework as described in ITIL V3. The maturity framework is aligned with the Software Engineering Institute Capability Maturity Model® Integration (SEI CMMI) and their various maturity models including the evolving CMMI-SVC, which focuses on the delivery of services.

### 10.1.1 Initial (Level 1)

The process has been recognized but there is little or no process management activity and it is allocated no importance, resources or focus within the organization. This level can also be described as 'ad hoc' or occasionally even 'chaotic'.

| Vision and steering | Minimal funds and resources with little activity<br>Results temporary, not retained<br>Sporadic reports and reviews |
|---|---|
| Process | Loosely defined processes and procedures, used reactively when problems occur<br>Totally reactive processes<br>Irregular, unplanned activities |
| People | Loosely defined roles or responsibilities |
| Technology | Manual processes or a few specific, discrete tools (pockets/islands) |
| Culture | Tool and technology-based and driven with a strong activity focus |

Table 10.1 PMF Level 1: initial (source OGC)

### 10.1.2 Repeatable (Level 2)

The process has been recognized and is allocated little importance, resource or focus within the operation. Generally activities related to the process are uncoordinated, irregular, without direction and are directed towards process effectiveness.

| Vision and steering | No clear objectives or formal targets<br>Funds and resources available<br>Irregular, unplanned activities, reporting and reviews |
|---|---|
| Process | Defined processes and procedures<br>Largely reactive process<br>Irregular, unplanned activities |
| People | Self-contained roles and responsibilities |
| Technology | Many discrete tools, but a lack of control<br>Data stored in separate locations |
| Culture | Product and service-based and driven |

Table 10.2 PMF Level 2: repeatable (source OGC)

### 10.1.3  Defined (Level 3)

The process has been recognized and is documented but there is no formal agreement, acceptance or recognition of its role within the IT operation as a whole. However, the process has a process owner, formal objectives and targets with allocated resources, and is focused on the efficiency as well as the effectiveness of the process. Reports and results are stored for future reference.

| Vision and steering | Documented and agreed formal objectives and targets<br>Formally published, monitored and reviewed plans<br>Well-funded and appropriately resourced<br>Regular, planned reporting and reviews |
|---|---|
| Process | Clearly defined and well-publicized processes and procedures<br>Regular, planned activities<br>Good documentation<br>Occasionally proactive process |
| People | Clearly defined and agreed roles and responsibilities<br>Formal objectives and targets<br>Formalized process training plans |
| Technology | Continuous data collection with alarm and threshold monitoring<br>Consolidated data retained and used for formal planning, forecasting and trending |
| Culture | Service and customer-oriented with a formalized approach |

Table 10.3 PMF Level 3: defined (source OGC)

### 10.1.4  Managed (Level 4)

The process has now been fully recognized and accepted throughout the IT organization. It is service focused and has objectives and targets that are based on business objectives and goals. The process is fully defined, managed and has become proactive, with documented, established interfaces and dependencies with other IT process.

| Vision and steering | Clear direction with business goals, objectives and formal targets, measured progress<br>Effective management reports actively used<br>Integrated process plans linked to business and IT plans<br>Regular improvements, planned and reviewed |
|---|---|
| Process | Well-defined processes, procedures and standards, included in all IT staff job descriptions<br>Clearly defined process interfaces and dependencies<br>Integrated service management and systems development processes<br>Mainly proactive process |
| People | Inter- and intra-process team working<br>Responsibilities clearly defined in all IT job descriptions |
| Technology | Continuous monitoring measurement, reporting and threshold alerting to a centralized set of integrated toolsets, databases and processes |
| Culture | business focused with an understanding of the wider issues |

Table 10.4 PMF Level 4: managed (source OGC)

### 10.1.5  Optimizing (Level 5)

The process has now been fully recognized and has strategic objectives and goals aligned with overall strategic business and IT goals. These have now become 'institutionalized' as part of the everyday activity for everyone involved with the process. A self-contained continual process of improvement is established as part of the process, which is now developing a pre-emptive capability.

| Vision and steering | Integrated strategic plans inextricably linked with overall business plans, goals and objectives<br>Continuous monitoring, measurement, reporting alerting and reviews linked to a continual process of improvement<br>Regular reviews and/or audits for effectiveness, efficiency and compliance |
|---|---|
| Process | Well-defined processes and procedures part of corporate culture<br>Proactive and pre-emptive process |
| People | Business aligned objectives and formal targets actively monitored as part of the everyday activity<br>Roles and responsibilities part of an overall corporate culture |
| Technology | Well-documented overall tool architecture with complete integration in all areas of people, processes and technology |
| Culture | A continual improvement attitude, together with a strategic business focus. An understanding of the value of IT to the business and its ole within the business alue chain |

Table 10.5 PMF Level 5: optimizing (source OGC)

# 10.2  ISO/IEC 20000 for IT financial management

The relationship between IT financial and ISO/IEC 20000 has already been briefly introduced in 7.5.5. Here, we want to briefly summarize the contents of the standard inherent IT financial management, which is mainly discussed in clause 6.4 budgeting and accounting for IT services of part one and part two of the standard. Part one contains the SHALLs, those elements that are mandatory to be compliant and certified according to ISO/IEC 20000, while part two contains the SHOULDs, the good practices that should be adopted relating to the subject.

## 10.2.1 Content of SHALLs
Part one of ISO/IEC 20000 requires:
• budgeting and accounting for the cost of service provision
• existence of policies and processes
• sufficient detail of costs to enable financial control and decision making
• monitoring and reporting of actual costs against budget and forecasting
• assessment of financial impact of all changes through the change management process

Some important aspects can also be derived from the 'shall' concerning policies:
• budgeting and accounting for all IT components is required
• costs shall be either direct or indirectly apportioned to services

## 10.2.2 Content of SHOULDs
Part two of ISO/IEC 20000 recommends:
• full understanding of charging mechanisms by involved parties (when charging is performed)

- taking into consideration general accounting practices of the whole of the service provider's organization
- policies should define the level of detail of budgeting and accounting considering cost types to be managed, apportionment of overhead costs, granularity of the customers' business, rules governing the variances against budget, links to service level management
- the level of investment in processes should be based on the needs of the customers, service provider and suppliers of financial details
- budgeting should take into account planned changes to services and manage shortfalls if any
- cost tracking against the budget should provide early warning of variances
- decision about service provision should be based on cost effectiveness comparisons
- cost models should be able to demonstrate the costs of service provision
- accounts should demonstrate over and under-spending and the costs of low service levels or loss of service

## 10.3  CobiT and IT financial management

CobiT is a very popular and widely adopted control framework for IT governance, which has now reached version 4.1. IT governance is the responsibility of executives and the board of directors, and consists of the leadership, organizational structures and processes that ensure that the enterprise's IT sustains and extends the organization's strategies and objectives.

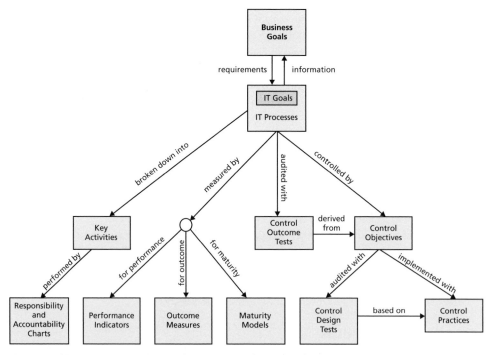

Figure 10.1 CobiT 4.1 components and relationships among them (source ISACA)

The key components of the model are processes. The framework identifies 34 of them, grouped in four domains:
- **Plan and Organize (PO)** – provides direction to solution delivery (AI) and service delivery (DS)
- **Acquire and Implement (AI)** – provides the solutions and passes them to be turned into services
- **Deliver and Support (DS)** – receives the solutions and makes them usable for end users
- **Monitor and Evaluate (ME)** – monitors all processes to ensure that the direction provided is followed.

For each process, CobiT provides useful information and inputs to control it and also, to some extent, to design. In particular, there are key activities, RACI (responsibility and accountability charts), performance indicators and a maturity model.

Some of the 34 processes are strictly related to IT financial management, in particular:
- PO5 Manage the IT Investment
- DS6 Identify and Allocate Costs.

### 10.3.1 PO5 Manage the IT Investment

This process is aimed at continuously and demonstrably improving IT's cost-efficiency and its contribution to business profitability with integrated and standardized services that satisfy end-user expectations. Activities performed are:
- maintain the program portfolio
- maintain the project portfolio
- maintain the service portfolio
- establish and maintain the IT budgeting process
- identify, communicate and monitor IT investments, cost and value to business.

If compared to the activity reference schema described in Chapter 4, the last two activities correspond to:
- investment evaluation
- annual budget
- budget review
- periodic forecast
- delta management

Management of portfolios is not a topic discussed in this book; it has been considered as part of strategic activities (see Figure 4.6).

### 10.3.2 DS6 Identify and Allocate Costs

This process is aimed at ensuring transparency and understanding of IT costs and improving cost-efficiency through well-informed use of IT services. Activities are:
- map the IT infrastructure to services provided/business processes supported
- identify all IT costs (e.g., people, technology) and map them to IT services on a unit cost basis
- establish and maintain an IT accounting and cost control process
- establish and maintain charging policies and procedures.

If compared to the activity reference schema described in Chapter 4, this corresponds to:
- periodic closure
- annual closure
- charging.

DS6 is also concerned with the definition and maintenance of the cost model. In this book, managing the cost model is spread among different practices and activities: policy management, IT financial management design and continual improvement. Defining the cost model is an initial and an ongoing activity of IT financial management.

Mapping the IT infrastructure with services has not been described in this book as it has been considered a task of configuration management, one of the core IT service management processes.

## 10.4 Techniques enabling improvement

### 10.4.1 Assessments

Assessments are the formal mechanisms for comparing the operational process environment to the performance standards for the purpose of measuring improved process capability and/or to identify potential shortcomings that could be addressed. The use of assessments has already been introduced in section 6.1 when discussing how to introduce IT financial management and, in particular, to understand and determine the initial situation. The use of best practices such as CMMI, CobiT or the process maturity framework described in section 10.1, or standards such as ISO/IEC 20000, is extremely useful to quickly identify the aspects to be assessed. Among frameworks, ISO/IEC 15504 provides a structured and complete approach for the assessment of practices. In particular, it can be used for the following purposes:
- by or on behalf of an organization with the objective of understanding the state of its own practices for improvement
- by or on behalf of an organization with the objective of determining the suitability of its own practices for a particular requirement or set of requirements
- by or on behalf of one organization with the objective of determining the suitability of another organization's practices for a particular contract or set of contracts.

The scope of the assessment can be limited to practice aspects or include people and technology. This will influence the number of attributes that will be considered for comparison with the target maturity model.

Assessments can be conducted internally (self-assessment) or by external people. Table 10.6 shows the advantages and disadvantages of each approach. Whatever the approach, assessments offer significant benefits:
- they can provide an objective perspective of the current operational practice state compared to a standard maturity model and a process framework. Through a thorough assessment, an accurate determination of any practice gaps can be quickly completed, recommendations put forward and action steps planned

- a well-planned and well-conducted assessment is a repeatable practice. Thus assessment is a useful management practice in measuring practice over time and in establishing improvement targets or objectives
- using a common or universally accepted maturity framework, applied to a standard process framework, can serve to support comparing the organization's process maturity to industry benchmarks.

| Using external resources for assessments | |
|---|---|
| **Pro:** | **Con:** |
| Objectivity<br>Expert ITIL knowledge<br>Brod exposure to multiple IT organizations<br>Analytical skills<br>Credibility<br>Minimal Impact to coperations | Cost<br>Risk of acceptance<br>Limited knowledge of existing environments<br>Improper preparation affects effectiveness |
| **Performing self-essessments** | |
| **Pro:** | **Con:** |
| No expensive consultants<br>Self-assessments available for free<br>Promotes Internal cooperation and communication<br>Good place to get started<br>Internal knowledge of environment | Lack of objectivity (internal agendas)<br>Little acceptance of findings<br>Internal politics<br>Limited knowledge or skills<br>Resource Intensive |

Table 10.6 Comparison of external versus internal assessments (source OGC)

There are some possible issues in performing assessments:
- an assessment provides only a snapshot in time of the practice environment. If the context is dynamic, it is probably not the main technique to be adopted for continual monitoring.
- The assessment can become an end in itself rather than the means to an end. Rather than focusing on improving the efficiency and effectiveness of practices through practice improvement, organizations can adopt a mindset of improving practices for the sake of achieving maturity targets
- assessments are labor-intensive efforts. Resources are needed to conduct the assessments in addition to those responding such as practice or tool practitioners, management and others. When preparing for an assessment, there should be an honest estimate of the time required from all parties
- assessments attempt to be as objective as possible in terms of measurements and assessment factors, but assessment results are still subject to the opinion of assessors. Thus, assessments are subjective and the results can have a bias based on the attitudes, experience and approach of the assessors
- without responsibilities in place for continual improvement and clear objectives, follow-up and corrective actions may remain still.

Assessments can be used as a starting point of the seven-step improvement process (Figure 6.4), replacing or reinforcing a Balanced Scorecard.

## 10.4.2 Auditing

Auditing is a term that can be used in several contexts. In financial management, it is normally interpreted as a systematic practice of objectively obtaining and evaluating evidence on assertions about economic actions and events to ascertain the degree of correspondence between those assertions and established criteria and communicating the results to interested users. In this context, audit is to be considered a financial (not IT financial) topic and is normally executed every year in many organizations, as it becomes a mandatory practice depending on the organization's size and local rules.

In the audit activity, always performed with appropriate segregation of duties and independence, the assertions about which the auditor seeks objective evidence relate to the reliability and integrity of financial and, occasionally, operating information. The examination of the objective evidence underlying the financial data may identify errors to be rectified and suggestions for improving the practices. This clearly applies to IT financial data and to IT financial management practices as well.

Another context where the term auditing is used is in information systems auditing. In this domain, auditing is a systematic and documented activity, performed by skilled people, with the objective to verify that the information systems of an organization are compliant with norms, internal regulations and/or policies. The auditing activity usually has two core objectives:
- to verify that information computed by systems is correct and complete
- to assure that information systems are reliable and secure.

Information systems audit is often part of a larger internal auditing department. The frequency of audits is dependent on the objectives and previously met problems but, typically, it is performed at least once a year. Information systems audit is focused on the systems used by the business and on the activities that are executed by the IT department to govern the provision of services. Information systems auditors generally use CobiT best practices to verify how well the information system is controlled. This is possible by means of CobiT's control objectives, which provide the critical insight needed to delineate a clear policy and good practice for IT controls. Included in the framework are the statements of desired results or purposes to be achieved by implementing the 214 specific and detailed control objectives throughout the 34 high-level IT practices. This includes the control objectives for IT financial management practices, detailed in processes PO5 Manage the IT Investment and DS6 Identify and Allocate Costs of the framework. CobiT provides a maturity model for processes and an approach to derive the relevant control objectives, starting from business goals and passing through IT goals. It also provides a complete set of metrics, helpful to measure performances of practices.

By means of CobiT, information systems auditing is able to understand and to agree with business management which controls for which IT practices should be implemented. Using these targets and verifying the status of implementation creates a concrete opportunity to improve IT practices, keeping them aligned with business objectives and needs.

## 10.4.3 Benchmarking

Benchmarking (also known as 'best practice benchmarking' or 'process benchmarking') is an activity used in management, particularly strategic management, in which different organizations evaluate various aspects of their practices in relation to best practices, usually within their own sector. This enables organizations to develop plans on how to adopt such best practices, usually with the aim of increasing some aspects of performance. Benchmarking may be a one-time event, but is often treated as a continual process in which organizations continually seek to challenge their practices.

Benchmarking can be focused on specific areas, for example IT financial management, and it involves cooperation with others as benchmarking partners learn from each other where improvements can be made. To use the benchmarking technique successfully, it is necessary to:

- ensure senior management support
- compare practices, not outputs – comparisons with organizations in the same sector are unlikely to identify the significant improvements that have been made elsewhere or overturn the conventions of the sector
- involve practice owners – their involvement encourages acceptance and buy-in by those who will be affected immediately by the changes required to improve performance
- set up benchmarking teams – as a benchmarking culture develops, people will apply the method as part of the normal way in which they manage their work
- acquire the skills – people who undertake benchmarking require a small amount of training and guidance; an experienced in-house facilitator or external consultant will probably be required to provide technical assurance and encouragement in the application of the method.

Benchmarking may involve several parties, depending on the scenario adopted: the customer (who pays for IT services), the user or consumer of IT services, the internal service provider, its suppliers and benchmarking partners. It can be applied at various levels from relatively straightforward in-house comparisons through to an industry-wide search for best practice. We will now explore the seven-step improvement process (Figure 6.4), executed by means of the benchmarking technique:

What should we measure?
- Draw up a preliminary list of potential benchmarking partners (these may be within the organization or outside).
- Within IT financial management, define the activities to be benchmarked (such as budgeting activity).
- Identify suitable Key Performance Indicators.

What can we measure?
- Check the availability of resources required for the study.
- Check the availability of benchmarking partners.
- Confirm the key performance measures or indicators.
- Agree the plan and its implementation.

Gathering and processing:
- Collect information about key performance measure or indicators.
- Compute and share benchmarking information among partners.

Analyzing:
- Confirm the best potential benchmarking partner and make a preliminary assessment of gaps.
- Establish contacts and visits, if appropriate, to validate and substantiate the information.
- Compare the existing practice with that of the benchmarking partner to identify differences and innovations.
- Agree targets for improvement that are expected as a result of adopting the benchmarking partner's ways of doing things.

Presenting and using information:
- Communicate the results of the study throughout the relevant parts of the organization and to the benchmarking partner.
- Plan how to achieve the improvements.

Taking corrective action:
- Identify and rectify anything that may have caused the organization to fall short of its target.
- Communicate the results of the changes implemented to the organization and the benchmarking partner.
- Consider benchmarking again to continue the improvement.

Benchmarking is a moderately expensive activity. The three main types of costs are visit costs, time costs (effort of people involved in data collection and analysis), benchmarking database costs (creation and maintenance of a database containing the data of all participants).

### 10.4.4 Six Sigma

Six Sigma is a methodology, existing since 1986, that can be used to improve any kind of practices, including IT practices. Sigma is a statistical measure of standard deviation from a 'normal' or statistical population. In lay terms, achieving six sigma of accuracy in the construction of a product adhering to Six Sigma methodology would translate into incurring no more than 3.4 defects per million opportunities. In some context, for example manufacturing, six sigma becomes a target to achieve as the number of executions of the activities is very high. In our domain, IT financial management, this is not applicable as the number of instances of activities is much lower (such as budgeting, performed once a year). However, the method may be applicable with more realistic objectives, especially when activities have a quantitatively relevant number of instances.

We will not enter into further details of the methodology, which may be found in literature (Boer, 2006). The key point is that Six Sigma can support the execution of the seven steps of process improvement (Figure 6.4) with a structured and clear set of activities and techniques.

### 10.4.5 ISO/IEC 20000

ISO/IEC 20000 is the first international standard for IT service management and is composed of two parts. Part one, Specification, defines the requirements for a service provider to deliver managed services of an acceptable quality for its customers. To be compliant with the ISO/IEC 20000 standard, these requirements *shall* be satisfied. Part two, Code of Practice, describes the best practices for service management within the scope of part one. These recommended practices *should* be adopted by a service provider.

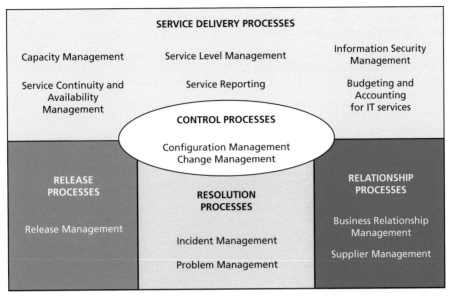

Figure 10.2 Service management practices of ISO/IEC 20000

Figure 10.2 shows the service management practices that are included in the standard. Many of these derive from ITIL V2 service support and service delivery practices. Two activities (budgeting and accounting for IT services), belonging to IT financial management, are included. In particular, the requirements for these activities are stated in section 6.4 of part one and the implementation guidelines in section 6.4 of part two. Since charging is an optional activity, the standard does not cover it.

The standard adds three important sections of requirements to those dedicated to the activities: planning and implementing service management, requirements for a management system and, finally, planning and implementing new or changed services.

The aims of the standard are multiple:
- to be used as a guide to procuring services
- to align the approaches of multiple IT services suppliers in a supply chain
- to benchmark
- as the basis for independent assessments
- to demonstrate the commitment to provide services that meet customer requirements
- to improve service through the effective application of practices to monitor and improve service quality.

As ISO/IEC 20000 contains some IT financial management activities, in particular budgeting and accounting, it can be used for many of the aims above listed in these domains.

The standard is suitable to be required for suppliers of IT organizations in Scenario 1, and to be adopted by IT service providers in Scenario 2 and, especially, Scenario 3.

Section 7.4 has described a possible approach for continual practice improvement based on the Plan-Do-Check-Act methodology (the Deming cycle). Section 4 of the standard, 'Planning and implementing service management', is focused on the service improvement cycle, performed on the basis of the same methodology (see Figure 10.3).

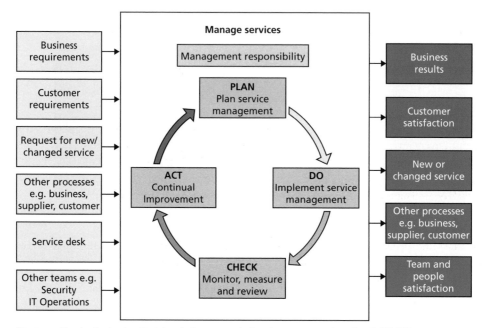

Figure 10.3 Plan-do-check-act methodology for improvement of service management practices in ISO/IEC 20000

ISO/IEC 20000 provides specific requirements (part one, section 4) and guidelines (part two, section 4) for each step of the Deming cycle, thus providing practical guidance in order to continually improve service management activities, including budgeting and accounting.

# Appendix A. Basic concepts for IT service management

A major aspect and benefit of ITIL is that it provides a common glossary and standard jargon that can be used across the IT service management industry. ITIL terminology is predominantly used in this book.

## A1. Good Practice

Good practices such as ITIL, which have been adopted by many, can be used as a solid basis for organizations that want to improve their IT services. A good approach is to select widely available frameworks and/or standards, such as ITIL, CobiT, CMMI, PRINCE2® and ISO/ IEC 20000. All of these can be applied to many different real-life environments and situations. Training is also widely available, making it much easier to develop staff with the required knowledge and skills.

Proprietary knowledge is often claimed to be good practice, however it is often customized for the context and needs of a specific organization. Therefore, it may be difficult to adopt or replicate, particularly where multiple suppliers are involved, and therefore it may not be as effective in use.

## A2. Service

A service creates value for the customer. ITIL describes a service as follows:

A **service** is a means of delivering value to customers by facilitating outcomes the customers want to achieve without the ownership of specific costs or risks.

Outcomes (or outputs) are made possible by the performance of tasks. They are often limited in what they can achieve by a number of constraints. Services enhance performance and can reduce the pressure of constraints. This increases the chances of the desired outcomes being realized.

ITIL V3 has the concept of a Service Portfolio and The Service Catalogue. The Service Portfolio includes all services that are in development, in live use, or retired. The Service Catalogue represents the services that are available to the customers.

## A3. Value

Value is the core of the ITIL service concept.

From the customer's perspective **value** consists of two core components: **utility** and **warranty**. Utility is what the customer receives, and warranty is how it is provided[1].

Another way of looking at this is to consider the following:
- Utility = fit for purpose. Does it meet the specification?
- Warranty = fit for use. Will it perform, will it be available when required?

## A4. Service management

ITIL describes service management as follows:

**Service management** is a set of specialized organizational capabilities for providing value to customers in the form of services.

## A5. Systems

ITIL describes the organizational structure concepts which proceed from system theory. The service lifecycle in ITIL V3 is a system; however, a function, a process or an organization is a system as well. A definition of a system is the following.

A **system** is a group of, interrelating, or interdependent components that form a unified whole, operating together for a common purpose.

*Feedback* and *learning* are two key aspects in the performance of systems; they turn processes, functions and organizations into dynamic systems. Feedback can lead to learning and growth, not only within a process, but also within an organization in its entirety. Within a process, for instance, the feedback about the performance of one cycle is, in its turn, input for the next process cycle. Within organizations, there can be feedback between processes, functions and lifecycle phases. Behind this feedback is the common goal: attaining the customer's objectives.

## A6. Processes versus functions

The distinction between functions and processes is important in ITIL. So what exactly is a function?

---

[1] The concepts utility and warranty are described in the ITIL version three book "Service Strategy".

A **function** is a subdivision of an organization that is specialized in fulfilling a specified type of work, and is responsible for specific end results.

Functions are independent subdivisions with capabilities and resources that are required for their performance and results. They have their own practices and their own knowledge body.

And what is a process?

A **process** is a sequence of interrelated or interacting activities designed to accomplish a defined objective in a measurable and repeatable manner, transforming inputs into outputs.

Processes convert inputs to outputs, and ultimately into outcomes. They use measures to assist control and as feedback for self-improvement. Processes possess the following characteristics:

- They are **measurable** because they are performance-oriented.
- They have **specific results**.
- They provide results to **customers or stakeholders**.
- They **respond to a specific event** – a process is indeed continual and iterative, but is always originating from a certain event.

Changing to a process based structure in an organization often shows that certain activities in the organization are uncoordinated, duplicated, neglected or unnecessary.

When arranging activities into processes, you should not use the existing allocation of tasks into an organizational structure as a basis. Instead, start with the **objective** of the process and the **relationships** with other processes. As the definition states, a process is a series of activities carried out to convert input into an output, and ultimately into an outcome; see the ITOCO model (Input-Throughput-Output-Control-Outcome) in Figure A.1.

The **input** to a process describes the resources that are used and changed or consumed by the process. The **output** describes the immediate results of the process, while the **outcome** describes the long-term results of the process in terms of meaningful effect. **Control** activities are used to ensure that the process achieves the desired output and outcomes, and complies with **policies and standards.** Controls also regulate the input and the **throughput**, ensuring that the throughput or output parameters are compliant with these standards and policies.

These individual processes are built together into process chains. These show what inputs goes into the organization, and what the outputs and outcomes are. They also provide suitable monitoring points to check the quality of the products and services provided by the organization.

The standards for the output of each process must be defined, so that the complete **chain of processes** in the **process model** meets the corporate objective. If the output of a process meets the defined requirements, then the process is **effective** in transforming its input into its output. To be really effective, the outcome should be taken into consideration rather than focusing on the output. If the activities in the process are also carried out with the minimum required effort and cost, then the process is **efficient**. It is the task of process management to use **planning and control** to ensure that processes are executed in an effective and efficient way.

Each process can be studied separately to optimize its quality. The **process owner** is responsible for the process results. The **process manager** is responsible for the realization and structure of the process, and reports to the process owner. The **process operatives** are responsible for defined activities, and these activities are reported to the process manager.

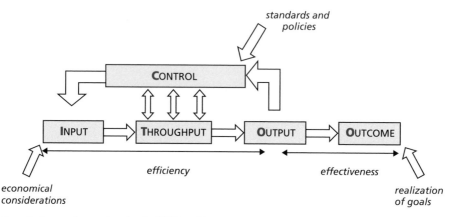

Figure A.1 Process diagram, based on the ITOCO-model[2]

Processes are composed of two kinds of activities: the activities to realize the goal (operational activities concerned with the throughput), and the activities to manage these (control activities). See Figure A.1. The control activities make sure the operational activities (the workflow) are performed to time, in the right order, etc. (For example, in the processing of changes it is always ensured that a test is performed *before* a release is taken into production and not *afterwards*.)

According to the ITOCO model:
– processes have inputs and outputs
– they can be adjusted by means of feedback and comparison against standards
– they can be rendered more specific by conversion to procedures and work instructions
– various roles are distinguished in relation to processes (e.g. owner, manager, executor).

## A7. Process models

The **process model** is at least as important as the **processes** because processes must be deployed in the right relationships to achieve the desired effect of a process-focused approach. There are many different process models available. A master process architecture should be defined before individual processes are designed.

A **process architecture** identifies the processes and process clusters, their interdependencies and interactions, their relationship to the IT organization structure, and the IT process-supporting application architecture.

---

[2]   Source: Foundations of IT Service management, based on ITIL V3. Van Haren Publishing, 2008.

Organizations should use standard methodologies for creating process diagrams. In-house developed methodologies are often difficult to interpret in an unambiguous manner.

The Business Process Modeling world offers various methods to create process diagrams, such as the Unified Modeling Language (UML), the Business Process Modeling Notation (BPMN), and the Business Process Execution Language for Web Services (BPEL-WS). Other systems design approaches can be used to create process diagrams such as the CCTA/OGC SSADM or the USA DOD IDEF methods. Figures A.2 and A.3 are examples of the BPMN method.

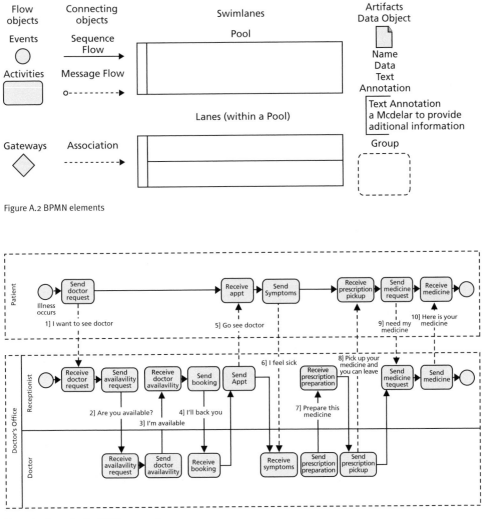

Figure A.2 BPMN elements

Figure A.3 Example of a BPMN process diagram

When described this way, it is easier to visualise and therefore manage a process. This is particularly true when processes are brought together in a process chain. Note that ITIL does not give much attention to creating these process chains.

An organization no longer stands out because of its unique IT management processes, but because of the extent to which these processes are truly controlled. It is therefore critical that organizations consider and build their own efficient process chains for IT service management, adopting and adapting the standard processes contained in available good practices.

In practice, there are many process models available in the form of supplier-based products. Unfortunately, the details of most of these models are not publicly available. This means that many organizations turn to developing their own based on the available non-proprietary schemas included in publicly available frameworks such as CobiT and ITIL V3.

## ISO/IEC 20000 clustering
ISO/IEC 20000 imposed clear clustering on its practices, see Figure A.4. The operations practices are out-of-scope in ISO/IEC 20000.

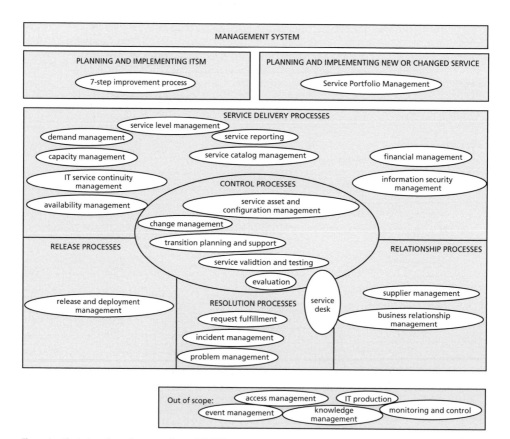

Figure A.4 Clustering of practices according to ISO/IEC 20000

## ITIL V3 lifecycle clustering
The lifecycle concept of ITIL V3 consists of five phases in IT service management control. Each of these phases describes several practices ('processes'), functions and 'miscellaneous activities'. Many of these practices are applied across more than one lifecycle phase, see Figure A.5.

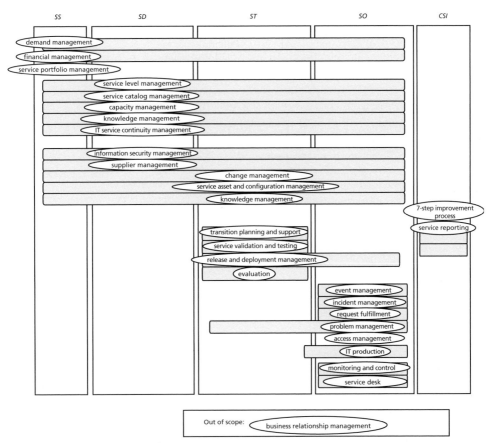

Figure A.5 Clustering of practices according to ITIL V3

# A8. Processes, procedures and work instructions

The management of the organization can provide control over the quality of each process using data from the results of each process. In most cases, the relevant **performance indicators** and standards will already be agreed. The day-to-day control of the process is then left to the process manager. The process owner will assess the results based on a **report** of performance indicators against the agreed standard. Clear indicators enable a process owner to determine if the process is under control, and if implemented improvements have been successful.

Processes are often described using **procedures** and **work instructions**, in accordance with the ISO 9001 Quality management System model (Figure A.6).

*A **procedure** is a specified way to carry out an activity or a process.*
*A procedure describes the 'how', and can also describe 'who' carries the activities out. A procedure may include stages from different processes. A procedure can vary depending on the organization. A set of **work instructions** defines how one or more activities in a procedure should be carried out in detail, using technology or other resources.*

Figure A.6 Process documentation in the ISO 9001 Quality Model[3]

It can be difficult to determine whether something is a function or a process. A good example of a function is a service desk, a group of people executing the same set of processes, normally in the same department. A good example of a process is change management, where multiple people are involved who generally work for different departments. A practical guideline, based on ISO 9001, is to consider the contribution of people, process and technology to the subject. A process would only cover activities, a procedure would involve the people factor, and a work instruction would also involve the technology (see Figure A.7).

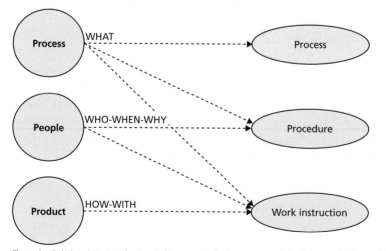

Figure A.7 Relations between the People/Process/Product paradigm and the ISO 9001 Quality Model[4]

3   Tricker, R., 2006. ISO 9001:2000 The Quality Management Process. Van Haren Publishing.
4   Source: Hoving, W. and J. van Bon, 2008. Functions and Processes in IT Management. In: J. van Bon (ed.), IT Service Management, global best practices, Volume 1, pp 363-384. Van

In practice, it is not the process that instructs the people in an organization on a day-to-day basis, it is the procedure and the work instructions. Processes only show how the logic in a procedure is constructed, but they don't tell you who should do what/when/how. However, if you don't understand your processes and build your procedures from those processes, then procedures will often be inconsistent with related and interconnected procedures. Also, the reason for the design of a procedure will not be clear. This means that – before you can construct or improve a set of procedures that determine your effectiveness and efficiency – you must have your process system in place, and people must understand its basics.

## A9.   Process and line in a matrix organization

The hierarchical structure of functions can lead to the creation of 'silos' in which each function is very self-oriented. This does not benefit the success of the organization as a whole. Processes run through the hierarchical structure of functions; functions often share some processes. This is how processes suppress the rise of functional silos, and help to ensure an improved coordination in between functions.

Organizations manage their activities from two perspectives: **process management** and **line management**. An organization using process management structures its activities in a neat series of processes, so that 'floating' or 'orphan' activities are eliminated. This way, the structure of the organization enforces the need to follow the processes. And since processes are generally accepted as the efficient and effective way to organize activities, this will support the organization's performance.

An organization using line management will also manage their activities in organizational structures: teams, departments, sections, business units. These structures are normally ordered along some kind of hierarchy. This way, the organization makes sure that it is clear how activities are allocated to organizational responsibilities.

If an activity is sufficiently important, it can be managed as part of one of the defined processes, or it can be managed from the organizational line. It is possible, and increasingly common, for activities to be managed using both of these perspectives, creating the **matrix organization**. It is important to establish to which extent an activity is managed from the process perspective and/or from the line perspective. Figure A.8 illustrates the Process Management Matrix, demonstrating how staff can be managed from different perspectives. Each individual organization can vary the extent to which it uses these two control mechanisms according to its own preferences.

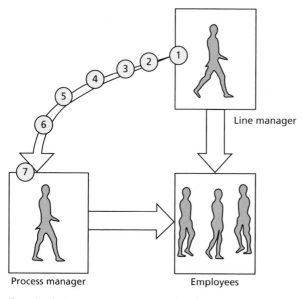

Figure A.8 The Process Management Matrix[5] (PMM)

According to the Process Management Matrix (PMM), the mix of the two 'pure' control models can be described in seven positions:

- **The pure line organization** – Often represented as the familiar rake or tree structure. All responsibilities are cascaded from the top down; interconnection between different lines are not recognized. The line manager is responsible for controlling their team, which consists of staff or other line managers. The performance of the organization is the sum of the performance of the departments. As such, the department's result is a direct responsibility of the department managers.

- **The line organization recognizes some processes** – In terms of control, this organization is still a pure line organization. One characteristic of this variant is that it recognizes patterns in the activities of different departments that lead to positive results. By laying down these patterns in a process description, it determines which activities must be executed, their order, and the quality criteria with which they must comply. The recognized processes are often cross-departmental. In this variant, the management of the department executing the activity and the staff involved bear exclusive responsibility for correct communication and collaboration.

- **Tactical process management** – In this variant, the organization not only recognizes process-based relationships in the activities that it executes. In addition to variant two, it also decides to make someone responsible for the creation, maintenance, and reporting for the process. A key feature of this variant is that someone is appointed to this position of **process owner.** They own the process description and the manner in which the process is executed. As a result, the line management is no longer exclusively responsible for the control and results of the organization. The added value of the correct execution of well-structured processes and the negative consequences of their failure must be demonstrated not only by the process setup, but also – and especially – from the reports.

- **Operational process control** – In this variant the process management, in addition to the responsibilities from variant three, is also tasked to monitor the correct execution of the defined process setup. In this case, 'correct' means that the process is executed according to the process description, and within the constraints of the agreement with the customer. 'Monitoring', however, does not mean correcting the execution, but detecting deviations and, if necessary, escalating this information. This means that the process management must be aware of the manner in which process activities are executed. It must also report (possible) deviations from the prescribed operating method or SLAs to the stakeholders, and inform them of the situation.
- **Operational process direction** – Sometimes the organization may decide to strengthen process control by granting the process management a mandate of direction. The main characteristic of this variant is the transition in who decides and who escalates. In variant four, the staff or manager decides whether he will follow the suggestion of the process management. If the process management does not agree with the choice, it must decide whether it wishes to involve higher levels of the organization in the conflict or will accept the decision made.
- **Operational and content direction** – While less obvious, it is possible to *also* authorize process management to decide which department – and which persons in that department – must execute activities. As a result, process management is allowed to influence content-related aspects. The process management selects the most suitable department and staff member in view of the situation. In this variant, the line management's role is virtually reduced to *resource management*. The line manager must ensure that the department has adequate resources with sufficient knowledge to execute the activities. In this variant, process management decides on deployment of the resources.
- **Full process direction** – This is primarily a theoretical variant. It is the last step in allocating more responsibility to process management. This variant allocates the responsibility for resource management to process management. The result is 'process departments', meaning that all activities that must be executed for a process are executed by resources from those departments. In fact, it returns the organization to the start because it boils down to full management along one single dimension, just like the pure line management in the first variant.

For an employee, it is important to understand how these 'competing' management forces are balanced, to prevent conflicts in the prioritization of tasks. This problem grows even more severe if the same employee is also directed from a third perspective: **project management**. In PMM it is highly recommended that project management follows the balance of line and process management, running projects 'over these lines' instead of adding another competing perspective.

## A10. Process and maturity

There are two mainstream "schools" of maturity thinking. They are based on different interpretations of the term "maturity":
- **Capability maturity** – explaining how well certain activities are performed. Examples are CMMI, SPICE, the Test Process Maturity Model, the Project Effectiveness Maturity Model (PEMM), Luftman's Business IT Alignment model, and Nolan's growth model. Basically, all of

these models describe process capability levels, expressing how well processes are performed.
• **Value chain maturity** – explain how well an organization is able to contribute to a value chain. Examples of the value chain maturity school are the KPMG World Class IT maturity model (see Figure 1.12), and the INK Management Model (based on EFQM).

Combinations can also be found, e.g. in the Gartner Networking Maturity Model.

According to the quality model of EFQM (European Foundation for Quality Management, see Figure A.9), the road to 'total quality' passes through the phases *product-focused, process-focused, system-focused, chain-focused,* and *total quality-focused* ('utopia'). This means that, before being able to realize a state of continuous improvement, the organization must first have control over a number of aspects. The phase in which the organization becomes skilled in managing *processes* is crucial in the maturity approach. The organization cannot focus on systems and chains until these processes are under control.

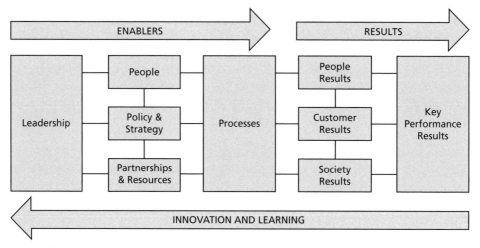

Figure A.9 The EFQM Quality Model[6]

The CMMI model (Figure A.10) also deals with the extent to which organizations control their processes. The continuous representation, for instance, is expressed through the stages *Incomplete Process, Performed Process, Managed Process, Defined Process, Quantitatively Managed Process* and *Optimizing Process.* The CMMI staged representation also defines maturity in terms of the extent to which the organization controls its processes.

---

6    The EFQM Excellence Model is a registered trademark of EFQM

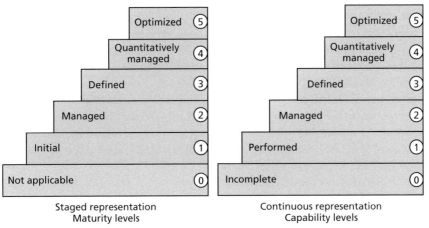

Staged representation
Maturity levels

Continuous representation
Capability levels

Figure A.10 CMMI, a maturity model for process management[7]

Processes are *internal* affairs for the IT service provider. An organization that is still trying to gain control of its processes therefore has an **internal focus**. Organizations that focus on gaining control over their systems in order to provide services, are also still internally focused. The organization is not ready for an **external focus** until it controls its services and is able to vary them on request. This external focus is required to evolve into that desirable customer-focused organization. This is expressed in the value chain maturity model (Figure A.11).

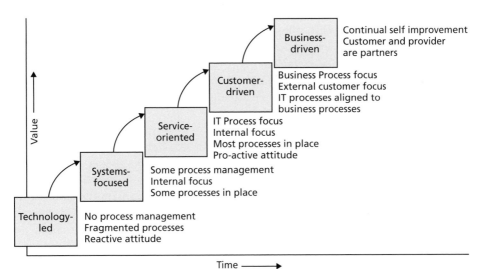

Figure A.11 Maturity in the value chain[8]

---

[7]  Capability Maturity Model and CMMI are registered in the U.S. Patent and Trademark Office by Carnegie Mellon University
[8]  Bosselaers, Theo, Mark Griep, Joost Dudok van Heel, Joachim Vandecasteele and Rob Weerts, 2000. The Future of the IT Organisation. In: J. van Bon (ed.), World Class IT Service Management Guide 2000. Ten Hagen & Stam Publishers, The Hague

Because organizations can be in different stages of maturity, IT managers require a broad orientation in their discipline. Many organizations are now working on the introduction of a process-focused or still have to start working on this. Process control is a vital step on the road towards a mature **service-oriented** and – ultimately – **customer-driven** organization.

In the last twenty years, ITIL has made an important contribution to the organization of that process-focused approach. The development started in North-Western Europe and has made progress on most other continents in the last decade. On a global scale and in hard figures, however, only a minimal number of organizations have actually started with this approach – and an even smaller number have made serious progress at this point. The organizational change projects that were thought to be necessary to convert to a process-focused organization were not all entirely successful. The majority of organizations in the world clearly require access to good information and best practices concerning the **business processes of IT organizations**. Fortunately, that information is abundant. The ITIL V2 books provide comprehensive documentation on the most important processes, while ITIL V3 adds even more information.

## A11. Core processes of a service provider

ITIL V3 acknowledges the difference between functions and processes: functions (organizational capabilities) make use of processes (repeatable strings of activities). In ITIL, the description of such functions may cover *activities* that are not covered in the description of the relevant processes.

As explained previously, what ITIL calls a 'process' does not always follow the above given definition of what a process is. One solution to this is to consider the twenty-six ITIL 'processes' as twenty-six ITIL 'practices'. For example, in ITIL Capacity management covers a range of activities that cannot be ordered as a logical and repeatable sequence of activities. As such, the ITIL context describes a capacity management practice (CMP) or function rather than a capacity management process.

By definition, the structure of a process is in fact a series of activities that are placed in a logical order: a **workflow**. This workflow is controlled by means of the **control activities**. These control activities make sure the operational activities are performed in time, in the right order, etc. (e.g. in the change management process it is always made sure that a test is performed *before* a release is put into production and not *afterwards*).

Like any other kind of service organization, an IT service provider has only a very limited set of **frequently repeated basic processes** or process groups:
- Four processes are concerned with **effectiveness**:
  - You **agree** with your customer what you will deliver ['*contract management*'].
  - You **deliver** what you have agreed ['*operations management*'].
  - You **repair** anything that goes wrong ['*incident management*'].
  - You **change** your service if this is required by your customer or by yourself ['*change management*'].

- Two processes are concerned with **efficiency**:
  - You **know** what you use to deliver your service with ['*configuration management*'].
  - You **adjust** (to) conditions that may prevent you to deliver tomorrow what you have agreed today, proactively eliminating risks that would prevent this ['*risk management*'].

This goes not only for an IT service provider, but for other service management fields as well. Imagine a catering service provider, the national post, or any other service provider: they all will perform these same basic tactical and operational processes.

For an IT organization:
- **Contract management** will cover areas of responsibility such as service level management, supplier management, business relationship management.
- **Operations management** will cover the activities required to realize the operation of the IT service, when the service is not down or changed. This would normally cover the planning and execution of all operations activities, including the monitoring of all services and components, which is the bulk of the IT provider's activities.
- **Incident management** covers anything that needs to be done for the repair of services or components.
- **Change management** covers anything to be done for actually changing an IT service or component.
- **Configuration management** covers all activities for providing accurate information on all infrastructure components which the organization uses to deliver their services.
- **Risk management** covers all proactive management activities that make sure that the organization will be able to deliver all Quality of Service (QoS) parameters that were agreed with the customer (in terms of capacity, performance, finance, etc.), while conditions are continuously changing.

Of course, an IT organization will have some kind of **strategic process** above this list. However, strategic activities do not usually get caught in process descriptions. First of all, the frequency of these activities is relatively low, so the short term repetitive nature is missing. And second, C-level managers (CEO, CFO, CIO, etc.) in strategic positions do not usually consider their activities as being standard and commoditized. The Service Strategy book in ITIL is a good example: although many activities are described, it is not possible to find a clear strategic process in the book.

# A12. Setting up functions in the service provider's organization

Looking at the provider's organization, and at documented best practices, we can recognize a large number of functions. Each of these functions uses one or more of the core processes.

Functions can have different formats, including:
- **an infrastructure format** – focused on managing a part of the Information System: e.g. the application, the network, the database, desktops, desktops, servers, mainframes, telephony, database, data, system software, middleware, power, climate, etc. Examples of well-known

functions are Application Management (Team), Network Management (Team), Database Administration.
- **a service quality format** – focused on managing a quality aspect, e.g. availability, continuity, security. Relevant functions can be Availability Management (Team), IT Service Continuity Management (Team), Security Management (Team).
- **an activity format** – focused on managing one or more specific activities (processes). Relevant functions can be Change Management Team, Configuration Management Team, Requirements Engineering, Service Desk.
- **an organizational format** – focused on organizing responsibilities in departments according to criteria such as size, region, skills, specialism. Examples of functions can be the EMEA Business Unit, Team West, Corporate Headquarters.

A function can of course also be a mix of any of these – and other – formats. Finding the optimum organizational structure is a balancing act: which functions are most important to the organization, which processes are essential, how is management along the function dimension (also known as "the line") and along the process dimension balanced?

You may now recognize the following examples of regular functions:
- **Capacity Management** is an <u>infrastructure function</u> that uses a set of basic processes:
  - for realization of the capacity of the agreed services at the agreed rate/demand, this function uses operations management
  - for repairing capacity issues it uses incident management
  - for changing capacities it uses change management
  - for agreeing on capacity aspects it uses contract management
  - for proactive actions re capacity issues it uses risk management
  - for the knowledge of which capacity carriers are deployed in which parts of the enterprise infrastructure it uses configuration management
- **Security Management** is a <u>service quality function</u> that uses a set of basic processes:
  - for realisation of the security of the agreed services at the agreed rate/demand, this functions uses *operations management*
  - for repairing security issues it uses *incident management*
  - for changing security it uses *change management*
  - for agreeing on security aspects it uses *contract management*
  - for proactive actions re security issues it uses *risk management*
  - for the knowledge of which security measures are deployed in which parts of the enterprise infrastructure it uses *configuration management*
- **Service Desk** is an <u>activity function</u> (call handling) that uses a set of basic processes:
  - for the operational support of calls (service requests) according to the agreed services at the agreed rate/demand, this function uses *operations management*
  - for handling incident calls it uses *incident management*
  - for handling change calls it uses *change management*
  - for agreeing on call handling performance it uses *contract management*
  - for proactive actions of call handling issues it uses *risk management*
  - for the knowledge of which service infrastructures are deployed in which parts of the enterprise it uses *configuration management*

- **Corporate Headquarters** is an <u>organizational function</u> that uses a set of basic processes:
  - for realisation of the agreed services at the agreed rate/demand, this function uses *operations management*
  - for repairing service issues it uses *incident management*
  - for changing services it uses *change management*
  - for agreeing on service levels it uses *contract management*
  - for proactive actions on service issues it uses *risk management*
  - for the knowledge of which service infrastructures are deployed in which parts of the enterprise it uses *configuration management*
- Network Management, Application Management, Data Management, Financial management, Workload Management, Print Management, Knowledge Management, etc. will now all be recognized as variations to the themes above.

If these functions would be perceived as processes, this would require descriptions in terms of logical sequences of activities, inputs and outputs, feedback mechanisms, etcetera. The fact is that the functions listed above are not normally described in those terms, and that thus the function interpretation is more realistic than the process interpretation.

The number of functions that can be defined is endless: a function can be defined on each service attribute that is agreed upon. Common paragraphs in an SLA deal with familiar QoS's like availability, capacity, cost and continuity (see Figure 1.1). As a consequence, we will find availability management, capacity management, financial management and continuity management functions in that organization. But if the organization also agreed to QoS's for performance, reliability, maintainability, scalability or others – you may expect to find functions like performance management, reliability management, maintainability management, scalability management and others. These functions would then all use the six basic processes for their activities.

# Appendix B. Sources

Bannister, F. (2004). *Purchasing and Financial Management of Information Techology.* Butterworth-Heinemann.

Brynjolfsson, E. (1998). *Beyond the Productivity Paradox*, Communications of the ACM.

Brynjolfsson, E. and Hitt, L. (1996). *Paradox Lost? Firm-Level Evidence on the Returns to Information Systems Spending*, Management Science, (41).

Boer, S. d. (2006). *Six Sigma for IT Management.* Van Haren Publishing.

Brigham, E. F. and Ehrhardt, M. C. (2005). *Financial Management: Theory and Practice (11e).*

Brooks, Peter, Jan van Bon and Tieneke Verheijen (2006). *Metrics for IT Service Management.* Van Haren Publishing.

CSC (2001). *Critical Issues of Information Systems Management.* 14th Annual Survey of I/S Management Issues.

Hammer, M. And Champy, J. (2003). *Reengineering the Corporation: A Manifesto for Business Revolution (Collins Business Essentials).* HarperCollins.

Hitt, L., Wu, D., and Zhou, X. (2002). "ERP Investment and Productivity Measures", Journal of Management Information Systems, (19).

Kellar, Gregory M. And Akel, Anthony M. (March, 2003). *The competitive benefits of IT investments: a two industry comparison.* Journal of the Academy of Business and Economics.

Kotler, P. (1997). *Marketing Management. Analysis, Planning, Implementation adn Control.* Prentice Hall International, Hemel Hempstead.

Lanen, N. and Anderson, S.W. and Maher M.W. (2008), *Fundamentals of cost accounting*, McGraw-Hill/Irwin.

McKinsley and Company (2002). *US Productivity Report. 1995-2000.*

Office of Government Commerce (2001). *ITIL Service Delivery.* The Stationery Office.

Office of Government Commerce (2000). *ITIL Service Support.* The Stationery Office.

Office of Government Commerce (2005). *Managing Successful Projects with PRINCE2.* The Stationery Office.

Office of Government Commerce (2007). *Service Strategy.* The Stationery Office.

Office of Government Commerce (2007). *Service Design.* The Stationery Office.

Office of Government Commerce (2007). *Service Transition.* The Stationery Office.

Office of Government Commerce (2007). *Service Operation.* The Stationery Office.

Office of Government Commerce (2007). *Continual Service Improvement.* The Stationery Office.

Silvius, G. (2008). *Does ROI matter? Insights in the true business value of IT* article from *IT Service Management Global Best Practice* book. Van Haren Publishing.

# Index

## A

Accounting. . . . . . . . . . . . . . . . . .11, 13, 14
Accounting center . . . . . . . . . . . . . . . . .108
Accounting model . . . . . . . . . . . . . . . . .142
Accounting systems . . . . . . . . . . . . . . . .115
Accruals . . . . . . . . . . . . . . . . . . . . . . . . .57
American Institute of Certified Public
      Accountants (AICPA). . . . . . . . . . . .153
Anchor values. . . . . . . . . . . . . . . . . . . . .151
Annual activities. . . . . . . . . . . . . . . . . . .159
Annual budget . . . . . . . . . . . . . . . .44, 167
Annual closure . . . . . . . . . . . . . . . .58, 173
Apportioning . . . . . . . . . . . . . . . . . . . . .57
Assessment. . . . . . . . . . . . . . . . . . . . . . .200
Asset items . . . . . . . . . . . . . . . . . . . . . . .69
Asset management . . . . . . . . . . . . . . . . .69
Auditing. . . . . . . . . . . . . . . . . . . . . . . . .202

## B

Balanced Scorecard. . . . . . . . . . . . . . . . .102
Balance Sheet Statement. . . . . . . . . . . . .143
Benchmarking . . . . . . . . . . . . . . . . . . . .202
Book value . . . . . . . . . . . . . . . . . . . . . . .70
Budget . . . . . . . . . . . . . . . . . . . . . . . . . .49
Budget approver. . . . . . . . . . . . . . . . . . .109
Budgeting. . . . . . . . . . . . . . . . .11, 13, 14, 44
Budget owner. . . . . . . . . . . . .45, 77, 85, 109
Budget owners . . . . . . . . . . . . . . . . .52, 55
Budget requester. . . . . . . . . . . . . . . . . . .77
Budget review. . . . . . . . . . . . . . . . .49, 170
Business plan . . . . . . . . . . . . . . . . . . . . .38

## C

Capacity management . . . . . . . . . . . . . . .68
Capacity plan. . . . . . . . . . . . . . . . . . . . .69
CFO . . . . . . . . . . . . . . . . . . . . . . . . . . .79
Change. . . . . . . . . . . . . . . . . . . . . . . . . .158
Change management . . . . . . . . . . . . . . . .67
Charging . . . . . . . . . . . .11, 15, 62, 108, 174
Chief Financial Officer. . . . . . . . . . . . . .77
Chief Information Officer . . . . . . . . . . . .77
CIO . . . . . . . . . . . . . . . . . . . . . . . . . . . .79

## D

Classification . . . . . . . . . . . . . . . . . . . . .122
Communication. . . . . . . . . . . . . . . . . . .106
Configuration items . . . . . . . . . . . . . . . .69
Continual improvement. . . . . . . . . . . . . .99
Controls. . . . . . . . . . . . . . . . . . . . . . . . .160
Controls for accounting . . . . . . . . . . . . .161
Controls for budgeting. . . . . . . . . . . . . .161
Controls for charging. . . . . . . . . . . . . . .162
Controls for forecasting . . . . . . . . . . . . .161
Controls for pricing . . . . . . . . . . . . . . . .162
Cost apportioning model . . . . . . . . . . . .130
Cost-benefit analysis. . . . . . . . . . . . . . . .151
Cost elements. . . . . . . . . . . . . . . . . . . . .123
Cost model. . . . . . . . . . . . . . . . . . . . . . .122
Cost object. . . . . . . . . . . . . . . . . . .123, 130
Cost plus . . . . . . . . . . . . . . . . . . . . . . . .138
Cost pool . . . . . . . . . . . . . . . . . . . . . . . .130
Costs . . . . . . . . . . . . . . . . . . . . . . . . . . .25
Cost types . . . . . . . . . . . . . . . . . . . . . . .122
Cost units. . . . . . . . . . . . . . . . . . . . . . . .123
Customers . . . . . . . . . . . . . . . . . . . .19, 23
Cycles. . . . . . . . . . . . . . . . . . . . . . . . . . .139

## D

Daily activities . . . . . . . . . . . . . . .157, 158
Delta management. . . . . . . . . . . . . .53, 171
Demand management . . . . . . . . . . . . . . .53
Deming cycle (Plan-Do-Check-Act). . . . . .27
Depreciation . . . . . . . . . . . . . . . . . . .57, 70
Design . . . . . . . . . . . . . . . . . . . . . . . . . .95
Direct allocation. . . . . . . . . . . . . . . . . . .124
Direct cost . . . . . . . . . . . . . . . . . . . . . . .123
Discounted Cash Flows (DCF) . . . . . . . .149

## E

EBIT . . . . . . . . . . . . . . . . . . . . . . . . . . .144
EBITDA . . . . . . . . . . . . . . . . . . . . . . . .144
EBT. . . . . . . . . . . . . . . . . . . . . . . . . . . .144
Ethical issues . . . . . . . . . . . . . . . . . . . . .153
Evaluating investments. . . . . . . . . . .13, 15
Event-process-chain model. . . . . . . . . . . .32
External focus. . . . . . . . . . . . . . . . . . . . .219

## F

Financial accounting . . . . . . . . . . . . . . . . . .10
Financial controller . .47, 52, 77, 79, 83, 109
Financial management for internal IT
    departments . . . . . . . . . . . . . . . . . . . . .12
Financial management for internal
    IT service providers . . . . . . . . . . . . . . .13
Financial management for SAM . . . . . . . .73
Financial manager . . . . . . . . . . . . . . . . . .109
Financial periods . . . . . . . . . . . . . . . . . .141
Financial plan. . . . . . . . . . . . . . . . . . . . . .34
Financial planning . . . . . . . . . . . . . . .13, 14
Forecasting. . . . . . . . . . . . . . . . . . . .14, 170

## G

GAAP requirements . . . . . . . . . . . . . . . .142
General accounting . . . . . . . . . . . . . . . . . .10
General Accounting System (GAS). .115, 179
Goal of financial management . . . . . . . . . .11

## I

IFRS. . . . . . . . . . . . . . . . . . . . . . . . . . . .142
Implementation . . . . . . . . . . . . . . . . . . . .96
Indirect allocation . . . . . . . . . . . . . . . . .124
Indirect costs . . . . . . . . . . . . . . . . . . . . .123
Institute of Internal Auditors (IIA) . . . . . .153
Institute of Management Accountants
    (IMA). . . . . . . . . . . . . . . . . . . . . . . . .153
Internal focus . . . . . . . . . . . . . . . . . . . . .219
Internal Rate of Return (IRR) . . . . . . . . .151
Investment appraisal. . . . . . . . . . . . . . . .147
Investments evaluation . . . . . . . . . . . .39, 165
IRR . . . . . . . . . . . . . . . . . . . . . . . . . . . . .39
ISO/IEC 19770-1\
    2006. . . . . . . . . . . . . . . . . . . . . . . . . .72
ISO/IEC 20000 . . . . . . . . . . . . . . . .10, 204
IT financial manager . . . . . . . . . . . . . . . .81

## K

Key Performance Indicators (KPIs). . .28, 103

## L

Level of resistance. . . . . . . . . . . . . . . . . .106

## M

Management . . . . . . . . . . . . . . . . . . . . . . .24
Management accounting . . . . . . . . . . . . . .10
Management Accounting System
    (MAS) . . . . . . . . . . . . . . . . . . . . .115, 179
Managing deviations . . . . . . . . . . . . . .13, 15
Market price. . . . . . . . . . . . . . . . . . . .40, 62
Metrics. . . . . . . . . . . . . . . . . . . . . . . . . .165
Monthly activities. . . . . . . . . . . . . . . . . .158
MoSCoW. . . . . . . . . . . . . . . . . . . . . . . .182

## N

Net Present Value (NPV) . . . . . . . . . . . . .149
Notional charging . . . . . . . . . . . . . . . . . .62

## O

On-going costs. . . . . . . . . . . . . . . . . . . . .26
Organization . . . . . . . . . . . . . . . . . . . . .109

## P

Passive cycle . . . . . . . . . . . . . . . . . . . .17, 57
Pay-back period . . . . . . . . . . . . . . . . . . .150
Periodic closure . . . . . . . . . . . . . . . .57, 172
Periodic forecast . . . . . . . . . . . . . . . . . . .50
Pilot. . . . . . . . . . . . . . . . . . . . . . . . . . . .97
Planning. . . . . . . . . . . . . . . . . . . . . .34, 170
Pricing . . . . . . . . . . . . . . . . . . . . . . . . . .40
Process-focused. . . . . . . . . . . . . . . . . . . .218
Profit center . . . . . . . . . . . . . . . . . . . . . .108
Profit & Loss statement . . . . . . . . . . .47, 144
Project board . . . . . . . . . . . . . . . . . . . . . .92
Project management team . . . . . . . . . . . . .92
Project manager . . . . . . . . . . . . . . . . . . . .92

## Q

Quarterly activities. . . . . . . . . . . . . . . . .159

## R

RACI charts. . . . . . . . . . . . . . . . . . . . . . .77
Reconciliation . . . . . . . . . . . . . . . . . . . .142
Recovery center . . . . . . . . . . . . . . . . . . .108
Regulatory compliance. . . . . . . . . . . . . . .153
Reporting. . . . . . . . . . . . . . . . . . . . . . . .140
Return On Invested Capital (ROIC) . . . .148

Return On Investment (ROI). . . . . . . . .148
ROI . . . . . . . . . . . . . . . . . . . . . . . . . . . .39
Roles . . . . . . . . . . . . . . . . . . . . . . . . . . .77
Roll-out . . . . . . . . . . . . . . . . . . . . . . . . .98

**S**

Scenario 3 . . . . . . . . . . . . . . . . . . . . . . .22
Service attribute . . . . . . . . . . . . . . . . . . .223
Service Improvement Plan (SIP). . . . . . .103
Service level management. . . . . . . . . . . . .68
Setup costs . . . . . . . . . . . . . . . . . . . . . . .25
Six Sigma . . . . . . . . . . . . . . . . . . . . . . . .204
Software asset management . . . . . . . . . . .72
Stakeholders . . . . . . . . . . . . . . . . . . . . . .23

Statement of Requirements (SoR) . . . . . .181
Strategic business planning. . . . . . . . . . . .34

**T**

Target price . . . . . . . . . . . . . . . . . . . . . .42
Tools . . . . . . . . . . . . . . . . . . . . . . . .18, 177
Transfer price . . . . . . . . . . . . . . . . . . . . .62
Type of document . . . . . . . . . . . . . . . . .142

**U**

Users . . . . . . . . . . . . . . . . . . . . . . . .19, 23

**W**

Weekly activities. . . . . . . . . . . . . . . . . . .157

# Other leading ITSM Books

Van Haren
PUBLISHING

## Metrics for IT Service Management

A general guide to the use of metrics as a mechanism to control and steer IT service organizations, with consideration of the design and implementation of metrics in service organizations using industry standard frameworks.

**€39.95** excl tax

**ISBN 978 90 77212 69 1**

## Six Sigma for IT Management

The first book to provide a coherent view and guidance for using the Six Sigma approach successfully in IT Service Management, whilst aiming to merge both Six Sigma and ITIL® into a single unified approach to continuous improvement. Six Sigma for IT Management: A Pocket Guide is also available.

English
**€39.95** excl tax

**ISBN 978 90 77212 30 1**   (english edition)

## Frameworks for IT Management

An unparalleled guide to the myriad of IT management instruments currently available to IT and business managers. Frameworks for IT Management: A Pocket Guide is also available.

English
**€39.95** excl tax

**ISBN 978 90 77212 90 5**   (english edition)

## IT Governance based on CobiT 4.1: A Management Guide

Detailed information on the overall process model as well as the theory behind it.

English
**€22.50** excl tax

**ISBN 978 90 8753 116 4**   (english edition)